Heart of War

Heart of War

SOLDIERS' VOICES

FROM THE

FRONT LINES

IN IRAQ

DAMON DiMARCO

CITADEL PRESS
Kensington Publishing Corp.
www.kensingtonbooks.com

CITADEL PRESS BOOKS are published by

Kensington Publishing Corp.
850 Third Avenue
New York, NY 10022

All Kensington titles, imprints, and distributed lines are available at special quantity discounts for bulk purchases for sales promotions, premiums, fund-raising, educational, or institutional use. Special book excerpts or customized printings can also be created to fit specific needs. For details, write or phone the office of the Kensington special sales manager: Kensington Publishing Corp., 850 Third Avenue, New York, NY 10022, attn: Special Sales Department; phone 1-800-221-2647.

First printing: April 2007

10   9   8   7   6   5   4   3   2   1

Printed in the United States of America

Library of Congress Control Number: 2006935125

ISBN-13: 978-0-8065-2814-4
ISBN-10: 0-8065-2814-1

Dedicated to U.S. Veterans of War.

Also to Doug Martin, USMC,
A high school teacher and athletics coach,
husband, father of two,
Vietnam veteran, and citizen

Who taught me about discipline, history,
and the great value
of paying attention.

✷

In a true war story, if there's a moral at all, it's like the thread
that makes the cloth. You can't tease it out. You can't
extract the meaning without unraveling the deeper meaning.
And in the end, really, there's nothing much
to say about a true war story, except maybe "Oh."
—Tim O'Brien, *How to Tell a True War Story*

War is merely the continuation of state policy by other means.
—Karl von Clausewitz

CONTENTS

WE WERE GOING HOME . . .
2nd Class Petty Officer Christopher L. Siddall ("Doc")—combat medic—
U.S. Navy Reserve, attached to Charlie Company, 1st Light Armored
Reconnaissance Division, USMC. Age 35.

The Truth (?) Behind Jessica Lynch

THE MATURITY COMBAT TEACHES
Sergeant Jason Adamiec—U.S. Marines Golf Company, 2nd Battalion,
2nd Marines. Age 24.

CFLCC ROE Card

ROADSIDE BOMBS, JORDANIAN WHISKEY, AND SERIOUS QUESTIONS
FOR PRESIDENT BUSH
Sergeant Chad Vance—Oklahoma Army National Guard,
1245th Transportation Company. Age 31.

SETTING THE RECORD STRAIGHT
Sergeant Jim Joraleman—327th Infantry Regiment,
101st Airborne Division. Age 25.

HUMAN NATURE IN A WAR ZONE
Staff Sergeant Justin MacEwen—U.S. Army, 513th Military
Intelligence Brigade. Age 32.

Acknowledgments

UNITED STATES MILITARY
CHAIN OF COMMAND

In time of war, all activated branches of military service fall under a chain of command that reads, from the top down, as follows (the names of leaders serving during the invasion of Iraq have been provided):

THE PRESIDENT OF THE UNITED STATES
COMMANDER-IN-CHIEF
George W. Bush

SECRETARY OF DEFENSE
Donald Rumsfeld

THE JOINT CHIEFS OF STAFF
Gen. Richard B. Myers, chairman

ARMY CHIEF OF STAFF
Gen. Eric K. Shinsecki

AIR FORCE CHIEF OF STAFF
Gen. Michael E. Ryan

CHIEF OF NAVAL OPERATIONS
Adm. Vern Clark

COMMANDANT OF THE MARINE CORPS
Gen. James L. Jones

COMMANDER, U.S. SPECIAL OPERATIONS COMMAND
Gen. Charles R. Holland

POINTS OF CLARIFICATION
ON THE BRANCHES OF UNITED
STATES MILITARY SERVICE

THE FIVE FIGHTING BRANCHES OF U.S. MILITARY SERVICE are the army, marine corps, navy, air force, and coast guard. Each branch has a full-time active-duty component, as well as a federal reserve component.

THE COMMANDANT OF THE U.S. COAST GUARD reports to the chief of naval operations during times of war or whenever the President so directs.

THE NATIONAL GUARD (AIR AND ARMY BRANCHES). The National Guard structure offers a cost-efficient alternative to maintaining a large standing military force. National Guards are state militias controlled by governors who have the right, under individual state laws, to call members of the National Guard into statewide service. However, guard units are not considered a branch of the armed forces unless federally activated.

Each of the 50 United States as well as Guam, Puerto Rico, the District of Columbia, and the U.S. Virgin Islands possess their own Army National Guard. With the exception of Guam and the Virgin Islands, they each also possess an Air National Guard.

THE INDEPENDENT READY RESERVE (IRR). Traditional enlistment terms for the armed forces are three, four, five, and six years. Terms of service for active duty range from two to six years. But all soldiers have a statutory eight-year military service obligation (MSO), which is established at the time of entry into military service (active or reserve).

What does this mean? Simply put, if a soldier completes a six year hitch in the army—for example—he can still be called upon by the IRR for the next two years to fill personnel gaps in the active or reserve army. These gaps have most recently been caused by the war in Iraq.

Mandated by Congress under Title Code 10 of the Department of Defense, the IRR is—in essence—a group of veteran soldiers who have completed their terms of service in either the active or reserve service. These soldiers are not new recruits. They are seasoned, experienced soldiers who contribute significantly to army readiness with relatively little preparation and installment time.

Presidential Reserve Callup Authority (PRCA) is a provision of a public law (U.S. Code, Title 10 (DOD), section 12304) that provides the President of the United States with a means to activate, without a declaration of national emergency, not more than 200,000 members of the Selected Reserve and the Individual Ready Reserve (of whom not more than 30,000 may be members of the Individual Ready Reserve). This callup may not last more than 270 days and must meet the support requirements of any operational mission. Members called under this provision may not be used for disaster relief or to suppress insurrection.

In early May 2004, the U.S. Army Reserve's Retention and Transition Division began contacting Individual Ready Reserve soldiers who had a remaining balance of time under their MSO. This effort was intended to match the skills of IRR soldiers with units in their local areas, thereby enhancing the readiness of the Army Reserve. On June 30, 2004, the army announced plans to order 5,600 soldiers in the Individual Ready Reserve to active duty for possible deployment with the next operations Iraqi Freedom and Enduring Freedom rotations. The soldiers called would have thirty days from the date their orders were issued to take care of personal business before reporting to a mobilization site, officials said. Their orders would call for eighteen months of active duty, a term which could be extended for a total of twenty-four months if needed.

This is not the first time the U.S. Army has used the IRR to fill its manpower needs. During the Gulf War, more than 20,000 IRR soldiers were mobilized and deployed.

THE UNITED STATES SPECIAL OPERATIONS COMMAND (USSOC) is a branch of service diversified from the regular branches in that it employs small, specialized units that focus on strategic or operational objectives, either directly or indirectly related to military actions. These objectives are often politically sensitive and therefore require well-equipped, tactically elite forces to accomplish them lest mission failure damage U.S. interests and prestige. The principal missions of U.S. Special Ops include: combating terrorism, foreign internal defense, psychological operations, civil affairs, the counterproliferation of weapons of mass destruction, special reconnaissance, and unconventional warfare. U.S. Special Operations Forces are comprised of units from the Air Force Special Operations Command; Army Special Operations Command; Marine Corps SOCOM Detachment -1; and Naval Special Warfare Command.

Heart of War

STEPPING OUTSIDE THE WIRE

⁂

Senior Airman Anthony Modica[*]
WASHINGTON AIR NATIONAL GUARD, ASSIGNED TO THE 381ST EXPEDITIONARY SECURITY FORCES UNIT IN KUWAIT

Modica, age 23, tells me that the air force runs in his blood. "It was my dad's life, so it became mine, too," says Anthony. "And I don't regret a minute of it. The military has given me many incredible experiences."

Anthony's home unit is the 140th Security Forces Unit of the Washington Air National Guard. The 140th has an F-15 fighter wing attached to it, which provides homeland security by flying combat air patrols throughout the American northwest. At the time of this interview, Anthony attended a large state university as a full-time student, earning his bachelor's in international studies. He also worked part-time for Sears, Roebuck and Company in their loss-prevention department. Two weeks prior to speaking with me, Anthony proposed to his girlfriend, Winona. The couple plans to marry in 2006.

I

People have a misconception about the air force. Everyone thinks we're in the rear with the gear. I've read half a dozen books on the Middle East and Operation Iraqi Freedom, and noticed a total lack of information regarding the participation of the air force. We aren't always sitting behind computers or flying over battlefields dropping bombs. I was in the military police. I did everything from escorting convoys and running reconnaissance missions to making felony arrests overseas. I contributed.

The general public doesn't understand that Air Force Special Ops guys have hunted Osama bin Laden *and* Saddam Hussein. Actually, I don't think the general public understands what the air force does at all. Well, guess what? I was there in the beginning. I was there before it began, I watched the war start. Rear with the gear, my ass.

[*]Some names, units, and locations have been changed at the individual's request to protect privacy.

My unit got to the AOR [area of operations] on November 6, 2002. We were originally sent to Ali Al Salem Air Base in Kuwait on ninety-day orders to support Operations Southern Watch and Enduring Freedom. Southern Watch had a simple goal: protect minority Shiites living in southern Iraq from any Iraqi forces, tanks, helicopters, soldiers, you name it, who were stupid enough to cross the No-Fly Zone.[1]

Ali Al Salem sent out air patrols every day for years to enforce the zone. When we left the States, everything was business as usual. The media had just begun to disclose the White House's deliberations over an invasion. There was a lot of smoke on the burner, but no fire. Then debates started raging in the UN over a Coalition Force attack on Iraq, and we noticed a rapid increase in base activity. That was January 2003. After that, the whole region turned upside down.

I spent my first four months pulling base security. I worked the gates, did body searches on incoming personnel, stood watch in the guard towers, that kind of thing. One of the places I guarded was a pretty high-level communications bunker. We did a lot of force protection for dual-country nationals who came onto the base serving food in the mess halls and so forth. We'd search their persons and vehicles for weapons, explosives, paraphernalia, anything that shouldn't be there. Pretty routine four months. Our THREATCON[2] never left Bravo. Alpha's normal, Bravo is increased awareness, Charlie's high alert. Delta essentially means you're under attack, so Bravo was fine by me.

I got bored, though. I wanted to grab people by the nose and kick 'em in the teeth, but here I was pulling guard duty in thirteen-hour shifts inside the wire. Check IDs, raise the security arm, vehicles pass through, lower the security arm, that's that. I'd joined the air force to do this? I felt underutilized. So I applied for the most active unit I could find on the base, a team called Viper, basically a bunch of cops who did op-based reconnaissance, security escorts, surveillance of suspected operatives, and patrols outside the wire. I figured the only downside would be that maybe I'd get shot at, but it was better than the boredom.

I've thought about it a lot and I've come to a decision. I didn't join Viper out of bravado. I just wanted to use my skills. If you're a doctor,

---

1. The Thirty-third Parallel served as the UN-mandated No-Fly Zone in southern Iraq.
2. U.S. Command Central developed the Threat Condition scale to determine the defense condition of the United States homeland and assets abroad. It differs in purpose from the Defense Condition (DEFCON) scale that determines the military's posture in preparation for war.

what would it be like to not use your skills? You go through four years of college, four years of medical school, rounds, internship, specializations—for what? To *not* save people's lives? How depressing is that?

Viper was an air force unit, but a lot of Viper guys had been with the marines, the army, the rangers,[3] and special forces. These were heavy hitters whose job was to operate outside the wire without any support. Viper worked closely with American special forces and the British Royal Air Force regiment. It was a pretty big deal, but I'd only been in the air force for a year. I was a rookie, so they were reluctant to assign me. I applied every day to get assigned to Viper and got turned down each time.

Finally, four months later, they accepted me into the program. I wouldn't be manning the guard posts anymore, I'd be outside the wall, way beyond the everyday, dancing in unknown territory. It wasn't until I joined Viper Flight that I realized how serious the American mission in the area was.

There's a big difference inside and outside the wire. When you're inside, you feel safe. You allow yourself to relax and feel comfortable, like you're at home. You take it for granted that a barrier of barbed wire and some guys posted in guard towers will protect you. Who could possibly threaten the safety of a United States military installation? You don't admit to this kind of thinking, but that's what's going on inside your head. Everybody does it. We all have our cherished illusions.

Trust me, it's a false sense of security. It goes away fast the first time you step outside.

I remember the first time I rolled out the gate with Viper. My blood started pumping so hard and I couldn't even tell you why. The unknown, I guess. Just leaving those walls behind. Suddenly, the only idea roaming through my head was that I had no idea what would happen to me. Anything could happen at any moment. We drove a little further out and suddenly I felt my stomach tightening as the base fell further and further behind, along with all the stuff you took for granted. There aren't

---

3. Like all special operations forces, U.S. Army Rangers report to the Joint Special Operations Command (JSOC) when in hostile or war situations. Rangers spearhead the Army's Special Op forces. They deploy by land, air, or sea at any moment to anywhere in the world, and specialize in rapid infantry assault, night fighting, and airfield seizure. Rangers have taken part in every major combat operation since the end of the Vietnam War. They are often supported by the 160th Special Operations Aviations Regiment—also known as the "Night Stalkers"—a unit that uses high-level state-of-the-art aircraft and equipment to assess conditions from the air.

any toilets in the empty desert. They don't serve hot meals in the bad-lands. You're out there with whatever you bring with you. You're out there with each other and that's it. You're alone, you're vulnerable all of a sudden, and it's frightening.

If you're not the kind of person who can imagine danger lurking around every corner, that's okay. The landscape outside the wire would tip you off. It's barren, scorched earth, blasted by war. Munitions and the burnt-out shells of vehicles left over from the original Gulf War dot the terrain. There are land mines, unexploded RPGs [rocket-propelled grenades], and occasional corpses. All these things are dead, but they still retain the power to kill. I was on patrol with Staff Sergeant Vasquez one time when we ran over a land mine. Thankfully, it didn't go off.

There were other, more alive dangers, too. When you're inside the wire, watching TV during downtime, you don't stop to consider some-one's out there, watching you, keeping the base under constant surveil-lance. But they are. They always are. Al Qaeda operatives. Someone who's never met you but hates your guts all the same and wants to attack you. They'll wait, and they'll wait until the time is right. One of our jobs on Viper Flight was to deter that.

One time, our patrol stopped four Kuwaiti nationals who were trying to break into our perimeter. We got into a high-speed vehicle pursuit with them and chased them all over the desert until they wrecked their car. Three turned out to be Kuwaiti military personnel. The fourth was a Kuwaiti police officer. They claimed they were lost—obviously not true. We arrested them. Because of international agreements, we had to hand them over to the Kuwaiti Ministry of the Interior police, but not before we'd found some falsified documents on them.

Another Viper Flight member used this evidence to track down a cache a couple miles from Ali Al Salem. He handed over what we'd found to plain clothes detectives from the Office of Special Investiga-tions. These agents confiscated the cache, which turned out to be weapons and more falsified documents. Then the cache bust led to the arrest of a man on Kuwait's Top Ten Most Wanted list, and that arrest, in turn, led to the arrest of other criminals, including Kuwait's number one terrorist, a guy who the Kuwaiti departments of State and Defense had been dogging for years. When it was all said and done, our arrest of the four initial perps led to the arrest of twelve high-level al Qaeda operatives, all of whom wanted nothing more out of life than to kill American citizens.

Recently I was awarded the air force Commendation Medal for being a link in that long chain. Which I have to say is pretty cool. See, when you're inside the wire, you never get a chance to do anything like that. In fact, I sometimes wonder if I'll ever have a chance to do something that worthwhile in my life again.

Viper Flight was divided into details 1 through 4, and members rotated through each team according to a schedule. Each team was geared toward a specific tactical purpose. Viper 1, for instance, was responsible for protecting the base's Coalition gates, which were manned by Kuwaitis, Brits, and Americans. Viper 1 also protected Echo 1, which was a gate for American use only. Viper 1 drove an up-armored Humvee with an M-60 machine gun mounted on the back. The guy manning the 60 also had a 9 mm Beretta sidearm—that was usually me. The Humvee driver had an M-16.

Viper 2 drove a regular four-door Humvee—no armor. The driver and gunners had M-16s, but the gunner's rifle came equipped with an M-203 grenade launcher for use on special occasions.

Viper 3 was the most dangerous detail. Viper 3 hung out south of the base along Highway 70, a major route that connects Saudi Arabia, Kuwait, and Iraq. There's tons of traffic along that road, especially during the month of Ramadan. You're exposed to a constant stream of foreign nationals who come bombing down the highway in a variety of vehicles; you never knew where they were coming from or what they wanted. Viper 3 rode in what's called a Barvee—a light Humvee with no doors, no roof, it's totally open to the elements but man, it's really fast. The driver for Viper 3 had his M-16. The gunner carried an M-249.

Pulling duty on Viper 4 meant that you were the shift supervisor. Command and control. Your job was to coordinate the other units. Viper 4 always had a senior NCO[4] on duty, and whatever they wanted to arm themselves with was fair game.

---

4. A senior noncommissioned officer (NCO) in the air force would be a soldier ranked E-7 master sergeant.

II

Something unusual began to happen in February. On the first of the month, our population at Ali Al Salem was, at maximum, 2,500. That included Kuwaitis, British, Americans, soldiers, cooks, and cleaners. Then, suddenly, troops started coming in out of the woodwork. By February 28, the population exploded to 12,500. Something was up.

When we first arrived in Kuwait, engineers were busy building a place called Camp Commando, a facility that lay kitty-corner to our base. I remember because we were rookies back then; we got assigned to set up C-wire[5] around the new perimeter. The new bodies coming in quickly filled up Camp Commando. It wasn't nearly enough. Personnel kept coming in so fast we had to literally stack people on top of one another, dicks to assholes, pardon my language.

Helicopters began landing. Truck convoys of navy Seabees[6] and army wreckers stopped in. Suddenly, six thousand marines found themselves crushed in with six thousand army personnel who, in turn, were packed on top of the air force. The chow hall was packed, the bathrooms became inaccessible, you couldn't jump on a computer to check e-mail. Forget all about trying to call home. It was life in a tuna can, with everyone shoving each other for elbow room.

The camp crime rate skyrocketed. Incidents of petty larceny broke out all over the place. There were assaults galore as soldiers lost patience with one another and started fixing problems with their fists. At one point, a team of navy SEALS stole an incredibly expensive piece of air force equipment. The piece they took was radar equipment that allowed us to perform the primary mission of Ali Al Salem, monitoring the skies for incoming attack. The theft forced us to shut down operations for at least a day, maybe longer. The base commander issued an immediate order to have the SEALS arrested and sent to his office. Air force cops found them, slapped cuffs on them, took them in and did all the paperwork, but everyone knew they'd only get slaps on the wrist.

---

5. Concertina wire—barbed wire or razor wire extended in a spiral for use as a barrier, often posted atop fences.

6. Officially the United States Naval Construction Force. The term "Seabee" derives from "CB" (Construction Battalion). The original Seabees organization was created during the Second World War, when civilian construction workers and engineers were recruited by the navy and placed under the leadership of the navy's Civil Engineer Corps. Since that time, Seabees have performed an impressive array of civic reconstruction, such as rebuilding roads, schools, orphanages, and public utilities in remote parts of the world, war-torn countries, and underdeveloped nations. Their arrival is often perceived as a gesture of goodwill to leaders of foreign nations.

Think about it. We were on the brink of war. SEALS are valuable U.S. government property, too valuable to waste by putting them in jail, no matter what they've done. The military's got 6 to 10 million dollars invested in their training. The SEALS knew it, too. Apparently these big, stocky guys were sitting in the post police station, handcuffed together, laughing like the whole thing was a colossal joke. They couldn't believe somebody'd had the nerve to arrest them.

As it turns out, their commander came down to the police station and met with our commander. I don't think anyone really knows what they talked about behind closed doors. The SEALS were released, the equipment got reinstalled, and everyone just shook their heads. We didn't dwell on it for too long. We all had other things on our minds.

It was obvious that war was approaching. On top of all the military personnel, we began to notice members of other agencies floating around, the CIA, the DIA [Defense Intelligence Agency],[7] FBI, probably the NSA [National Security Agency],[8] you name it. We figured this out when the FBI came to investigate the Failaka Island[9] incident. You can tell spooks by the way they conduct themselves.

Spooks have a professional demeanor, but it's not a military demeanor. Spooks drive different vehicles, too, usually up-armored Chevy Suburbans, and they all look like Jack Ryan.[10] They all wear sunglasses and khaki pants with khaki vests over polo shirts. They're conspicuously inconspicuous. Without divulging too much information, I can also say that you could tell which spooks worked for the CIA because

7. According to their official Web site: "The Defense Intelligence Agency is a Department of Defense combat support agency and an important member of the United States Intelligence Community. With over 7500 military and civilian employees worldwide, DIA is a major producer and manager of foreign military intelligence. We provide military intelligence to warfighters, defense policymakers and force planners, in the Department of Defense and the Intelligence Community, in support of U.S. military planning and operations and weapon systems acquisition."
8. According to their official Web site: "The National Security Agency/Central Security Service is America's cryptologic organization. It coordinates, directs, and performs highly specialized activities to protect U.S. information systems and produce foreign intelligence information. A high technology organization, NSA is on the frontiers of communications and data processing. It is also one of the most important centers of foreign language analysis and research within the government."
9. The Failaka Island incident occurred on October 8, 2002, when a marine detachment practicing urban warfare on this island off the coast of Kuwait was attacked by two Kuwaiti gunmen. One marine was shot and killed, another was shot and wounded. The Kuwaiti government called the incident a terrorist attack. The FBI has sole investigative powers in the event that American citizens are killed.
10. The CIA character in Tom Clancy novels (e.g., *The Hunt for Red October, Clear and Present Danger,* and *The Sum of All Fears*) who, in the film versions of the books, has been played by actors Alec Baldwin, Harrison Ford, and Ben Affleck, respectively.

they were the guys conducting a very specific type of aerial reconnaissance from the base, using unmanned aircraft.

Troops from the chemical warfare department came in and taught us the procedures for biochem combat. Medic teams came in to refresh us on how to bind wounds and stop bleeding. A day before we were supposed to leave for home, the air force extended our tour indefinitely. You didn't have to be a rocket scientist to figure out that something big was about to happen.

I was in my tent watching Fox News on my day off. We had sheets strung up to cordon off private sleeping areas and I was alone in my bunk. The president came on and gave his speech to the nation. He basically told Saddam Hussein and his sons that they had forty-eight hours to surrender or leave the country. It's our way or the highway. And it was one of those moments when you feel the apple in your throat grow large. Your mouth tightens up. You begin to think, *Within two days I will be at war. I will see combat. I will be afraid. I already am afraid.* You have that sensation like you're falling over the edge of a cliff and there's no way to stop it. Your life is about to change dramatically.

Then, just as suddenly as they all came in, the marine and army units began to move out. Many of them went north and began setting up sites along the Kuwait-Iraq DMZ [demilitarized zone]—Camp Pennsylvania, Camp New York, and so forth. Once war was declared, ten thousand soldiers might leave while seven thousand more came in behind them. The cycle became nonstop throughout the month of March. After that, as quickly as it all started, everything got quiet again. By then we were in the thick of it.

You know what I'd want people to know? That fear you have when you think you're going to get killed or seriously injured. I'd like people to really appreciate that because there's nothing else like it. Until you've felt it, you really don't know what it's like to be over there.

For us, the war started on March 19. That night, I was out on patrol with Senior Airman Mike Lucans. The war was already in full swing. Tomahawk cruise missiles[11] shot out over the Persian Gulf, there were

---

11. BGM 109 Tomahawks are all-weather submarine or ship-launched land-attack cruise missiles. They are highly survivable weapons that cannot easily be detected by radar, due to their low altitude flight and small-width cross-section. Several varieties of Tomahawks exist, but their general specifications include subsonic flight at 550 miles per hour over a 600-nautical-mile range, carrying a 1,000-pound conventional warhead or submunitions dispenser.

distant explosions, flashes of light, but everything was silent at Ali Al Salem. In fact, it was the quietest night we'd had in a while. Eerie quiet.

Mike and I got off work at six A.M. and he said to me, "Tony, man! Damn! I bet the shit's gonna hit the fan during our sleep cycle." I laughed and said, "You're probably right." At noon, I was still asleep, like everyone else who'd pulled night duty. The PA system kicked in all of a sudden, waking us up, and a female said, "Attention on Site! Attention on Site! Alarm Red! MOPP 4, Bunker Now! I say again: Alarm Red, MOPP 4, Bunker Now!"

"Alarm Red" means the base is under attack. "MOPP 4" means you're at warfare-level mission-oriented protective posture, sustaining a chemical attack. "Bunker Now" means the missiles are incoming at that very moment. This is not what you want to hear when you're coming out of a dead sleep.

I had all my gear set up so I was ready to grab it and run. When I heard that call, my heart stopped. My buddy, Senior Airman Dellmar, started yelling, "Up, up, up! Everyone up! We're under attack!" It was a blind rush. I grabbed my gear and bolted out the tent before I realized I'd forgotten my gas mask, and what's the point of MOPPing up if you don't have your gas mask?

I ran back in and grabbed it, fifty pounds of gear in my arms now, turned, and staggered back out into the confusion. People were running around in boxer shorts, combat boots, and nothing else. Soldiers staggered into each other in a mad panic. Helicopters were taking off. Aircraft were scrambling. Shouting. Cursing. Orders screamed out left and right. You could see the panic in everyone's eyes.

I was right behind Dellmar and we were running toward the bunker over by guard tower Tango 3, near the base perimeter. It's hard to describe that sensation. Like you're running from a monster that wants to eat you, and no matter how hard you run, you're not running fast enough, you're *going* to get eaten. Everything slows down at the same time as adrenaline flushes through your system and makes you high. Dellmar and I were en route to the bunker as these streaks started tearing toward us from the sky and impacting maybe five kilometers outside the base. Five kilometers isn't far at all when you're dealing with nuclear or biochemical weapons. Not nearly far enough.

You have just enough time to think, *They're trying to kill us, those sons of bitches are trying to kill us!* The missiles would come in and hit the earth. You'd feel the concussion first, so strong that it felt like someone cracked you across the knees with a stick. You had just enough time to think, *That's what they do from more than a mile out?! What do they do when they land right on top of you?!* Your legs wobbled. You nearly fell down. But you ran. And you ran. And you jumped into the bunker. Safe.

Or was it? I put on my gear and crammed on in. Soldiers were stuffed up against each other, center of the afternoon, over 120 degrees, stifling. People were puking in their masks. Automatically you think they're suffering from a nerve agent, you don't stop to think that it's just an anxiety reaction. The missiles have captured your imagination and held it, spellbound.

You start to sweat, you start to shake. You panic and fight to keep your breathing regular. You suddenly know for a fact that you'll be trapped inside that suit for the rest of your life, and you realize that getting hit by a bullet or shrapnel isn't the biggest fear in war, not nearly. The biggest fear is the insidiousness of fear itself: *Will they nuke me? Will a gas leak in and stop my heart? What can I do? I'm defenseless here. We're all, every one of us, defenseless.*

This is, by far, the worst feeling I've ever had in my life. After it's all over, the peace that comes on is weird. You feel like you're floating. Like you've died. But you're alive. You're happy. So happy that you don't care about anything else. Just the fact that you're still breathing. There's nothing else in the world but breathing. And everything is beautiful. Just beautiful.

III

When I left for Kuwait, I was a young, dumb airman. The way I saw it, I'd joined the best branch of the military. Air force soldiers are smart. They live good lives. Marines are jarheads, the army's retarded, and navy guys are all queers—that was the mentality. Everyone who hasn't gone into combat has it. They think their branch of the service is the best, and that's a luxury you can afford until shit starts to really happen. I'll never again make fun of another service member, regardless of their branch or country. I learned the hard way that we all bleed the same.

On the night of March 23, 2003, I was on Viper 3 with Sergeant Bertram and two other marines whose names I forget now. We were four days into the war and we'd experienced an endless amount of SCUD[12] and surface-to-surface missile attacks. We were exhausted. I remember one of the towers called in to say that they'd seen a missile launch, the ordnance was now in flight—they wanted our visual confirmation from the ground. That's how things were over there. Everybody was always calling someone else to see who could figure out what the hell was going on.

It was dark out. People started popping flares to get a look at what was going on in the sky. I caught sight of the missile somewhere out over the Persian Gulf, somewhere in that hot zone where the countries of Kuwait and Iraq meet. I knew a plane was involved because I saw more flares begin to pop, a different type. Planes release flares like that when they're trying to fool the targeting systems of enemy missiles. The flares act as decoys and the missiles fly astray. But not this time. There was a bright flash, and a *Boom!*

I picked up the radio and said, "Tango 2, this is Viper 3. Confirm explosion. Something just got shot down. Over." We were happy as hell. We thought it was an enemy aircraft, an Iraqi plane that wouldn't be dropping bombs or conducting reconnaissance or misbehaving anymore. The next day, we found out one of our Patriot flights had mistakenly shot down a British Tornado, killing the pilot and the radar intercept operator. Somehow the IFF [identify friendly or foe][13] system had malfunctioned and that was that.

Our British colleagues were not happy with us at all. They didn't say anything. Not a word. How could they? It was war and stupid things happen. Friendly fire happens. We were all disheartened. But the looks on their faces. Not angry, not sad. Just stone. That's what made me real-

12. SCUD missiles are Russian-manufactured short-range tactical ballistic surface-to-surface ordnance. Originally deployed by the Russian military during the 1960s, the missile was originally designed to carry either a 100-kiloton nuclear warhead or a 2,000-pound conventional warhead over ranges from 100 to 180 miles. Additionally, SCUDs could carry chemical or biological warfare agents. According to Norman Friedman in *Desert Victory—The War for Kuwait* (Naval Institute Press, 1991): "The Iraqis modified SCUDS for greater range, largely by reducing warhead weight, enlarging their fuel tanks and burning all of the fuel in the early stages of the flight (rather than continuously) . . . [Modified SCUDS were] structurally unstable and often broke apart in the upper atmosphere. That further reduced its already poor accuracy, but also made the missile difficult to intercept, since its flight path was unpredictable." Different types of SCUDS could be fired from either mobile or static sites.

13. A Patriot site sends a coded signal to all targeted aircraft, which the aircraft responds to with its own signal that identifies it as a nontargetworthy asset. The malfunction of that signal could convince a missile that a friendly aircraft is, in fact, enemy.

ize that I was no better than anyone else out in the desert. Your mind wants to break things down into digestible units. He's a marine, so he must be a dumb killing machine. He's not American, so he can't understand me. Bullshit. The uniforms may be different, but we're all the same when it comes to bleeding.

Three weeks into the war there was this general in southern Iraq who commanded a SCUD missile brigade, a real asshole who kept lobbing missiles at us on a regular basis just to make himself giggle. Our intelligence couldn't find his location—somewhere out of Basra, certainly—but he'd cover his tracks after every launch and disappear. Rumor had it he was launching his missiles from schools, a real scumbag.

After a while, it became less of a threat than it was purely annoying. I'd changed shifts by that point, I was working the days. Myself, Sergeant Trium, and Senior Airman Dellmar were inside our tent getting ready to go back out—another day outside the wire—when a missile came in out of nowhere. No siren, no warning. Just the *whisssssh* of the incoming and the *whisssh-phooosh BANG* of the intercepting Patriot missile. The damn thing exploded maybe six hundred meters over our heads.

The explosion was so loud, so tremendous, that it picked all three of us up and threw us back down. Again: this is not a good way to start your day. Absolute fear kicked in. It all happened so fast and so close that the first thing to run through my head was *terrorist attack.* I thought somebody had driven a car bomb onto the base and blown it up. Our buddy, Sergeant Samper, was—impossibly—still asleep in his bunk. I shook him out of bed screaming, "Get the fuck up! Up! We're under attack!" Poor guy. You should've seen the panic on his face. I'd pulled him out of a dead sleep.

Again, we ran for the bunkers. I don't know about the other guys, but my ears were ringing hard from the concussion. Later on I found out I'd lost fifteen decibels of hearing in my left ear. We're running fast as bits of metal missile debris, rained down from the sky. Another moment where you figured, *Well, this is it.* Another moment to practice saying goodbye.

Later on I found a guidance fin from that SCUD sitting on the ground, smoldering. Dog teams came through to sniff for chemical traces and found nothing. But nobody picked up this blasted piece of metal. It sat there for two days. I figured, I'm not gonna let that go to waste, so I took it. I'm a little surprised I got it back into the States. When it was time to leave the Gulf, a couple of days before the war ended, I put it in my bag as if it was a shirt or a pair of pants.

We're not supposed to bring home war souvenirs. But this wasn't a gold-plated AK-47, it was a hunk of charred metal that had almost taken my life, and it meant something to me though it's hard to describe what. Coming out of the Gulf, customs was done by military cops and there's a creed among us: you sanction your own. They didn't blink when they saw the hunk. They didn't say a word.

Customs in the United States? Not much different. One guy asked me, "So, what's this?" He pointed to the fin. "It's nothing," I said. "Just a piece of metal." That seemed good enough for him. Right now, it's on the kitchen table in my home. I don't know what else to do with it.

Know what? I was excited to tell you about all this because I think this book is a really good idea. You hear about the army and you hear about the marines. I want to reiterate: no one ever hears about the air force's contribution to this war. Thanks for letting me tell my story. But let me say one last thing: right now I live in the Pacific Northwest, which is one of the most liberal places in America. They hate our government and they hate everything the military stands for. It's a really tough place for me to live right now. Veterans get treated like—how do I say this? Like a bastard version of Vietnam vets.

The other day I had my car vandalized. I had military stickers on it and some asshole trashed it. They took a key and scratched FUCK YOU into the paint. They took a lighter to my air force bumper sticker. This was the day after I'd proposed to my girlfriend. It sure ruined the moment. One moment I'm happy because I've asked the woman I love to join me for the rest of my life. The next, somebody lets it known that he hates my guts for I don't know what.

Ninety-five percent of the professors at my university preach the Liberal Left point of view. I don't have a problem with that. It's a wonderful thing that we have an open discourse on political views in this country. But the constant protests . . . the constant derogatory comments. I'm taking eighteen credits this semester and I'll take eighteen next semester so I can graduate in June and get the hell out of this school. The students are worse. We entertain debates all the time and these kids—I'm the same age, but I have to call them *kids*—they talk about the war as if they've been there. They have this misconception that we're decimating the Iraqi infrastructure and I have to point out to them that there *is* no infrastructure in Iraq. The only person who had infrastructure was Saddam, and he could afford it because he embezzled his people's money, stole their food, killed indiscriminately, and took what he wanted.

No, we didn't find any weapons of mass destruction. But I've ridden out on British patrols and seen mass graves out in the middle of nowhere in the Kuwaiti desert. They had a bunch of little plastic bags set up to collect the indiscriminate bones of men, women, and children—people whom the world has forgotten. So go ahead. Split hairs. Saddam Hussein *was* a weapon of mass destruction.

I want to scream at these ignorant people. What you're seeing on TV today isn't a complete picture of the war! CNN and MSNBC focus on the number of casualties, but the United States military has done some wonderful things in the Middle East. We've saved children. We run convoys of school supplies. We feed people. We've liberated an entire country. I know it's the same old thing you hear every day from the president and vice president. But it's all true. I've been there and I've seen what's going on.

It's not good enough for these students. They point to the Abu Ghraib scandal, cite Michael Moore, and call up isolated instances of misbehavior on the parts of certain American soldiers without stopping to consider that the military is exactly like society: you get a few bad apples in the barrel. When you boil it all down, the students at my school are content to treat vets like we're the tools of some giant right wing conspiracy. You know what? I *am* a tool. I'm *proud* to be a tool. A tool is something that's created to do a specific job and that's what happened to me. I was trained to perform and I did. I performed well. If anybody's got a problem with the war, that's fine, you're entitled to your opinion. But if you've got a problem with me? Step up to the plate. Walk a mile in my boots. After that you can explain to me why I deserve your ridicule, and if you can't? Then shut the hell up.

It's no wonder I crawled into a bottle when I first got home. I was expecting—I don't know. I guess I was expecting a parade. What a fucking idiot I was. Everyone here is fat and happy. They put yellow ribbon stickers on their bumpers, but they don't care about what's really going on over there. They don't want to care about what's really going on *anywhere*. They've never answered the call to serve their country. They've answered to Starbucks. They've answered to corporate America.

Listen to me, please. I don't need your backlash. I need your support. Please give me your support. I hope this book sends a message to people.

ON POINT

Specialist Jeremy Simon
U.S. ARMY, GHOST TROOP, 2ND SQUADRON,
2ND ARMORED CAVALRY REGIMENT

Age 23. A born-and-raised Texan, Specialist Simon was stationed in Kosovo prior to participating in the invasion of Iraq in March 2003. He speaks in an even tone chock full of understatements, and frequently uses derivations of the word "fuck" to make a point. Despite this, Simon comes across as a respectful man. During our interview, he frequently calls me "sir," when he has no reason to do so. He is a soldier and this is his habit.

Simon and his wife, Jackie, have been married for four years; they have one son, Ian, who is three years old. When asked if they plan to have any more children, Simon laughs. "Trust me," he says. "One is more than enough."

Specialist Simon was medically discharged from the army in October 2004. He and his family currently live in southeast Texas.

I

I talk to some folks about my job in Iraq and they think what I did was crazy. They're probably right. Ghost Troop is a light reconnaissance unit, a glorified military term for "scouts." When an army advances, we strike out ahead of them by anywhere from a single kilometer to thirty miles. Your job is to figure out what's in store for your troops. It's dangerous work. You're out there all alone, eighteen guys in six light Humvees, riding around on a strip of land that's about to explode. There's enemy up ahead and your own army behind. You're sandwiched in the middle while everyone's loading their guns getting ready to fire. You hope they don't start shooting while you're taking notes on the quality of roads, bridges, and terrain. You learn to take notes pretty quickly.

Sometimes we'd split into three smaller teams, two vehicles each, and go separate ways to cover more ground. That's when you really start to feel vulnerable, like gnats flying up a giant's nose. Gnats don't have a prayer in hell when it comes to defending themselves but they can be real fast when they want to be. Ghost Troop prized our speed above everything else. We didn't carry much in the way of weaponry so we could be light and quick.

It's a special sort of job, and you have to have the nerve for it. Me and the guys in my unit were real proud of what we did. We used that old motto a lot, the one that goes, "We the willing, Led by the unknowing, Do the impossible, for the Ungrateful."[14]

Our mission was to get out there and gather intel, as much as possible, then establish communication with the troops behind us and radio updates on what they could expect to find on the road. We used maps and a compass rather than computers, because satellite imaging won't tell you if a bridge can support a passing tank battalion. It can't eyeball potholes in a road and say, "Nope, no way the Bradleys[15] can get through here." You can have all the newfangled equipment in the world. Bottom line is some things have to be done the old-fashioned way.

We didn't have any structural engineers with us, those personnel arrive when the troops push forward. We pretty much eyeballed everything and sent a best guesstimation as to what infrastructure could support the invasion. Which meant we asked ourselves questions like, Is this road wide enough to handle LAVs [light armored vehicles]?[16] Is that bridge strong enough to support the weight of armored units? Later on, if an engineer says, "Whoa, wait a minute! You can't drive a tank

---

14. This quote's been attributed to various sources, most of them naval, though it's been embraced by members of all branches of the military. Many versions exist. Whether in verse or in prose, the complete text reads: "We the willing, led by the unknowing, are doing the impossible for the ungrateful. We have done so much for so long with so little that we are now qualified to do anything with nothing."

15. The Bradley fighting vehicle has seen various incarnations throughout twentieth-century American warfare. The newest series (the M2A3 and the M3A3) carries far more sophisicated weapons systems than its "battle taxi" predecessors of the M113 variety. The new Bradleys are designed to safely transport infantry to critical battlefield locations, provide fire support to cover dismounts operations, and destroy enemy tanks and other vehicles that may threaten infantry troops on board. To assist with these operations, the Bradley relies on its main weapon, the M242 25 mm "Bushmaster" chain gun; a M240C 7.62 mm machine gun mounted to the right of the "Bushmaster," and TOW antitank missiles, which are effective at a range of nearly 4 kilometers and travel at a speed of nearly Mach 1 en route to a target.

16. One of several varieties of 8 by 8 wheeled combat, combat support, and combat service support vehicles. They tend to be 6.39 meters long and nearly 2.5 meters high—depending on what sort of pintle mounts have been equipped. Their crew consists of a driver, gunner, commander, and six troopers. LAVs are all-terrain, all-weather vehicles that carry a variety of weaponry depending on their particular tactical designations.

across that bridge!" well, that's their ball game. At that point they either send out bridge layers or Command alters the course of the march toward another route we've recommended. That's the way it's supposed to work, at any rate. In "Shock and Awe," engineering support didn't arrive until the invasion had been under way two full months. Another fucked-up situation we saw over there. One of many, I assure you.

Scouting keeps you on your toes. We used fake tactics a lot. Bob and weave. Move at night. Run, run, run. Look around. Never stay in the same place longer than you have to. Stop. Hide out and pull security during the day. Don't sleep. You can't ever sleep.

I went the first five days of the invasion on about three hours' sleep. I started hallucinating—not visualizing entities or anything, it was more like I got slap happy and out of character. My vision blurred. I felt disembodied. Finally my sergeant ordered me to get some rest. I wanted to climb in the back of the truck to stretch out, but we had weapons in the back. The Hummers were equipped with TOW missiles, .50 cals, 240 Bravos. My truck had an MK-19 automatic grenade launcher.[17] Not comfortable. Eventually I huddled down in one of the seats and got my three hours. After that, I was good to go.

The Iraqis were trying to feel us out just as we were feeling them out. On our way across the terrain, we drove through a lot of tiny villages and took small arms fire. A few Iraqis found it amusing to climb on the rooftops of buildings and take potshots at us with rifles. I would classify these incidents as highly frustrating. We never got close enough for anyone to spray us down with automatic weapons fire and it's tough to hit a Humvee with mortars or missiles. There were incoming shells, but if they ever started dropping too close, we'd stomp the accelerator pedal, bob and weave, and get the hell out of there. Fast, fast, fast—that was the key. We kept pushing forward.

We didn't talk much. Mostly we listened. When we did speak, it was to make a joke to keep everyone alert or to say something practical like,

17. Probably referring to the MK-19 40 mm machine gun, a weapon with a firing rate of 350 grenades per minute that are effective to ranges of over 2200 meters. This system was developed by the U.S. Navy during the early '60s and notably deployed in Southwest Asia during Desert Storm where it devastated enemy infantry. The shells from this gun pierce armor up to two inches thick, kill personnel within five meters of impact, and wound personnel within fifteen meters of impact.

"Up there, look ahead. Watch out for that." Sometimes we talked about the fucked-up information we'd gotten from Command before they sent us out on this fucked-up mission. They'd pretty much told us, "Well, we really don't know what's going on out there, so y'all go get us some information." That's fucked up. Sometimes we talked about home, which kept everyone sane.

Scouts are a select group of people. There's only eight to ten light recon brigades in the entire army, maybe six hundred soldiers plus support elements that handle command and control bullshit. By that I mean officers who sit in the rear saying, "Do this, do that" over a radio, while we're getting shot at.

The highest rank in my platoon was Sergeant First Class, Kevin Mock. He was the best! He got us through a whole bunch of shitty situations. Fucking flawless. He pushed us when we needed pushing, kept our morale up. When you're that far forward, the biggest danger is allowing yourself to get even a little complacent, and Sergeant Mock wouldn't have it. He followed the book to the letter and enforced safety standards, which seemed petty but kept us alive. He insisted on weapons care, for instance. Our guns had to be spotless at all times, which is a tough trick to pull off in a desert with sand flying around all over the place.

Sergeant Mock split his MREs[18] with any soldier who needed more food. He gave up his water ration—that's like giving somebody a piece of your life when you're in the desert. I remember he gave one guy a pair of socks. Anything he had was ours. We all shared things, but Sarge? Man, Sarge was so far above and beyond the call, I don't know how to describe it rightly. No bones about it, we were *his* soldiers and he was gonna make sure that every single goddamn one of us walked off that landing strip when the plane touched down home.

When I say that things were fucked up over there, I want to qualify it. For example, ROE was *very* fucked up. Throughout the invasion, my

18. Meals ready to eat—designed to sustain an individual engaged in heavy activity such as military training or combat when normal food service facilities are not an option. MREs are totally self-contained rations consisting of a full meal packed in a flexible meal bag lightweight enough to fit into uniform pockets. Each bag contains an entrée such as meatloaf with gravy, chicken with cavatelli, beefsteak with mushrooms, jambalaya, and more. Side orders such as clam chowder, potato sticks, minestrone stew, and refried beans are also included in each MRE, as well as a desert, sauce packets, accessory pills, powdered beverages, utensils, and flameless heat sources.

unit's ROE [rule(s) of engagement] was, "If you see somebody with an AK-47, you can't shoot right away. You have to wait for him to point the weapon in your direction, then you're clear to open fire."

Unfortunately, the Iraqis had already figured this system out. They sent out decoys. You'd have one guy walking down a side of the street with his AK slung over his shoulder. He draws your attention but he doesn't attack so what can you do? Nope. Sorry. You can't fire at him. While you're keeping an eye on that guy, another guy would sneak up behind you and shoot. Which means you're finally clear to open fire if you live.

We found this out the hard way a couple of times. Finally we made a habit of maintaining 360 security[19] but even then, we were vulnerable. We'd watch the decoys, take a couple shots from the real shooters, and pretty much say, "Fuck this. Time to haul ass to the next point and hope we avoid further enemy contact."

But when I say ROE was fucked up, I don't just mean getting shot at, that's part of the job, you expect it. No, I mean a month after the invasion started, we were assigned to scout for Charlie Company, Third Brigade, Eighty-second Airborne Division. Which meant we'd roll into a town, secure a point, pull security, and wait for the infantry to arrive.

Eighty-second Airborne—those guys are a premier unit. They're one of the best-funded divisions, they get top-of-the-line equipment, body armor, and weapons. Working with them was weird. Call it a difference in perspective. See, my unit snuck around a lot and tried like hell to use intelligence to avoid combat at all costs. These guys were *looking* for it. They *wanted* it. Those fuckers are like trained pit bulls. You point to a hill and say, "Take it," that's what they'll do. Some people call that hard core. I call it really fucking stupid. I think the reason my unit didn't suffer too many casualties is because we'd think first, then act. None of this "shoot first, ask questions later" crap. Hell, shooting was always the last resort.

As it turns out, Eighty-second Airborne was given different ROE. They had permission to shoot anyone wearing combat boots. So if a guy came at you wearing a fucking man-dress[20] but you could see combat

19. A watch perimeter focused out in all directions, 360 degrees.
20. A dishdasha, traditional Islamic garb.

boots poking out the bottom, boom. He's dead on sight, no questions asked. The guys in my unit found this a little extreme. A lot of the people in those villages were poor. They hadn't had shoes at one point. Maybe they'd pulled their boots off dead soldiers just to get some decent footwear. Anyway, weren't we there to win the hearts and minds of the Iraqis and free them from this fucking despotic ruler who'd oppressed them for forty years? But here we had a bunch of assholes running around shooting people who wore combat boots just because they didn't have any other shoes. Hypocrisy at its finest. The guys in the Eighty-second bragged about it, too, especially in Al Samawah.[21] They were like, "Yippee! We're killing this and we're killing that!" Some of those people might be innocent. Assholes.

Don't get me wrong, I was a soldier, too. I'd kill anybody for the right reasons, the life of my friend or my brother. But you don't set yourself loose in a foreign country and run around murdering people. I don't know what that is. The point I'm trying to make is not everyone's ROE was the same over there. Another bullshit lie that's been fed to the masses like candy.

II

The saddest thing I saw over there. A couple months after the invasion, we pulled up to a school yard in Sadr City, Baghdad. By that point, we were running routine scout patrols in and around the city. We were still out on point, but at least the war was over and we knew who'd won. There was a bunch of locals, hundreds of them gathered around this suitcase sitting in the playground. By that point, we'd been assigned an interpreter[22] so we had him ask them what was the matter.

The translator spoke to the people and relayed this: the people thought there was a bomb in the suitcase. They were afraid to approach it, so we pulled security and cordoned off the area. The suitcase was bulging at the sides. Whatever was inside was really packed in tight. One of our men crept up to examine it. We were all incredibly tense. He didn't

---

21. A town 280 kilometers southeast of Baghdad. Its population was 124,400 in 2002.

22. On the subject of interpreters, Specialist Simon says, "A lot of units had them by that point—they were often former school teachers and one guy we had—his name was Morfa—he was a former Iraqi artillery officer. Basically, it was August, the invasion was over. It was fucking hot as all hell and the more educated Iraqis—the ones who could speak English, for instance—were coming to us to offer their services."

see any signs of explosives or detonation apparatus so he leaned down and unzipped it.

A little girl's body rolled out. She was six years old, maybe seven. She had brown hair and she'd been dismembered. The crowd let out a gasp. For a moment, nobody said anything. After that, I don't know. People were screaming, I guess her family. Everyone started yelling and screaming in Arabic. Wailing. Madness.

We snapped to, tried to control the peace. Called some medics from one of our forward observation bases and they put the pieces in a body bag. We gave the bag to one of the tribal leaders so the people could handle everything according to their culture and religion. This was a calling card that basically told the locals, "Letting your child go to school is dangerous, see?" Let them go to school and this might happen, see? That's the kind of people who ran that country.

I don't know what else to tell you. That was a pretty fucked up day. To do that to *anybody* is insane, but to do it to a little girl? That's beyond—I don't know.

That summer we pulled a lot of foot patrols through Sadr City, still scouting, still walking point, setting up forward perimeters on main roads with good entrance points and holding them 'til troops arrived behind us. We moved in small groups and never penetrated too far into the city at once. Small groups are more vulnerable, so we took everything in tiny bites, making sure we could pull back toward help if shit got heavy. Sometimes, to make ourselves feel better, we'd put guys up on the rooftops to catch a bird's-eye view. We weren't trained snipers, it was anybody who raised a hand when we asked, "Who can shoot real good and climb?"

The people of Iraq watched us from the streets. They hung out of windows, following us with their eyes. Nobody moved, everybody just watched. Moving took too much energy in that heat. Summertime in the desert. One time we checked the temperature with a thermometer. It was 132 degrees.

That wasn't good enough, though. A joker in my unit grabbed a meat thermometer off the cooks and stuck it in his flak vest while he pulled foot patrol. When he took it out, it read 160. Another time we walked patrol for what seemed like forever and I got back to the Humvees, collapsed from total dehydration. They pumped six IVs into me before I started feeling right again. One hundred and sixty degrees. That's fucking hot.

We tried to keep good humor between us. We didn't laugh very much since nothing was really ever funny over there, but sometimes things happened that made you grin, and you'd like that very much. You took a grin wherever it came from, no questions asked.

Like one time, this Iraqi guy came driving down the road in the oldest, most fucked-up car you can possibly imagine. No hood. No roof. Bald tires, black smoke pouring out a tailpipe that's so low to the ground it's sending out sparks. When he gets up close, he flashes you the biggest smile you've ever seen in your goddamn life and waves at you like he's king of the world. I don't think I ever saw somebody so happy to drive such a rotten piece of shit. Come to think of it, that time we *did* laugh. We laughed because it was crazy.

When we were off duty, which wasn't often, we played a lot of cards. Spades, mostly. I could hold my own fair enough, but I had nothing on this dude from Seattle, Washington, Dayton Barry from Ghost Troop, third platoon. Dayton was a real smart guy and I guess he'd always played cards. He could whoop anybody in the unit anytime he wanted. Never bragged about it, either—well, once in a while he did. He was quiet if he didn't know someone, but he'd open up if you hung out around him.

We smoked a lot, in fact, we smoked our asses off. I couldn't believe how much we smoked, but it passed the time. Also, it kept the flies and the mosquitoes away, an added bonus. So we sat around bullshitting each other. Told lies. Joked about everything and tried to forget about the bullshit we were going through. The jokes were stupid, but that didn't matter. What mattered is we told them. With everything going on around us, it mattered we were still alive to groan at the bad ones and say, "That sucked."

We saw a lot of kids over there and most of the time they seemed real happy, which made us feel good. Kids're incredible when they're the age where they haven't figured out what sad feels like. We'd mess around with them and say things like, "*Ish da! Ish da!*" which means, "Go away!" They'd giggle and run away five or ten feet but come right back. It was hide-and-seek for them. We were their toys; they'd follow us all over the place.

As a rule, I guess you could say that anytime we thought we were helping the people it made us smile, brightened our spirits. But then the reality would set in that we weren't really helping them at all, we were just breeding more terrorists. That's all that's happening in that country, trust me.

Why do I say that? You have to understand who these people are, how their culture operates. They have a faith, a belief system based on revenge and martyrdom. Think about this: You're a small kid and your dad gets killed by Americans. You loved your dad, you thought he was a great guy. Well, shit, what happens next? You hate Americans, it's that simple. But these people, they're not the kind of folks to do anything half-assed, I assure you. When they get the urge to act on something, they do it, no questions asked. When they cry "jihad," believe me, they fulfill it.

See, this is what I think happened over there: America broke a trust. We said to these people, "We're here to help you." But really, how can we? We don't have the manpower, the funds, or the knowledge to help them the way they need to be helped. Face it, the whole war was a pre-emptive strike that happened for reasons I don't think we'll ever get clear on. The only people who might have an inkling are the people who sent us there. No. I am not in favor of this administration at all.[23]

III

I was medically discharged from the army for two reasons. One, I developed asthma. All my life, I never had it but I noticed I had difficulty breathing during Basic. I got a case of pneumonia in Basic and after that I was never really the same. Basic was just one big gaggle-fuck of disease, anyhow. You've got all these guys walking around, smashed in, living together, bivouacking, not showering. Who knows who's got what. Then I got to the desert, where the heat and the blowing sand bothered me so much I had to wear a face mask. Sometimes I felt fine. Other times I didn't. Adrenaline's a motherfucker. It lets you get things done in the moment but you answer for them later on.

---

23. The administration of U.S. President George W. Bush.

Second reason: I was in a car wreck and hurt my back severely. One day we were returning from patrol on a quiet night. I was in a small convoy, two tanks from the 237th Armored pulling up the rear, two Humvees in front. We were moving down the road in a standard column, four, maybe five kilometers from the base gate. We heard gunshots.

Everyone tracked the sound and shouted, "Contact north! Contact north!" Next thing we saw the flashing lights of Iraqi cop cars speeding toward us, two of them chasing this beat-up orange-and-white SUV jeep taxi that's hauling ass, driving on the wrong side of the road, straight toward us with its lights off.[24] The first thing that went through my mind? Car bomb. No question about it.

The SUV slowed down for a moment, hesitating. The cop cars closed the distance. Then, the SUV's driver stomped his gas and rocketed toward us, which was all we needed to see. Everyone in the Humvees opened fire with their M-16s. Pure instinct.

As best we could tell later on, after everything cooled down, this guy getting chased stole the SUV. The police saw him do it and engaged in pursuit. We knew what happened after that. This is what the Iraqi cops told us had happened, but really? Who knows what the hell was going on? The police in that country were a corrupt bunch of liars, to a man. It's entirely conceivable they just didn't like the guy for some reason and decided to take him out, end of story.

A bunch of M-16s can tear up the chassis of a car pretty good, punch holes in it, twist it, shred it into ribbons. The driver never had a chance. Bullets punched through his windshield and opened him up like a bag full of blood. The car must have been doing sixty when we shot it, and it started to slow down a little. Unfortunately, dead men don't drive so well. The jeep kept coming and collided with my Humvee head on, going about forty miles an hour. I was in the gunner's hatch of my vehicle and the collision snapped my back. My lower spine crushed itself against the ring of the gun turret and my body jackknifed over, folding me in half backward.

---

24. Specialist Simon says, "I noticed a lot of cars in Iraq were painted orange and white. I gathered from our interpreters that Saddam Hussein didn't like having a city full of different-colored cars. So a lot of vehicles ended up with this orange-and-white scheme. There were a lot of taxis in Iraq since most people couldn't afford cars, and all the taxis were painted orange and white, too. The police cars chasing that taxi were newer make—really new. They were painted white and blue."

Iraqi police don't give a fuck about anything. I never saw any of them do their job, they just stood around posing a lot. I don't know if they were scared to commit themselves to anything or if they'd resigned themselves to the fact that they held down the only paying jobs left in the country. I guess I'd get lazy, too, if I had money coming in to support my family, I was armed, and no one could challenge my authority.

After the smoke had cleared, the police were incredibly cool about the incident. Their attitude was like, "Well, see what happens? Another one of these dumb kids? Big fucking deal." They left the shot-up SUV right there in the middle of the street and went on with their business. From what I heard, it was days before they sent a tow truck out to pick it up.

Meanwhile, me and the guys were a little rattled by what happened. Our superiors kept telling us over and over and over again that we'd done the right thing, You have to protect your life and the lives of your fellow soldiers in a war zone. Turns out I was the only one who got hurt. They evaced me via FLA[25] and admitted me to a tiny hospital, where the doctors checked me out and gave me some muscle relaxants to ease the spasms. I stayed the night. For the next three days I was ordered to relax. I wasn't allowed to go out on patrol, which was fine by me. After that, it was business as usual.

But this is how fucked up the army is. Clearly I had sustained my injury during combat. A superior of mine said, "I'm going to start the paperwork to get you your Purple Heart."[26] I told him, "Well, you know, I wasn't shot or anything." To which the guy said, "Uh-uh, that's not how it works. Shit happens, you sustained an injury. You got fucked up? You deserve the medal." Apparently not, though. I was denied my Purple Heart. Word came back down the line that my injury was a bullshit reason to justify the award. To which I said, "Okay, I could understand that point of view." Again, it's not like I got shot.

Later on, though, I bumped into an officer whose name I won't utter

---

25. Field land ambulance—rather like a Humvee equipped with stretchers in the back.
26. An American military decoration. Originally created as the Badge of Military Merit by George Washington, the Purple Heart was the first military award made available to the common American soldier. It is now the oldest military decoration in service in modern armies throughout the world. Currently, the Purple Heart is awarded to members of the U.S. armed forces who are wounded by an instrument of war in the hands of an enemy. It is bestowed posthumously to the next of kin for soldiers killed in action, or as a direct result of wounds sustained in action.

here. This guy got a Purple Heart from a scratch he sustained on his arm when an Iraqi kid threw a rock at him. No shit. It wasn't even a combat situation. Get this, he got *scratched*. Here I had to kill some guy by splattering his brains across the front seat of his car to keep myself and my buddies alive. I got my spine twisted into a fucking pretzel and this guy gets hit with a rock and goes, "Ouch." Congratulations, you just won the Purple Heart. Fucking officers.

To this day, I still go to physical therapy. Looks like my back won't ever be right again, but I guess that's just the way it goes. Shit. Looking back on it now? I don't want their damn medal, anyway.

I didn't ask to be discharged, it just became more and more noticeable I couldn't keep up with PT anymore. I couldn't run with my guys; my breathing choked up and I'd fall behind. It got so bad that the army sent me to see a doctor who examined me and shook her head. She said, I'm going to start proceedings for a medical discharge. Mind you, I didn't say no. By that point, I was ready to go home. I'd served four of my six-year contract. I'd seen enough of the army and Iraq and all of it. I felt like I'd been fucked over too many times.

In Kosovo, for instance, before the war. My Kosovo posting was fucking bullshit. The army's been established there since '99 or so, and all my unit did was man guard towers on a base where nothing happened. Who were we guarding against? I understand that region had problems a few years back, but there sure as hell wasn't anything going on while I stood watch. The Russians were pulling out, the Greeks were gone. Nobody else in the so-called Coalition was sticking around and, in my opinion, keeping American armed forces in a place like that is an incredible waste of taxpayer money.

I wasn't back from Kosovo three months before they shipped me out to Iraq for thirteen more. The long deployments took a toll on my wife. I mean, hell, the army wasn't my life, my *family* is my life. I want to see my son grow up. I want to be there when he starts to change. I see it all very clearly now, family's the only thing that matters in life. When the army offered discharge, yeah, I took it. Gladly.

I work for the Texas Forest Service now, dispatching crews to handle forest fires whenever they pop up. In southeast Texas, we've got a lot of pine trees and oaks that spark from time to time. We get a few grass fires, too. It's a good job and I feel like I'm doing something useful and important. In Iraq, I didn't feel that at all.

Okay. Last thing. What I'd really like people to know is this: do your best to weed through all the bullshit the media's feeding you about this war. I'm talking about MSNBC, CNN, the networks. They've got their own agenda. They're trying to sedate the American public by keeping things muted. They know that if Americans got wind of some of the things really happening in Iraq, there'd be outrage and revolution here in the United States. Revolution. I honestly believe that.

I've actually noticed some things that've led me to believe this is already happening. People are getting fed up. They've been fed shit their whole lives through a shit tube the government's had them hooked up to since we were little kids. Listen to me. The government doesn't have all the answers. The government's *hiding* a lot of answers and creating more problems. I want to tell people this: Get away from the mainstream news. Invest your time wisely. Pull information from organizations like Free Speech TV, *Democracy NOW*, they give pure commentary on what's going on in Iraq. Benjamin Franklin said, "The first responsibility of every American is to question authority." Please. Don't turn away from what's really going on.

CONVOY RUNS

✯

Specialist Tina Garnanez
EMTB [EMERGENCY MEDICAL TECHNICIAN BASIC] WITH THE 557TH GROUND
AMBULANCE COMPANY, ATTACHED TO THE FIRST INFANTRY DIVISION

Famously known as the Big Red One, First Infantry Division is the oldest continuously serving division in the U.S. Army. Before deploying to Iraq, Specialist Garnanez, age 24, was stationed in Germany and Kosovo. She hails from Farmington, New Mexico, a town of about 41,000 people, where oil, gas, and mining form the major industries.

An AK-47 fires a devastating round that will totally destroy human tissue. The amount of blood and bandages needed to stop a wound was staggering. I'd carry a stretcher off the ambulance and work to keep my focus, head up, firm grip, legs moving forward. The soldiers on the litters were covered with blood and screaming. It was all I could do to not get upset.

I had to change uniforms a lot. Every time I helped the wounded come off convoys or helicopters, the soldiers' blood would spill right off and stain my clothes. That's part of the job, but it's very unsettling.

I joined the army right out of high school in 2000. I come from a lower-income, single-parent household and I needed money for college. I figured the army was a pretty good place to go in, do four years, get the money, and get out. When I joined up, there was no September 11th, no Saddam, so I figured I'd be safe. As it turned out, I got deployed to a war zone.

We landed in Tikrit. My unit was tasked to work as the medical team for local firefighters, but we also pulled hospital duty and responded to calls as you'd expect EMTs to do in the States—base emergencies, city emergencies, and so forth. The only real difference was that, because we worked in a war zone, we frequently responded to mass casualty incidents. There was also a level of impact difference. You could go two years working in Farmington and not see what I saw working two days in Iraq. You don't see a lot of bullet wounds, IED [improvised explosive device] wounds, and shrapnel in New Mexico.

A typical day started by waking up to loud booms. I always wondered if it was enemy mortars, controlled explosions, or what, and I never got an answer to that. Suffice it to say that morning explosions were the norm in Tikrit. I'd pull on my uniform and wonder what was going to happen to me that day. Would the assignment I pulled put me in harm's way? I was always conscious that this could be my last day on earth. That thought and many others crossed my mind all the time, especially in the morning.

Pulling fire station duty was a good thing because I'd report for duty and sit around waiting for an alarm, which didn't happen frequently. Hospital duty was pretty much the same thing, you hung around and waited for somebody to say, "You're needed here." But then there were convoy days. They were the worst. I dreaded convoy days, because that meant we'd have to drive out into the country, completely vulnerable, moving targets in the middle of the Sunni Triangle.[27]

Essentially, we rode as medics for transportation units delivering supplies from base to base. We drove an army ambulance, which was a modified Humvee with a thing like a camper hatch on the back. The hatch had four litters which you could swing up into position. With the litters down, you could double your passenger capacity and fit eight bodies seated on benches.

You couldn't expect the ambulances to be armored. Sometimes we got lucky, though, and they'd let us use a model with armored doors. We scrounged up any materials we could and made do. Sandbags piled onto the floorboards kept IED blasts from coming up from below and taking

---

27. The so-called Sunni Triangle, a roughly triangular area of Iraq that lies northwest of Baghdad mostly inhabited by Sunni tribesmen, the group to which Saddam Hussein and most of his senior personnel belonged. For the sake of ease, one could imagine an upright triangle whose lower eastern point is in or around the city of Baghdad, whose lower western point is in or around the city of Ramadi, and whose upper point lies in or around the city of Tikrit. The Triangle contain the cities of Samarra and Fallujah. Immediately following the invasion in 2003, the Sunni Triangle became a hotbed of armed, anti-Coalition opposition. The Sunni Triangle, however, should not be confused with the Triangle of Death, a Sunni- and Shia-dominated area south of Baghdad that became the staging ground for heavy combat in the late autumn and early winter of 2004.

our legs off. We ran Kevlar blankets under and over the seats in case shrapnel hit us at midsections. We hung them in the back, too, to give our patients protection. But I should reiterate that this was all a best-case scenario. Sometimes we went out in a vehicle that didn't have any protection at all.

We were jam-packed with life-saving equipment. We carried C-collars [cervical collar], which are those thick braces used for neck injuries, and blankets for casualties. We had Sked devices, these durable plastic sled-like contraptions that unfold neatly from a case; you use them to drag wounded bodies here and there. We had our aid bags which were full of bandages, IV fluids, needles, QuikClot,[28] tourniquets, knives, penlights, BP [blood pressure] cuffs, stethoscopes, the works.

It's standard procedure for medics to travel under international Red Cross markings so we had placards on the sides of the Humvee that operated like flaps. With the flaps open, our medic insignias were displayed, huge red crosses on white fields. With the flaps down, you couldn't distinguish our vehicle from the others in the column. There was a big debate over whether we should travel with the flaps opened or closed, but to understand that argument, you had to try crawling inside the mind of the enemy.

Clearly, the open flaps set us apart from the rest of the group, making us potential targets. But no, some people argued, "insurgents won't shoot at medical personnel." "You're joking," said other people. "You think these people really follow the Geneva Conventions? They behead American civilians and post the footage on the Internet." The way they saw it, they'd want to take out the medics first. Do that and there's no one left to help the wounded.

Personally, I agreed with that line of thinking. From what I saw, the Geneva Conventions didn't translate well in Tikrit. Eventually, we opened and closed the flaps according to orders from Command. That's what happens in the army; you follow orders. But I have to tell you: Every time we traveled with open flaps, I was terrified. To me, it was a clear invitation for someone to shoot at us.

---

28. A brand-name hemostatic agent for sterile treatment of traumatic wounds. QuikClot comes in packets as a fine powder, which, when sprinkled on open wounds, rapidly arrests high-volume blood loss.

Convoys ranged from fifteen to twenty vehicles. Most vehicles were big diesel eighteen-wheelers; driven by TCNs [third-country nationals].[29] Between every five of these, we'd have a gun truck provided by the transportation unit. Our ambulance always brought up the rear.

Don't ask me what was in the eighteen-wheelers; nobody ever told me and I never asked. We responded to orders by showing up at the appointed time, checking our equipment, and falling into the convoy. The logistics of what we hauled never became clear to me. I wondered from time to time, but it wouldn't have made any difference if it was paper or plutonium.

It was a nerve-racking job. When my unit received convoy orders, everyone held their breath to hear who got assigned. If it wasn't you, you heaved a big sigh. If you were selected, you just kept on holding your breath. You didn't want to let it out cause you knew you'd need it in the desert.

Whenever I was selected, I went through a little preparation ritual. I made sure I had pictures of my family with me, and made sure I had proper ID in case anything happened. Then it was all about packing up the vehicle, making sure that my partner and I carried all the proper supplies. My hands would shake a lot when I was packing. It was tough to keep from thinking, *Okay. I'm going to die today. Relax, I'm going to die.*

Before EMTs reported for their assigned duty, everyone in my unit would get together and hug. We said, "I love you" and "Hurry back safe. Let me know when you get in." If you were lucky enough not to be sent out, you'd see the assigned soldiers off then sit down to wait. In many ways, that was worse, the waiting. You'd go about your duties trying to put your mind on other things but you always found yourself asking people, "Is so-and-so back yet? Have you heard from him or her?" When medics came back alive, we'd repeat the good-bye ritual. Everyone gathered around and hugged, only this time we'd say, "I love you. Good to see you. Thanks for coming back in one piece."

My company had roughly 380 soldiers, but we all weren't stationed together. We had one platoon in Al Asad, another in Balad. We must've had three platoons total in Tikrit, about eighty soldiers. With everyone

---

29. According to Garnanez, "The drivers could have been Iraqis, Kurds, Turks, who knew? They were from the region, that's all we knew."

so spread out, we always wondered what was happening to our friends. The 557th was a pretty tight group. We hated not knowing what was going on with other members of our family assigned to other regions.

We ventured further out from time to time, but our convoys mostly went to small bases within the Sunni Triangle—Mosul, Balad, Kirkuk, and a few other locations. The longest trip was to Mosul, which took about four hours. On average, we'd join convoys two weeks out of every month. That's a lot of driving under adverse conditions, by which I mean we took a constant barrage of fire from AK-47s, RPGs, and IEDs. I can think of only one or two convoys where something *didn't* happen. Peaceful drives were shocking occasions.

The enemy capitalized on the fact that we were way out in the open with very little protection. They knew the land well and set up very effective assaults. They'd fire from sand dunes flowing by the side of the highway. They'd blast us from the rooftops and windows of buildings we passed near. They placed IEDs under tiny rock piles by the side of a road and detonated them with cell phones to block us from going over bridges or down certain roads. I hate to admit it, but the insurgents were very creative. I was always a little astounded by how clever their ambushes could be. Basically, convoy jobs became about climbing into a truck which sometimes had a huge target painted on it, and driving directly into enemy territory so we could get shot at.

How did I keep from going insane? When I wasn't on duty, I read a lot, I painted, I wrote letters. I'm a practicing Buddhist, so I meditated and tried to keep my thoughts positive, tried not to become bitter. As I saw it, the biggest temptation would be to view the Iraqis as enemies. Even while they were shooting at us, I tried to see them as people. To embrace any other point of view would have consumed me with hatred or anger, and I didn't want to do that, not to another person and not to myself. Buddhists have strong beliefs against doing harm.

My partner and I took turns driving. We listened to the convoy over the army-band radio and played our own music through a little stereo system we'd rigged up. It wasn't loud and it wasn't clear, but it was better than listening to the engine and waiting to get shot at. We had excellent blues on tap—Muddy Waters, B. B. King, Janis Joplin, and Jimi Hendrix. Luckily, my partner and I had similar tastes. Deciding what music to play was the same as you'd do here in the states if you're going on a long drive. We'd laugh, share stories, get to know each other, and take turns playing DJ.

You kept your eyes peeled, though. Didn't matter if you were driving or not. You scanned ahead, you scanned side to side. You checked the rearview mirror for any signs of activity. Any little motion, anything at all could set up an attack. Weapons were kept locked and loaded from the moment we left the base gates.

My first near-death experience on a convoy happened like this. We were coming home, cruising along, playing Jimi Hendrix. Everything looked good. My partner was driving and I noticed a decrepit old building creeping up on us off to my left. I thought, *Hmmm, that looks like a good place for ambushers to hide.* The next thing I knew, something exploded in front of our vehicle.

I don't remember what came first, the bright orange flash leaping up from the side of the road or the roar. The next thing I knew we were driving through a cloud of dust and smoke. A tornado of shrapnel and dirt slammed against the windshield. I closed my eyes because I thought, *This is it. I'm dead.* But when I opened my eyes again I heard a voice screaming over the wail of Jimi's guitar. "Go, medics! Go, go! Get outta there!" It was the convoy chief on the radio. My partner was screaming, "What was that? What was that?" He was out of his mind with panic, we both were. He punched the accelerator and the ambulance shot forward. The whole column was picking up speed now, trying to get away.

The shock started to wear off and my senses leaked back in. I could feel my heart pounding in my chest, and that's when I first realized, *Aha! I'm not dead, otherwise my heart would have stopped.* "Shit," I said. "Oh, shit." Then—it's funny how the mind works. My thoughts spun instantly into medic mode: Airway, breathing, circulation, stop the bleeding. I thought the vehicle in front of us had been hit so I had a full plan ready in seconds. I'd leap from our vehicle and start pulling the wounded out of the truck in front of us.

As it turned out, the blast had come from an IED. The bomb had gone off dead center in the gap between us and the truck in front of us. If we'd been traveling any slower, it would've killed the lead truck. Any faster, it would've killed us. The convoy went two or three miles further down the road before stopping to make sure everyone was okay. We got lucky, everyone was fine. My partner and I didn't say another word to each other until we got home. We drove two hours in silence. What could we say? We were both trying to process the fact that we'd nearly died.

It wasn't until we were back on base with the gates closed behind us that my partner looked at me and said, "You took that really well. You didn't scream or anything." I said, "Thanks. You, too." And that was it.

I was fortunate. Despite all the fire we took, no convoy I rode in suffered any casualties. Other medics weren't so lucky. The stories I heard when people got back to base. A lot of times we'd sit there, listening. When someone was finished, the only thing you could think to say was, "Wow."

Like the one where this Hummer in a convoy drove right over an IED. The blast demolished the right front tire. No Kevlar blankets on that trip; the explosion went up through the floorboards and hit the female soldier sitting in the passenger seat.

The convoy stopped and the medics started up the column. By the time they arrived, soldiers had already pulled the female and her partner from the vehicle. They were lying on their backs in the road. When the medic moved in to treat her, he could hear her saying, "That's okay. I'm fine. No, really. I'm good."

The medic said, "I've got to treat you," and he moved closer. "No," she said. "Check my partner." The medic said, "Somebody's with him already, I'm here to take care of you." But she kept saying she was fine. "Don't worry about me, I know I'm gonna die."

The medic looked down at her and thought, *What is this woman talking about?* He couldn't see any wounds. He knelt down and began his assessment.

We're trained to do what we call a sweep. Start at the head, insert your fingers under the patient's body, pull them out to check for blood. If you don't find any, keep moving down the body, moving to the neck, the shoulder blades, the torso, and so on. The medic didn't find any blood until he got to her pelvis. Then he rolled her over, and that's when he saw that her entire back side was gone. No flesh at all. Blood pouring out all over the place.

"It's okay," the woman said, "I know, I know. It's okay."

It was such a big wound. There was nothing he could do. I'm glad I didn't have that case.

Some wounds can be treated. You put a tourniquet on limbs, apply QuikClot and bandages for most everything else, though you have to be careful with sucking chest wounds, spurting blood, and head trauma.

Some wounds can't be treated. Like when you meet a soldier from a different company and strike up a conversation. Just like that, you've made a new friend. Maybe you're into the same music, or maybe you grew up near to one another. You've got the same favorite baseball team. You share stories, pull pictures out of your wallet and pass them around. For a moment, you share everything. Their kids become your kids, you live a little sliver of their life. You shake hands and promise to keep in touch. You mean it, too. Then the convoy moves on and everyone gets on with their business.

A few weeks later, you're working with that company again. You don't see your friend around anywhere so you ask, "Hey, where'd he go?" The look on everybody's faces says it all. "Last week," they say. "In a convoy. He didn't make it. I'm sorry."

No matter how many times this happens, it never seems right. *No, you think. How can that be? I was just talking to him, seems like yester-day.* For a while, you're confused. Then it sinks in and you start breathing again and that's it. They're not here anymore. That's what a war is, people disappear, just like that. It makes no sense at all, it could be you. Time to go back on duty.

The Iraqis we saw as we drove through towns didn't seem to care we were there. They'd stare at our vehicles passing by; some didn't even look at us, they just went about their business. I never saw a smiling child, they all looked desperate, they'd approach us for food. Some of the children looked very angry. They'd flip us off as we drove by and I always wondered if they actually knew what that gesture means. At any rate, we weren't welcomed with roses.

I think that might have had a lot to do with the fact that we were in the Sunni Triangle. Saddam was a Sunni; he was born in Tikrit. These people had been his power base. Not anymore. All over the region, we saw statues of Saddam, murals painted on the sides of buildings, every-thing fashioned in his likeness. It was insane, like he was some kind of god. Many of these works had been defaced by gunshots and explosions, but whether that was our doing or the Iraqis, I don't know.

I noticed the violence escalated during my year in-country. When we first arrived, some places in our region were safe—Kirkuk, for instance, or Mosul. Each convoy that went out filed a report when it returned. The results of those reports were marked on a big map we kept of the triangle. Pins would be added to mark the hot zones, and each pin had a little note attached to it that said things like, IED ATTACK, 2 SOLDIERS DEAD, then a date when that occurred. When I first arrived, that map was mostly blank. By the time I left, it was covered with pins. You could hardly see the map at all.

I find it interesting that the war began in March of 2003. In May of 2003, President Bush declared the end to all major fighting; 198 American soldiers had been killed. By January 2006, that number was up to two thousand two hundred and something.[30] How is that possible if all major fighting was finished?

What is violence in the first place but an escalation of anger? Because of my Buddhist beliefs, I could sympathize with the Iraqi people. Look at how they might have viewed us. Here come the Americans. We enter their country, destroy everything, then drive up and down the streets threatening to kill anybody who dared do what we did. A lot of our soldiers had no respect whatsoever for Iraqis. They called them "towel heads" and reduced them to stereotypes. Then they'd go out on missions and shoot at a farmer's livestock, robbing him of sustenance. It was all a big joke to them.

What good does that do? How could anyone conscience that sort of action? How would that feel if someone destroyed your livelihood? Your daily bread? Your means of putting food on the table for your family? But these soldiers would laugh and say, "Ha-ha, that was so cool. I just wasted that old man's sheep!" That disgusted me.

On the same day the helicopters came to take my group home, a bomb attack took out a troop dining facility in Mosul. A lot of soldiers were killed. So no, I don't believe the White House and the Pentagon when they say things like, "Everything's under control." From what I saw over there, they're lying through their teeth, and I'm sick of it.

―――――――

30. On January 17, 2006, the official Department of Defense number of soldiers killed in Iraq was, 2,205.

No, I'm not in favor of this war. I believe it's illegal and immoral, a bunch of lies from start to finish. It's nothing but the greedy agenda of a few who speak for the many. A lot of soldiers I served with felt the same way, but among soldiers there's this attitude of resignation. It's like, "Well, that's what we're here for and there's nothing we can do." Speaking your mind isn't part of a soldier's job. You swallow your feelings and go about your business. Other soldiers and I would air our concerns in small groups, but the moment someone who outranked us walked by, we'd clam up. Dissension or free thought invites higher-ups to make things bad for you.

Now that I'm out of the service, I've made it my mission to speak out. This war isn't about what they say it's about. It's not about terrorism or spreading freedom and democracy—if it was, I'd be all for it. Honestly, I feel it's about oil. I've read enough and seen enough at this point to think that it couldn't be about anything else. I hear people listing reasons why the war is right, and all I hear are rationalizations. I can't wrap my head around that, the fact that everyone's kidding themselves while a country is burning.

Since I got home, I've been protesting. I go to rallies and vigils, I speak at schools and universities whenever someone asks me to. Sometimes I do radio and TV interviews. And every Tuesday afternoon from four P.M. to five, I join two or three other people and we stand out in the street of our home town with signs that say IRAQ VETERANS AGAINST THE WAR. Sometimes we list the current death toll and write HOW MANY MORE? Some people honk and wave, but a lot of people flip us off and yell, "Get a life!" which I think is ridiculous. I have a life. I lived part of it in Iraq. I saw what I saw. Did you?

I was on a Bring Them Home Now bus rally headed for Washington, D.C., and we stopped in some small Southern town. This woman walked right up to us. She read our signs, then she got this queer look on her face. She looked up at me, and with all seriousness she asked, "Is that war still going on?" I couldn't believe my ears. I was like, Where has this woman been?

I'll say it again, some wounds can't be treated. Now that I'm home, I'll find myself driving downtown and it's hard. I'm watching the road, I'm watching the movement on the sidewalks, I take special note of people carrying packages, I'm constantly on edge. When I enter a room now, I always check my corners and note the exits. If I sit, I sit facing the door. I have nightmares, sure, but some of them happen while I'm wide awake.

Sometimes I can't sleep at all. If someone drops a plate in a restaurant, I'm halfway under the table before I realize it's not a hand grenade coming in through the window. Forget about fireworks on the Fourth of July. I tried to watch them this year and it freaked me out. The moment the flares started going off, all I could think about was enemy soldiers charging in. Call it post-traumatic stress disorder. Call it whatever you want. I'm not the same woman I was when I left.

I get angry like never before and I don't know how to change that behavior. I know it isn't normal and I want to shut it off. I want to get therapy through the VA, but when I sit down to do the paperwork, the forms ask questions like "What specific incident makes you believe you need help? Please list the date of the occurrence and a description of the details." I sit down with the very best intentions and start to answer. Then, in the middle of it all, I get overwhelmed. I have to put it away. I'll get to it next week. Or the next. Or the next. The process of reporting the problem reinforces the problem.

Then I watch them closing VA hospitals on the news, cutting back on vet benefits, and I have to shake my head. How can they do that? The army seduced all these young soldiers with glossy brochures and cool videos. They put them in a hot zone to get shot at and wounded, maybe even killed. If they were anything like me, those soldiers were in Iraq thinking, *Holy shit. This is nothing like my recruiter said it would be.*

They come home missing a limb, or they come home paralyzed. They come home maybe with nothing wrong on the surface, but there's always something there. Sometimes they don't come home at all. The government's actions make it clear that they just don't care and you think, *Wait a minute. I thought you loved me. You said if I did my job right, I'd be welcomed home with open arms and you'd take care of me.*

I'll say this for the army, they were smooth. They got what they wanted out of us, then they threw us to the curb. So where do we go from here?

THE BOMBING OF THE UN HEADQUARTERS AND A VERY UNLIKELY LIMOUSINE

✢

First Sergeant William von Zehle
411TH CIVIL AFFAIRS BATTALION, U.S. ARMY RESERVE, BASED OUT OF DANBURY, CONNECTICUT

Bill von Zehle, age 54, is a former Wall Street specialist clerk and retired civilian fire chief. Currently, he works as an antiterrorism instructor at the JFK Special Warfare Center and School. He's been married for thirty years to his wife, Emma, and together they have a twenty-one-year old daughter, Alexandra.

For those who don't know, this much should be stated: a Civil Affairs battalion advises unit commanders of their legal obligations under the Geneva Conventions to both enemy combatants and local civilians. Civil Affairs also conducts reconnaissance to designate no-fire zones that protect hospitals, schools, mosques, and places of antiquity—anything that cannot or should not be attacked. A Civil Affairs unit might also meet clandestinely with the local population to establish better relations with incoming American forces. These meetings often minimize civilian casualties and collateral damage.

I

In 1972, I was ROTC [Reserve Officer Training Corps] at Alfred University in upstate New York. My dad was very pro-military and my mother—at least for the duration of the Vietnam War—was not. The way things were going back then, I was likely going to be commissioned into the army and sent to Vietnam. But my dad had a friend in the military, a newly minted brigadier general, whom I contacted. I admitted I was confused about the war and mentioned that I was working for my college paper. Dad's friend said, "Well, I could probably get you over there on a press pass. That way you could see what's going on for yourself." So that's what happened. I got clearance to take a seventeen-day trip to Vietnam—strictly as an observer—so long as I paid my own way.

It was an eye-opening experience. I found myself riding convoys going up into the highlands. In ROTC, we'd done everything by straight and narrow military protocol, but there's a military term called "ground truth" and in Vietnam I began to learn what that meant. The soldiers I saw—well, their uniforms were anything but uniform. They wore cutoff jungle fatigue pants with T-shirts and bandanas wrapped around their heads. I saw very few officers or senior NCOs[31] in charge, everyone kind of ran their own thing. The whole operation was a far cry from the strict regimentation I'd been taught in ROTC.

Remember, this was 1972. America would be out of Vietnam by '73, so the Vietnamization process was in full force by then. Morale among the soldiers I talked to was bad. None of them wanted to be the last to die in a war the U.S. was abandoning. Everyone I talked to joked that Vietnamization was a euphemism for "losing the war with honor." The military was turning things over to the Vietnamese people and the Vietnamese people weren't ready. You need proof? Two years after we left, the enemy came sweeping out of the highlands and took Saigon.

I'm not proud of this, but when I got back home? I decided I wanted nothing further to do with the military. I dropped out of Alfred University and transferred to NYU. Since there wasn't an ROTC program within fifty miles of NYU, my contract with the corps was voided. But I was left with this massive guilt. I'd only completed three out of the four years for ROTC, and deep down I knew I hadn't fulfilled a commitment.

After college I worked for E. F. Hutton on the floor of the New York Stock Exchange. My parents had moved out of the city to suburban Westchester County, where I became a volunteer firefighter. I loved it. In fact, I loved it so much that my new wife finally asked me, "Do you really like working on Wall Street? If you enjoy being a firefighter so much,

31. Noncommissioned officers are enlisted soldiers (or sailors) who have been delegated leadership or command authority by commissioned officers. An experienced NCO corps is a very important part of a highly functioning Western-style army. Sergeants are well-known examples of NCOs.

why don't you go back, get another degree, and pursue it full time?" I think she probably meant it as a joke, but it made a lot of sense to me. So I went back to school and got an associate's degree in fire science from Westchester Community College. After that, I applied for career firefighter positions while I moved up the ranks as a volunteer. Eventually, I applied for a job as fire chief out in Michigan at a small department that had only two career firefighters. I got hired, so my wife and I packed up everything and headed northwest. For the next ten years I was chief of the Comstock Fire Department just east of Kalamazoo.

I met a friend out there, a police chief who served in an Civil Affairs Army Reserve unit. In 1984 he said, "Bill, why don't you join the reserve? We use all kinds of people with civilian skills in Civil Affairs—policemen, firefighters, hospital administrators, you name it." Well, that made a lot of sense to me, too. I felt like it gave me an opportunity to get closure on the military commitment I'd abandoned twelve years before. So I joined up with the reserve and I've been with them ever since.

My wife and I moved back east at the end of '87 to take care of my mom when her health started to fail, and I got a job as chief of the Wilton Fire Department in Connecticut, spent fifteen years there before retiring. Right after that, I got shipped to Iraq. I was serving as the operations NCO for my unit, so I was one of the first guys who received our orders. Hell, it wasn't the first time I'd been called for duty. I'd been to the Gulf War in '90–'91 and Bosnia in '95–'96. After 9/11, I had this feeling it wouldn't be long before we went out again because the regular military has a very limited Civil Affairs capability. There's only one active-duty CA battalion and something like twenty-four Reserve battalions. Obviously that one active-duty battalion can't cover the whole world. Anytime there's a conflict and you're in a Reserve CA unit, you expect to mobilize.

Once I got the orders, we implemented a plan for my unit and we premobilized in January of 2003. By February, we were down at Fort Bragg. In March, we shipped off to Kuwait, the jumping-off point to enter Iraq.

Civil Affairs evolved from the old World War II model of military theory where you go into a country *after* a war and set up a government. But in 1986, the Goldwater-Nichols Bill merged CA into the Special

Operations Command, so the mission of Civil Affairs changed significantly. Nowadays we'll frequently go into a region *before* an attack. During battles, we'll maneuver with combat battalions as if we're regular troops, but we're not regular troops, not really. Nowadays—in theory, at least—a team of four to six CA operators will accompany every maneuvering battalion going into a hot region. This way we can get to work immediately after the smoke clears. In a best-case scenario, we're able to prevent the destruction of civil assets before a single shot is fired.

A big part of CA's job is to win the hearts and minds of a local population. Unfortunately a lot of movers and shakers at the Pentagon don't really understand this. Case in point: just before the Gulf War ended, my unit was stationed in western Iraq, just outside of Basra. We were supporting the Third Armored Division. Now, Basra had about a half million people holed up in it, plus several Republican Guard divisions and a few more divisions of regular army. This was a very heavily fortified city.

On what turned out to be the last night of the ground war, a brigade commander of Third Armored came up with this brilliant idea. He wanted four Civil Affairs guys to jump into two unarmored Humvees and drive into Basra holding a white flag. He wanted us to ride right up to the mayor of Basra and inform him that, if he didn't declare Basra an open city, we'd roll right in and kick their asses.

Well. This didn't seem like a great plan to us. In fact, we thought it was a suicide mission. Don't get me wrong, we would have done it. We weren't like that Reserve unit you heard about, the one that refused an order.[32] No, we'd all written our last letters home, we'd made out our wills, we would have gone. But I'll admit we were actively trying to dissuade the commander when, fortunately, the cease-fire took effect the

---

32. Breaking news on October 16, 2004, indicated that up to nineteen members of a platoon from the 343rd Quartermaster Company—a reserve unit based in Rock Hill, South Carolina—were "under investigation" after they allegedly refused to transport supplies from Tallil air base near Nasiriyah to Taji, north of Baghdad. The particulars of this report changed over the next few days, but the soldiers maintained that their mission to transport contaminated, useless fuel through dangerous enemy territory in poorly maintained vehicles unequipped with proper armor plating was an inappropriate order. The incident sparked massive controversy over the state of command in an already controversial war. It also seemed to dovetail with a December 2003 letter to the Pentagon sent by army Lieutenant General Ricardo Sanchez, commander of U.S. forces in Iraq from mid-2003 to the summer of 2004. As disclosed by the *Washington Post*, Sanchez wrote of a severe lack of supplies and key parts for equipment vital to the overall mission. As well as noting how adversely the shortage affected his troops' combat ability, Sanchez called the problem so severe that, "I cannot continue to support sustained combat operations with rates this low."

next morning, shooting ended, and we never got outside the wire. Fine by me.

To offer a bit of comparison: everything I observed in the Gulf War went almost perfectly in accordance with what the army calls an "air-land battle," that is: a synchronization of air and ground forces. Then, after the war ended, the humanitarian side of things went pretty well, too. I found myself in southern Iraq providing MedCap missions; we'd go into these little villages and provide medical care and food. We weren't met with open arms, but the people tolerated us. Later on, they actually became very friendly—they'd bring *us* food, for instance. Iraqis by nature don't like to wait in line but there were sufficient supplies to go around. Loose ends got secured and things got done. We left the country in a fairly timely manner and I thought, *Okay. Mission accomplished.* I thought this latest war in Iraq would be similar to that. But it didn't go quite so well.

This time around we worked with the Third Armored Cavalry Regiment for six months predeployment. We'd built up a great relationship with them, a real understanding of how to work together. But then our orders changed last minute. We arrived in Kuwait and found out we weren't going to be working with Third Armored Cav at all, we'd be working with the Second Cav.

We arrived to the war theater, in March of 2003. Second Cav had moved out several days previous, so this turned out to be a tremendous pain in the ass. Not only did we have to play catch-up in a war zone, but—I reiterate—it's essential for CA units to have good relationships with the units they support. Tough to do when you're meeting one another for the first time after the shooting's started. Eventually, we caught up to the Second Cavalry in An Najaf[33] where the Imam Ali mosque[34] is, but that snafu should have been the first indication that things weren't going as planned. We inquired about the shift of assignments and were told that there hadn't been enough sea or air transportation to get the Third Armored into the war in time. As things turned out, they got stuck back in Fort Carson, Colorado.

---

33. An Najaf is considered an Islamic holy city and contains, among other sites of religious importance, one of the largest cemeteries in the world where, according to Imam Ali ibn Abi Talib—cousin to the Prophet Muhammad and fourth caliph (656-661)—any Muslim buried there shall enter paradise. Several notable prophets are buried in Najaf.
34. One of Shia Muslims' holiest shrines.

In Najaf, the members of my unit introduced ourselves to the local imams [Islamic clerics]. We were hoping to create a rapport. We'd strip off our helmets whenever we entered their presence, but we always stayed armed; we'd sling our rifles and keep our sidearms. We were soldiers, after all, and soldiers never surrender their weapons. By the same token, we never used them to threaten. Sometimes we'd go out on patrol with the active-duty guys who had a very different mentality. They'd sit in the turrets of their Humvees scanning the streets like the whole scene was about to become another Mogadishu. The U.S. regulars always had their weapons ready and the locals clearly resented that. We were always ready, too; don't get me wrong, it was a war zone. We just maintained our readiness in a less obviously threatening way.

In fact, one imam asked me, "Are you in the same army they're in?" He'd point to the regular army guys, then point to my CA troops who were all wearing boonie caps instead of helmets.

"Yes," I said, "same army." "But you're so different," the Imam said. "You come to us as friends, those men come as Crusaders." Which is just about the biggest insult you can get from a Muslim.

The point is that civilians could identify CA troops right away, and we encouraged that. We maintained all sorts of visual clues. We had tan trucks, for instance, whereas the active-duty troops had green trucks. And because of little distinctions like this, we were treated very well. My guys were treated as liberators.

The military part of our operation seemed to go well. About the only thing we found frustrating was the "Just in Time" supply system set up by Secretary Rumsfeld and his staff. "Just in Time" is a very common system in the civilian world. For instance, you don't keep huge stockpiles of material and food lying around your house, do you? Of course not. You get your supplies as you need them: you get them Just in Time. The higher-ups tried implementing this same system for the military. It didn't work; we always found ourselves running low on food, water, and bullets. By low, I mean that we routinely fell below our basic load, but it never got so bad that we ran out.

The supply situation eased off a bit once we started using Iraqi weapons. I had an AK-47 and a Makarov pistol, you could pick them off the bodies of dead Iraqis, which were lying around all over the place. Bodies frequently carried ammunition, too, so—no supply shortage there.

Plus Saddam Hussein had stockpiled ammunition all over Iraq. The entire country was basically one giant arms warehouse you could pick and choose from. Once we arrived in Baghdad, we found that schools had been converted into arms storage facilities. Of course, this violates the Geneva Conventions, but Saddam didn't seem to have any qualms. We found boxes and crates containing thousands and thousands of rounds for Soviet-made weapons stockpiled in the classrooms. Large shells like 155 mm artillery rounds were just lying around out in the open, take your pick.

I have to say, I liked my AK. Aside from the plentiful ammunition, they worked better in the desert than American-made rifles. M-16s tend to jam if you don't lubricate them properly. When you do lubricate them, the gun oil gets clogged up with sand and the mechanism jams anyway.

We stayed with the Second Cav all the way to Baghdad. The initial attack forces entered the city on the ninth of April; my group followed on the eleventh. We went in as two detachments of thirty-four people each. My detachment covered the eastern half of Baghdad; we were the first American presence in that region of the city. The other group covered the southwest corner.

It was deathly silent as our convoy rolled in. The Second Cavalry is a light cavalry regiment, so they were in Humvees instead of tanks or Bradleys. Saddam's spokesman had gone on TV while our tanks were rolling up to his back door and raved that Iraqi forces would drive the American infidels out. Obviously that hadn't happened. The local men, women, and children were standing on the streets of this major city, staring at our vehicles as we passed by. I think they were a little in shock.

Now an army guy never likes to give the air force credit. But rolling into Baghdad, you could see how amazing our precision bombing had been preceding the ground forces. Second Cav set up their headquarters in a former security compound where the main building had taken four direct hits from JDAM [joint direct attack munitions] bombs.[35] Imagine

35. JDAMs are not explosives themselves, but tail kits designed to upgrade existing inventory, thereby producing high-accuracy, all-weather, autonomous, conventional bombs. JDAM systems can be launched up to fifteen miles from a target, and guide themselves in using sophisticated computer programming. Once in the air, their trajectory is guided by satellite global positioning systems and a 3-axis inertial navigation system that, under conditions where the GPS signal's being jammed, can function as an autonomous guidance system. JDAM systems were developed by Lockheed Martin and Boeing (McDonald Douglas). The systems were given Operational capabilities from certain aircraft as early as 1997.

a three- or four-story building, and exactly on the center of each wall—north, south, east, and west—is a bomb hole. Also, we'd hit that building once on each side every five seconds, just to show the Iraqis what our firepower could do. The building was reinforced concrete so it was still standing, but it wasn't in great shape. You couldn't use it for anything, and everything inside it was destroyed. But other than to military targets, there wasn't a lot of damage to the city. That's quite an accomplishment. Baghdad didn't have any electricity when we pulled in, but other than that, it was just fine. Basically no different than any other large third-world city.

We started in with the "hearts and minds" campaign, which basically meant we started supplying food. We had electricians in my unit; one guy worked for KeySpan Energy Systems[36] and his team got the power grid running again for most of the country. Another guy was a lieutenant in the New York City Fire Department, he tried to get fire service going again in Baghdad. Point is, the people began to see results. That's the whole "hearts and minds" thing in a nutshell; that's what CA guys do. We show people that we're not really ogres, we're making lives better. Meanwhile Psychological Operations units handed out leaflets, only we don't really call them Psy Ops these days, the new name is IO [Information Operations].

Initially, most American forces were treated as liberators. In fact, there was a district on the east side of Baghdad called Saba Nissan, which means "seventh of April" in Arabic, that was the date that Saddam came to power. The locals renamed it Tissa Nissan, which means "ninth of April," the day our armies arrived. They did that to honor us, which gives you an idea that the "hearts and minds" campaign was going well. Then the looting started.

I think it was one of the largest mistakes that our government made, not to shoot the looters. Iraqis would come to our compound hollering, "You have to shoot the looters! They're ruining our country!" So my

---

36. A member of the S & P 500, KeySpan is the largest distributor of natural gas in the Northeast, with 2.4 million gas customers and more than 13,000 employees. KeySpan is also the largest investor-owned electric generator in New York State, operating Long Island's electric system while serving its 1.1 million electric customers, and the Ravenswood electric generating station in New York City. The KeySpan family of companies provides the Northeast with a broad range of energy and services for homes and businesses.

unit and the Second Cav went through the chain of command requesting
information from the Pentagon on how to proceed. Essentially, the orders
came back saying, "No, don't shoot the looters." That's a bad CNN moment. I'm sure it didn't come out of the Pentagon precisely like that, but
that's how it filtered down to us. Still, the decision was clear. We couldn't
shoot the looters. As a result, they stripped the entire country.

In fact, remember the movie *Star Wars?* The *jawas*, those little guys
running around scavenging everything they could in the desert? We
started calling the Iraqis *jawas* because, damn, they could strip an entire
building in a day. They took it all: wire, copper tubing, the furniture,
electrical fixtures, carpeting. When they got done with a building, there
was nothing left but a concrete shell. They were amazingly resourceful,
too. They'd burn the insulation off of wiring, melt it down, and sell the
copper. They even cut the power lines at night. You'd wake up in the
morning and there'd be no electricity because a couple of guys had
climbed the poles in the dead of night, cut the juice, and cut the wires
down to melt them and sell. Or they'd blow up the towers supporting
high-tension lines, with explosives they'd found lying around the country—thousands of tons of explosives. Remember, Iraq had maintained a
draft, so nearly everyone in the country had some form of military training. Lots of people could do rudimentary demolitions work, one of the
reasons we've got so many improvised explosive devices over there.

The biggest mistake we made early on was disbanding the Iraqi national military and police forces. See, after World War II, the U.S. converted the defeated German military into a constabulary. That is, we
took men who'd been Nazis six months before and retrained them into a
Western-style police force to keep order. But we didn't do that in Iraq;
we told those soldiers and policemen, "You're fired," and sent them
home. Now we had tens of thousands of formerly employed young males
with no income and nothing to do with their time, but they were trained
in the use of powerful weapons, which were just lying around loose in
massive quantities all over the country. Bad move. I believe this was another crucial error in U.S. policy. We didn't have enough people to protect the Iraqis, let alone ourselves. That was Paul Bremer's decision.[37] I

---

37. L. Paul Bremer served as the civilian administrator in Iraq. He headed postwar efforts to stabilize the
country until June 28, 2004, when he stepped down to hand over the reigns to an interim Iraqi government.
His controversial book detailing his experiences *(My Year in Iraq: The Struggle to Build a Future of Hope,*
with Malcolm McConnell, Simon & Schuster) was published in early 2006.

remember reading a statement he made recently in the news. Basically, he said that, in hindsight? Yeah. That hadn't been a good idea.[38]

By the way, some of the Iraqis took it upon themselves to shoot the looters. Because that's what really happens in a war zone, policy or no policy.

II

One area of Baghdad we were responsible for was called Sadr City. It was predominantly Shiite, with small Sunni and Christian enclaves sprinkled throughout. It became one of the big hot spots where Muqtada al-Sadr had his al-Mahdi army.[39] Up until the war, Sadr City was called "Saddam City," which is really ironic since it had about two and a half million people compacted into this really small area. It was such a hell hole, it made Mogadishu look good. The people had no water, no electricity, no city services like fire or police protection, and this was before the war! Saddam basically punished the Shiites because he was a Sunni. The Shiites were initially happy as hell when we arrived.

We weren't kidding ourselves, though. The Shiite goodwill toward us didn't have a whole lot to do with who we were or what we were doing. The Shiites just liked that they'd gone from having very little opportunity to being a resounding majority. They were no longer under the yoke of Saddam's Sunni administration. We freed them from oppression for the first time in twenty years.

On the other hand, the Sunnis had been on top for years thanks to Saddam's patronage. Suddenly, they found their power base destroyed. The other detachment of the 411th was working on the west side of town where they dealt with a Sunni population. Needless to say, that detachment didn't enjoy the same rapport with their locals that we did. In the Sunni mind-set, they'd gone from having everything to nothing because of America.

38. On October 4, 2004—speaking at an insurance conference in White Sulphur Springs, West Virginia—Bremer claimed that he found "horrid" looting going on when he arrived to head the U.S.-led Coalition Provisional Authority in Baghdad on the May 26, 2003. "We paid a big price for not stopping [the looting]," he said, "because it established an atmosphere of lawlessness." Bremer went on to state, "We never had enough ground troops." A senior Defense Department official immediately noted that Bremer had never asked for more ground troops and expressed annoyance that Ambassador Bremer appeared to be second-guessing the advice of military officials. Bremer clarified his remarks the next day, stating that he had meant to refer only to "the situation as I found it on the ground, when I arrived in Baghdad in May 2003, and when I believed we needed either more Coalition troops or Iraqi security forces to address the looting."
39. Believed to be the son of a Grand Ayatollah, Muqtada al-Sadr was approximately thirty years old when, leading a group of devout followers, he took control of the city of Najaf in early April 2004. Though accounts vary, the al-Mahdi army boasted somewhere between 2,000 and 10,000 well-armed soldiers as of late 2004.

Comparatively speaking, my team had very few problems in the areas we handled. Very few aggressive incidents, very few attacks on military convoys. I can't say we won the Iraqis' hearts and minds 100 percent, but we had a damn good track record. Despite the rough start we'd had with the Second Cav, we ended up building a great relationship. We attended daily meetings with the regimental commander and made every effort to cooperate. By and large, Second Cav really came to appreciate what we were doing. They didn't always like the *way* we did our jobs, but they appreciated it. Eventually they saw what we were doing as part of what needed to happen in Iraq.

But then, right after the war ended, the First Cavalry Division came in not long after the president declared that the war, or "major combat operations" I think is how he put it, was over. They set up shop and took over the show. Like I said, conventional forces often have tremendous concerns about the procedures followed by Civil Affairs and other Special Ops units. They just don't understand what we do. For instance, CA Command had no qualms whatsoever about my unit picking up AK-47s, but First Armored got serious heartburn over it. They got on our cases for all sorts of reasons, like our uniforms, for instance. See, folks in Civil Affairs don't care much for uniforms. For operational security reasons, we frequently don't wear name tags. One thing I learned as an antiterrorism instructor? Terrorists target family members. So we kept low profiles. We didn't give last names when doing interviews. I called myself "First Sergeant Bill," for instance, and left it at that.

It might sound like we were intentionally trying to flaunt authority, but to win the hearts and minds of a local population, you have to mingle. That's why in Afghanistan it's common to see our guys wearing army pants with a dishdasha on top, the local dress, what we called a man-dress. Technically, that's against regulations. But you're trying to blend in with the mujahideen[40] and win rapport. Some of our soldiers grew nonregulation moustaches because almost every Arab male has fa-

40. The term *mujahideen* (spelled variously) literally translates from the Arabic as "strugglers," plural for *mujahid*. There is no explicit link to religious context in the word's roots though the term has come to be associated almost exclusively with religious freedom-fighters. The most well-known and feared mujahideen were those that fought in Afghanistan against the Soviet invasion from 1979 to 1983, and the war that followed. These groups were well financed, armed and trained by the United States under presidents Carter and Reagan.

cial hair, it's his mark of masculinity. I grew a mustache, too. Like many Special Ops guys' mustaches, mine didn't meet army regulations and no one in the conventional forces' chain of command was thrilled about it, but what can I say? We didn't fall under the conventional forces' chain of command. The Arabs we worked with loved the mustache, that was what mattered. Chalk it up to a necessary breach of protocol.

Or look at it this way: working in Civil Affairs, you learn to behave like a beat cop in a city. A beat cop driving back and forth in a patrol car never grabs the chance to walk the streets. The people don't get to know him. They definitely won't get to know him if he stays hidden behind convoys of thirty or forty armored vehicles. No, you've got to go into the community, preferably on a daily basis. Meet with the imams and the people who'd formerly been elected officials in Iraqi society. Create a relationship. Articulate plans for change. First Cavalry didn't like it. They thought it was risky, and it was. But that's our job.

We never went out of our way to ignore regulations and we always tried to explain the rationale behind our behavior when asked. We never rubbed their faces in anything, either. When we'd go into First Cavalry Division Headquarters, we'd leave our AKs in the trucks. Still, First Cav started pulling out all these rules. They said, "All vehicles have to be equipped with crew-served weapons."[41] Well, my unit didn't have enough to go around, it's another reason we'd been using the AKs and RPK machine guns in the first place. We explained this to First Cav and their answer was, "Well, then you can't leave the wire." To which we said, "Okay. No sweat on our end." Being ordered to stay within the wire was like being ordered to go on vacation.

After a few days, though, the CA mission wasn't getting done. Things were falling apart. Relationships with locals require upkeep and we didn't want to lose them. As it turns out, there were a lot of Soviet-made crew-served weapons lying around all over the place. They were perfectly functional; they just weren't American made. We'd already been using a few, so we suggested that we be allowed to continue this protocol so we could continue our mission. First Cav wasn't thrilled. But we said, "Look, if you've got something better for us to use, fine. But

41. Essentially meaning machine guns. They're called "crew-served" because they're operated by a gunner plus a crewman feeding ammunition into the weapon.

until then?" They gave in after a few days. We remounted the Russian weapons on the backs of our trucks and got back to work.

I give First Cav credit, it takes a lot for an armored division to start thinking differently. Eventually they got us American guns, the M-249, what we call a SAW[42] Later on we recovered an M-2 .50 caliber machine gun from the insurgency. We were chasing a van full of suspected insurgents, and they threw this weapon out the door as they fled. We had it refurbished and made arrangements to use the gun on our cargo truck, even went so far as to install a rotating ring mount on the roof that we'd cannibalized off a destroyed Humvee.

We were out on missions every day. Normally our teams consisted of six people in two canvas-topped Humvees. For the first eight months or so, the Humvees weren't armored. We even took the canvas doors off them because it was easier to get in and out of the vehicles. Later on a Civil Affairs captain from another unit designed a homemade armor kit. Basically, the army bought sheet metal from Iraqi dealers and welded it together, spray-painted it, and welded it on the back of trucks in the cargo area. They also made these little fold-up half doors with steel plate on them. It wasn't real armor, but it looked good. We never personally tested it but, if nothing else, it was a placebo.

Placebos can actually work in tense moments, and we had a few. A lot of times, we'd wind up in the middle of a neighborhood where the people didn't like us. The Iraqis would start throwing rocks, and sometimes we'd get out and fire our weapons in the air to scare them off. Not pretty, but you had to set a precedent before things got worse. We were doing a lot of good things in Iraq, but it was still a war zone. We saw a lot of bad things, but the worst of them had to be the UN bombing.

III

My unit occupied a former aero-medical research facility about a hundred meters away from UN headquarters. Our base was called a CMOC, civil military operations center, a place where the local populace could come to report their problems. In other words, this building became the de facto city hall for eastern Baghdad, with the 34 members

---

42. Squad automatic weapon—a light machine gun.

of my portion of 411 serving as city administrators. When we took the building over, we found that it had a MIG-29 flight simulator. I have a pilot's license and, man, I really wanted to fire that thing up, I thought it'd be great fun to play with. But we could never figure it out. The machine was made in Baltimore, but all the manuals were in Arabic.

It was no chance thing that we'd placed our headquarters so close to the UN. My unit had actually occupied UN headquarters before they'd returned to Baghdad; we subsequently vacated it to give them the space. The UN mission had a lot in common with our own, so we developed a good working relationship. We met with UN officials on a regular basis.

In all of Baghdad, we were the only Civil Affairs unit based outside the wire. All other units lived within fortified base clusters. We chose to live outside for the same reason my unit did anything in Iraq, to earn a better rapport with the locals. This turned out to be true, but it also meant that we were essentially twenty people living on our own in a war zone with no backup in case we were attacked. We set up defensive perimeters. We had a wall, fences, concertina wire, and trip flares running all the way around. We had grenades and machine guns, the works. We armed ourselves well. In fact, we carried so much armament that one time we loaned 40 mm grenade ammunition to the Second Cavalry when they ran short.

August 19, 2003, four twenty-eight in the afternoon. I was in my office getting ready for a meeting. My desk faced a window which we'd replaced with tempered glass to blast-proof it. I was standing by my desk and had just put my helmet on. I bent down to pick up a sheaf of papers on my laptop when the bomb exploded.

If the blast had gone off two seconds sooner, I would have been looking straight into that window and flying glass would've turned my face into hamburger. The windows were supposedly shatterproof. Nope. The blast blew them out. I remember seeing an intense orange light, that was it. When I came to, I was on the ground with my back to the wall on the other side of the room. I must've flown something like fifteen feet through the air. First thing I noticed was my office was trashed, windows gone, papers flying around, a real mess.

I got up. I had shrapnel in my arm and leg and cuts all over my face and hands from flying glass. My initial thought was that some idiot had accidentally thrown munitions in the burn pit outside the building. See, there weren't any functioning garbage disposal facilities in Iraq; we burned all our garbage outside. And everyday we went out among the Iraqis, we'd see dangerous things lying around, like loose 155 rounds. Sometimes they'd even approach us and turn over weapons, which we'd hand over to EOD [Explosive Ordnance Disposal]. Well, my first thought was that some idiot had mistakenly thrown one of these live shells into the burn pits. But once I looked around the room and took in the damage, I knew it was something else.

I blew a call on my first sergeant's whistle, signaling all personnel to get to their defensive positions. Then I ran like hell to take my own.

In the event of an attack, we'd preestablished defensive positions for all personnel in my unit. When the bomb went off we did as we'd been trained to do, took those positions fast. It turned out that, along with myself, four or five CA soldiers had suffered minor shrapnel wounds. Notably, my own battle buddy[43] was—as we say—*hors de combat*. Out of action. The blast threw him thirty feet and knocked him unconscious. Aside from that everyone was fine.

My position was on the roof of a stair tower atop our two-story building. As soon as I got up there I saw what had happened. A truck bomb had detonated at the southwest corner of the UN building. It must have pulled into the driveway running between UN headquarters and the Baghdad Spinal Hospital. Where there used to be a parking area you could see this big smoking crater blown into the ground. There were burning cars surrounding the crater and debris all over the place. A lot of body parts, too, scattered everywhere by the blast. Some of them had landed on our building.

I've seen a lot of fires in my day, but I've never seen a blast like that. I'm not an EOD guy, so I couldn't estimate the size or type of explosion. Later on I heard them say 500 to 2,000 pounds of explosives. The UN building was made of reinforced concrete but it collapsed in upon itself. Fortunately, it wasn't on fire, not a major conflagration, anyway, though some of the building's contents were burning. In a way, we'd been lucky.

43. Sergeant von Zehle: "Everybody in the military has a battle buddy whom you're supposed to eat, sleep, breathe, and live with. My battle buddy had just stepped outside the building when the bomb exploded. He was thrown through the air about thirty feet and landed against a generator, knocked unconscious with a concussion. One of our other sergeants found him, threw him over a shoulder, and carried him inside."

It doesn't get real cold in Iraq, so any buildings that have heat get it from combination air-conditioner/heater units instead of natural gas. If they'd had natural gas piped into that building? I doubt anything would have been left standing.

The really sad thing? I'll probably get in trouble for saying this but—what the hell, it's public record. Three months earlier, we'd met with UN security personnel. At that meeting, I recommended that the UN should seriously look into shoring up Canal Road, a busy highway with three lanes running in each direction. You got to UN headquarters by turning off Canal onto an open, narrow driveway that ran between UN headquarters and the Baghdad Spinal Hospital, maybe twenty meters away. To me, the driveway came way too close for comfort. I suggested that the driveway made the UN vulnerable, and that a security gate could prevent vehicular bombs from pulling in and detonating.

The UN security chief had concerns about traffic flow. Canal was a busy road. He felt that setting up a gate to screen vehicles entering the driveway would cause a bottleneck on the highway as vehicles queued up. Fender benders, he said, were bound to occur. My answer to that was, I'd rather have a fender bender on Canal than a car bomb coming up the driveway. They didn't follow my recommendation. The first thing I thought when I got to my post and realized what had happened was, *Damn. Told you so.*

I bandaged my arm and pulled a piece of shrapnel the size of a knife blade out of my leg. Then I radioed my commander, Major Scott Hill, who was down at the central command post and told him what I could see from my perspective. Based on my civilian experience, I figured we'd need ambulances and rescue equipment. Body parts lying all over the place meant that there might be more people trapped inside the UN building. Major Hill then radioed the Second Cav to share information. They already knew something was up. Everyone in Baghdad heard the explosion.

I radioed Major Hill again and requested permission to do reconnaissance at UN headquarters. I wanted to see the extent of the damage. Major Hill granted me permission, along with Captain Caroline Pogge, an officer from our unit who's a civilian hospital administrator and understands mass casualties.

Before we left, I told Captain Pogge and Major Hill that I expected another attack. You learn this as an antiterrorism instructor; terrorists frequently blow something up, then wait a few minutes until everyone rushes in to help. Then they blow up a second bomb or have a sniper open fire to kill the rescuers. I told Captain Pogge, "Be prepared." Then she and I took off running.

There was an open stretch of ground between our building and the UN. Captain Pogge and I took the distance at a covered rush, maybe a hundred meters. She'd cover me with her M-16 while I advanced and hid behind what was left of a gate, or a pile of concrete. Then I'd cover her with my AK while she moved ahead and hid behind a piece of burning truck. Ten meters. Stop. Next person move up. Stop. Ten meters more. Stop. Next person, and so on, leap-frogging our way forward 'til we made it to the building after about a minute. We were the first U.S. troops to arrive on the scene.

Why did we go in when we expected a second attack? Because we're in the military. That's our job. It's one of the reasons I'm so annoyed with that Rock Hill transportation unit that refused its mission. They said it was suicide. Crap, it's suicide! My group went out every day for thirteen months in two vehicle "convoys" that were a lot less armored than their vehicles. You're not willing to do something dangerous? Don't join the military. The military is inherently dangerous.

Captain Pogge and I knew that a blast like that ceases to become a military matter and very quickly become a fire/rescue operation. We both had civilian expertise that could help. That's part of being in the military, too. Helping people. We wanted to go in and ascertain what resources we'd need to mount a rescue.

A gentleman in a UN baseball cap staggered around a side of the building and moved toward us. His clothes were torn. He was totally covered in dust and very shaken. I said, "Are you in charge?" And he replied, "Honestly, I don't know. I don't know where anybody is." He explained that there'd been a press conference going on in the main meeting hall. Then the bomb had gone off. "I don't know *who's* in charge now," he said.

"You are," I said. "What do you know?"

This man said he thought there were about twenty-five people injured. I relayed that information back to Major Hill, along with my recommendation that the collapse, based on my experience as a fire chief, would immediately require heavy rescue equipment and lots of lighting. I'd never been at a bombing site before, but the situation began to play out exactly as if we were handling an emergency at home. One minor difference: I was waiting for somebody to start shooting at me.

I set up a command post near a pile of brick rubble, car parts, and body parts. Standard fire service practice made me choose the location; you want your command post positioned on a corner of the building to allow for observation of two sides at once. You want it placed far enough away from the building's base to avoid any damage from further structural collapses. The quickest way to figure out this distance is to take the height of the building and divide by a third. I did the math and added a few feet, since Iraqi concrete isn't the highest-quality building material in the world.

Captain Pogge outranked me but she deferred command since I'd had more experience with this kind of operation. I made her the medical sector commander. She set up a triage site and tried to get a handle on how many wounded we had. We quickly found out that the guy in the baseball cap was wrong. We weren't facing twenty-five or thirty wounded. More like over two hundred.

I kept Major Hill advised of our findings and requested more resources. A lot of guys in our unit were cops, firefighters, or EMTs in their civilian lives. Plus almost everyone in our unit was a certified combat lifesaver, a unique military designation combining EMT and paramedic training. Everyone carried aid bags, too, full of IVs, trauma dressings, and stuff called QuikClot, which you pour on a gunshot wound to seal it instantly. All this stuff was about to come in very handy.

I'd broken the pin in my watchband while I worked, so I have to estimate the time. But about fifteen minutes after we got there, other army units began to show up. A soldier came up to me dressed in full body armor. I couldn't read his name tag with all his gear on. I looked up from what I was doing and he said, "Stand down, soldier, I'm in charge now." I started giving my assessment of the situation, plus a briefing on where our people were and what they were doing. That's standard fire service practice when transferring command. This guy didn't want to be bothered. He interrupted me. "First Sergeant? What don't you understand about this? I'm a colonel. You're a sergeant. I'm in charge. Go find something to do."

I started offering to stay and assist technically. I'd done this sort of work for thirty years; I thought I had something to contribute. But then another UN worker in a blue baseball cap approached me and said, "Sergio and Gil are trapped inside the building."

Sergio de Mello. I knew him, of course. We'd dined together on several occasions. But right then, in the midst of all that chaos, the name didn't register. Almost all the UN employees I'd met were foreigners. Many had strange-sounding names. I just said, "Where are they?" and this man walked me over to a pile of rubble on one side of the building. He pointed out this little hole maybe six by twelve inches across near the base of the building. The hole had formed where two overlapping slabs of rooftop concrete slid down and interlocked with one another. I switched on a penlight from my medical kit and looked in. I could see two people in a very dark, very confined space. They had rubble on top of them, but they were alive. I could hear both of them talking.

I knew we weren't going to get them out through that hole. No way. They had tons of concrete stacked above them. Often the best way to handle collapse rescues is to work the job from inside. So I said, "Okay. Show me how to get into this building."

The UN worker led me inside, and we climbed to the top of the third-floor stairs. He stopped there and refused to go any further. From that vantage point we could see how half the building had fallen off. The corridor we were in was exposed to the air. Whatever offices had been on that level had dropped to the lower floors in the collapse.

I walked out along a sort of ledge and sited on landmarks I could see outside until I got to above where I thought the two men might be. I looked down into the darkness of the collapse and saw sunlight shining though, which I took to be light from the hole in the wall I'd seen outside. I paused, and used my radio to call in to Major Hill. The building was still shifting, but I told him I was going in. I asked him, "If anything should happen, tell my wife and daughter that I love them." Part of me honestly didn't believe I was coming back out. The potential for further collapse was pretty good.

The space I was going to shimmy through was small, so I took off my body armor and gear. I left my weapon up on the ledge but kept my pistol on my belt. Then I started crawling headfirst down this slope of rubble canted nearly 80 degrees steep until I reached what would have been the second floor. Here the space widened out a little. There were several bodies in the void.

They were obviously dead. The bodies were covered in plaster dust and rubble, but I could tell some details. One had been a woman. I later found out these were the people who'd been meeting with Sergio de Mello in his office when the bomb exploded. I was able to turn around at that point so I continued the descent feet first. When I reached the bottom, I found the two people I'd been looking for.

As an EMT, you learn to introduce yourself at the site of an emergency. It helps relax people. So I said, "My name is Bill," and one guy said, "My name is Gil." He had an English accent. The other man said, "My name is Sergio." His accent sounded Spanish to me. I looked both of them over. Gil was pinned by rubble from his midthighs down. He lay in a two-by-two-foot space. The man who called himself Sergio was pinned from about his waist down. A slab had fallen over his body, leaving less than a foot of space over him.

There wasn't a lot of room to work in and I foresaw that under the circumstances the only one way to handle the situation was this: get the man named Gil out first and create access to Sergio.

I only had my penlight, so I radioed back to Major Hill at Command. I said, "I need more light." I also asked for some rope and a bone saw, which rescuers frequently employ as a hacksaw. I wanted the saw to cut away the reinforcing rods in the concrete rubble. Figured I'd get the bars out of the way in order to create access to Gil and Sergio. I never got the supplies. The regular army guys running around outside, the ones who'd just arrived, they'd commandeer the stuff from members of my unit who were trying to run it out to me. This happened more than once. The regular army guys outranked my crew and just took whatever they wanted. I have no idea what they used any of it for; maybe they put it to some good. But my feeling, then and now was, get your own damn supplies.

Rather than sit around waiting, I started Gil on an IV drip and took Sergio's vital signs. At that point, both men were talking. I could see that each had suffered plenty of superficial cuts on their faces from the blast. Internal injuries were another matter entirely, but there was no way to determine their extent under those circumstances. Of the two, Gil wasn't as severely pinned by rubble. Going from that alone, I predetermined Sergio to be the worse off. Both men were covered in bricks so I started to clean them up, pulling off debris. The confined space gave me nowhere to throw the rubble, so I sort of moved it around as best I could, trying to make them comfortable. I did this for maybe half an hour—again, my best estimation—when I heard someone yell down from above.

There were three soldiers up there now, and one of them yelled, "Can I help you?" The last thing I wanted down there was somebody who didn't know what he was doing. So I hollered back up, "You had any training for this?"

The guy shouted back, "I'm a New York City firefighter paramedic." Exactly what I was hoping to hear. I said, "Come on down." His name was Andre Valentine. He was a staff sergeant in a Reserve MP [military police] company.

The two other men with Valentine didn't have rescue training so I told them to stay put where they were, that we needed a rope plus something to haul up the bricks. We ended up using a woman's purse we found lying half-buried in the debris and what looked like the drawstring from a drapery or a set of blinds. Valentine and I loaded bricks into the purse, and the two guys up top would haul it out using the drawstring line. They'd empty the purse, throw it back down to us, and we'd do it all over again.

Valentine was great. He was smaller than me so he could wriggle in to where Sergio was. We probably worked for three hours to get those men out. It was frustrating, and it would have been exhausting but for the fact that our adrenaline was pumping so hard.

I'll give the army credit: they do a great job being an army. But they're not trained for collapse rescues. Normally people get the instinct to pull slabs off the wreckage from the outside, but that makes the rescue work much more dangerous. Valentine and I had Gil uncovered for the most part when somebody outside started moving stuff around and the bricks we'd pulled out slid back down on us. It didn't land us back at square one, but we were pretty damn close.

Time is your enemy in that kind of operation. In the fire service, we respect something called the Golden Hour. From the time a traumatic injury occurs, if you get a victim to a hospital within sixty minutes and they're still alive, they have a good chance of surviving. We were way beyond the Golden Hour with Gil and Sergio. Their vital signs were getting bad. Valentine and I kept pumping IVs into them. Men from outside handed new IV bags through the hole in the wall. A little later on, an air force medic showed up and threw down some morphine. Valentine gave morphine to Gil and I gave some to Sergio. At least they weren't in pain. I tried to keep both men talking because I didn't want them to slip into shock. Sergio started telling me about his family. He had two sons, he loved his wife, and so forth.

We kept digging, knowing that time was against us. Sergio died about fifteen minutes before we managed to get Gil out. It wasn't sudden. He'd been lucid when I arrived but as time wore on he started slipping away. At first, he'd answer all the questions Valentine and I asked. Then his responses became less coherent. You could tell he was moving deeper and deeper into shock. Eventually he died. There was nothing we could do.

Both of Gil's legs were extremely damaged but we were finally able to haul him out by putting him on something called a Sked, which is a kind of folding stretcher. We hauled him out feet first with a rope that finally arrived after a couple of hours. Eventually, doctors had to amputate both his legs, but Gil survived. He was transported to an army hospital in Germany. Later on, his wife called my wife to thank her for what I'd done. I still didn't know his last name but it turns out Gil was Gil Loescher, a senior UN official. His daughter went on to make a documentary on the bombing attack.

Here's the thing that annoyed me most about this episode: when I met Sergio de Mello down in that pit that day, I didn't know who he was but I could tell he was someone important. It was obvious from the questions he asked while he was lucid: "How bad are my injuries? How many people are hurt? Do we know what's happened? What's the extent of the damage?" This wasn't somebody used to taking orders, this was a take-charge kind of guy; he demanded to know how his people were. From this I gathered that he was somebody in a position of authority. I just didn't know at the time he was *the* man.

As the hours wore on, he said things like, "I'm not going to get out of here, am I?" Based on my American fire service experience I said, "Don't worry. We'll get you out. Both of you." But in America we would have had the tools to shore up the area. We would have had rope, stretchers, torches, winches, the works. We would have handled the situation very differently than we handled it that day. I really and truly believed we could get those two men out alive. I gave Sergio my word, and my word didn't work.

That night, back at the damaged CMOC, we were watching CNN on satellite TV and they flashed a picture of Sergio, the first time I realized who he was. So I wrote a letter to Kofi Annan[44] telling him everything Sergio had said to me. I addressed it to the secretary general and marked the envelope personal and confidential. The next day I handed it to the senior surviving UN employee, asking that it be delivered to Mr. Annan directly. It never got there. Somebody leaked it. Within twenty-four hours, the fact that I had written the note and Sergio's stoic actions had made the front page of the papers even though the actual details weren't yet known. Reporters from CNN, the *Washington Post*, the *New York Times*, and ABC News descended on me from out of nowhere.

I still won't mention what I wrote in the letter. Suffice it to say that Sergio de Mello was a complete gentleman up until the end. He asked about his wife and he asked about his family. When I told him the explosion had been a terrorist attack, he told me, "Don't let them pull the UN out of Baghdad. That's giving in to the terrorists. Please. Don't let them do that." The UN pulled out anyway. In my opinion, it was another tactical mistake in what had already become a long list.

My unit's building was so damaged by the explosion that we moved tables outside and continued our work from there. We met with the local

---

44. Kofi Annan became the seventh secretary general of the United Nations on January 1, 1997, his election following a bitterly contested U.S. veto of a second term for his predecessor, Boutros Boutros-Ghali of Egypt. Born in Ghana in 1938, Annan studied economics in Kumasi and earned a bachelor's degree at Macalester College in Minnesota in 1961. He did graduate work in Geneva and later earned a master's degree in management from MIT in 1972.

Iraqis during the day. Since we couldn't sleep in the damaged building at night we'd move to a compound of the Second Cavalry, an abandoned little hell hole that badly needed fixing up.

A few nights later, a little before eleven o'clock, a female sergeant came into my room and asked, "Which one of you is Sergeant von Zehle?" I raised a hand. "That's me."

She said, "You've got to follow me right away." I thought, "Uh-oh, this doesn't sound good." We went downstairs and next door to their command post. The soldiers there offered no explanations. They said, "Get into your battle rattle," which is an army term that means your flak jacket, helmet, weapon, and so on.

I said, "What's the problem?" My first thought being that something had happened to my wife or daughter. "What's going on?" But all they said was, "No idea, but we need to get you over to Second Cav Headquarters on the double." It was three or four miles away. They put me in a Humvee and off we went.

At Second Cav Headquarters, the regimental command sergeant major said, "Von Zehle, there's a phone call coming in, it's going to be for you." I said, "Who's it from?" Standing there with this pit in my stomach, still thinking something had happened to my wife or family.

But the soldier said, "The chief of staff of the army wants to talk to you. Now I'm thinking, "Aw, cripes. I really shouldn't have written that letter."

As it turned out, they were having trouble with the phone systems and they couldn't receive a call from the Pentagon at Second Cav. So they put me back in the convoy and drove me over to Baghdad Airport on the other side of town. By that point it was midnight and I was really upset. I figured the chief of staff of the army doesn't talk to NCOs unless they've done something really wrong. When we arrived at Baghdad Airport, I was greeted by Major General Dempsey, who commands the First Armored Division. He shook my hand and I blurted out, "I understand the army chief of staff wants to talk to me."

The general said, "No, he doesn't."

"Then I'm confused," I said.

"Not the army chief of staff, his *boss*, General Myers, chairman of the Joint Chiefs of Staff."

I'm thinking, *Oh God.*

Major General Dempsey took me into his office and sat me down in his chair, which had big stars emblazoned on the back. He got me a coffee and handed me a newspaper. It's not often that a sergeant in the army gets served coffee by a general. Then he turned to his aide, a colonel, and said, "Anything he needs, take care of it. I'm going to bed. I have to get up at four." And he left.

The phone they handed me was one of those jobs we call a STU phone—a satellite telephone unit that lets you talk directly to the President and so forth. It rang twenty minutes later. General Dempsey's aide looked at me and said, "Well, go ahead. Answer it."

I picked up the receiver and identified myself. It was Richard Myers, chairman of the Joint Chiefs of Staff. He said he'd heard about my letter, and I said, "Sir? Meaning no offense. But I'm a little pissed off the letter's content got leaked." The general laughed and said, "Well, then you don't understand how things work inside the Beltway."[45] He said that he'd read about the letter in the papers, then he'd heard about it again from his "boss"—meaning the President. So whether Kofi Annan told President Bush about the letter and President Bush leaked it, or Kofi Annan leaked it himself—who knows? Long story short, it was given to the press from someone at a very high level. General Myers wasn't calling to grill me at all. He was calling to thank me personally.

He said, "Look, Sergeant. There's no good news coming out of Baghdad right now. You and your letter are just about all we have."

I said, "Sir, I'm really not in the mood to talk to the media right now," and General Myers said, "I'm telling you: talk to the press."

"Sir, do I have to?"

"Yes."

I was given an order, so I followed it.

Now let me be clear: I don't deny that what I did was a good thing, that's not why I didn't want to talk to anyone. But you see, everybody I worked with in Iraq was doing good things on a daily basis. People put their lives on the line to make Iraq a better place all the time, but you'll never hear about them. And that got to me. That's wrong.

See, my CA unit did great stuff. For instance, Saddam had closed

45. In Washington, D.C.

down five hundred schools in Baghdad alone, there were no schools functioning in Baghdad when we arrived there. We got them up and running so kids could get an education. That never made the press. But that's important, don't you think? We got the power back on, we got water running again, we got the sewage working. No press. Or maybe it was on page 42 of the *New York Times* in a little teensy mention. I'm saying that only the bad stuff makes it into print, and sometimes not even that. The terrorist explosion on August 19 also took out the Baghdad Spinal Hospital next door. That was horrible, that was the only spinal hospital in the entire country. I never saw it mentioned once. I wanted to go to Iraq, do my job, and come home to a quiet life. August 19 of 2003 changed all that. Between August and the following April, nobody wanted to talk to my unit about anything but the UN bombing.

I've gotten a lot of medals in my career, and there are people in the army—one person in my battalion that I'm thinking of in particular—who go out of their way to get themselves medals. I don't care about them. I'm not into them. I didn't want the attention and I still don't. All this attention over me and Sergio de Mello? You know what? I didn't even save the guy's life. He died. In hindsight, I probably should never have gone down into that pit. I didn't succeed in what I set out to do.

What I did pales in comparison to Audie Murphy[46] or any of those guys, guys that won the Medal of Honor. The truth is that I did what I did because I happened to be there at the right time. Other guys in my unit would have done the same thing. They had the training, too. It just happened to be me.

IV

One last story I think you'll find interesting. I bought a white Mercedes Benz for 9,000,000 dinars off a wealthy Sunni businessman who'd prospered under Saddam. I happen to collect Mercedes. I was down in the Green Zone shortly after we arrived in Baghdad and I noticed this car, so I went over to take a look. The Sunni stuck his head out the window and spoke to me in perfect English with a British accent. He said, "What the hell are you doing?"

---

46. Audie L. Murphy was the most decorated American combat soldier of World War II. He received every decoration for valor that the U.S. his country offered, plus five decorations presented to him by France and Belgium. He died in an airplane accident in 1971.

I said, "I'm just admiring your car," and he said, "You want to buy it?" We started haggling over the price. The car was in good condition. The price he quoted, 9,000,000 dinars, was worth about $5,000 at the time. The Sunni said he'd purchased the car from the Iraqi government. It was bulletproof and had a lot of other neat features. But because he could see the way the wind was blowing in Baghdad, he was on his way out of Dodge. He'd decided to move to Jordan.

I wanted to make sure that I handled the purchase correctly, meaning the way the army wanted it handled. So I contacted the provost marshal's office and the judge advocate general [JAG]. I said, "I bought this car and I want to bring it home." They said, "Oh no. That violates General Order Number One."

There's a joke in the army that says General Order Number One basically prohibits anything pleasurable. No alcohol, no pornography, no *Playboy* magazines. You can't bring bayonets home or do anything that could remotely be considered dangerous or offensive to the local population. The JAG guy kept insisting that I couldn't bring the car home under General Order Number One but I kept saying, "Show me where it says I can't ship a car home." The way I read the rule, it didn't say you couldn't bring souvenirs home, it just said which souvenirs were prohibited, notably bayonets, guns, drugs, and Cuban cigars. I said, "Show me where it says you can't bring an automobile home?" Well, he couldn't.

So I was all clear with the army. So far so good.

I left the car at our compound when we had to abandon it. Being good at what they do, the Iraqis came in and stripped it. They took out the airbag, they tried to hotwire it. Then they tried to use a false key, which ended up breaking off in the ignition. They took all the papers and stole the license plates.

When my driver finally got the car to the border, the border guard looked the car over and said, "This is Saddam Hussein's car. There's no way that a private individual owns Saddam's car." This border captain told my driver there was only one white armored Mercedes in Iraq and therefore you couldn't get it across the border unless you filled out this special form. He took out a blank sheet of paper, wrote his name on it, and said, "This is the form. There's a thousand dollar fee for filling out this form." He wanted American money in hundred-dollar bills.

So the driver turned the car around and drove back to Baghdad. I'd bought the car at the end of April, by now it was already September. I e-mailed my wife and told her to wire $1,000 to the Rafadain Bank; I gave her the address. Then I had one of our interpreters go to the bank and withdraw the sum in hundred-dollar bills, which I put in an envelope and gave to the driver who set out once more. At the border, the captain apparently looked at the blank piece of paper, counted the money, said, "Yup, this form's all right." He stamped the piece of paper and let my driver through.

I'd contracted to have the Mercedes placed in a shipping container in Amman because I didn't want the car looted. From Amman it was sent to the port of Latikia, Syria. I've always been pretty good at geography but I didn't even know Syria had a port. Then from Latikia the car went to Pyraeus, Greece and from Greece it continued to Spain. Then from Spain to Port Elizabeth, New Jersey.

You know how they only inspect 5 percent of the cargo containers coming into the United States? Uh-huh, you guessed it. They chose to inspect mine. The dock in Port Elizabeth called me up and the woman on the other end of the line says, "Customs is going to inspect your container."

I said, "That's fine. Go ahead. It's got a car in it." The woman from the dock said, "There's a fee."

I said, "The government's charging *me* to inspect the container?" Apparently so. That cost another $760 and I still don't think it's right.

The container was still sealed when they opened it in Port Elizabeth, but the car inside had been further damaged. I knew the airbag had been taken after the UN bombing, but now the mirrors were missing, the radio was missing, all the electronic control modules were gone. In addition, there was evidence of damage to the right front end, and the hood had been replaced with another that had a different shade of white. It must have happened in Jordan, before the car was sealed into the container.

From soup to nuts I've sunk about $20,000 into the car, including shipping and conversion to U.S. specifications to satisfy Customs and NHSTA [National Highway Traffic Safety Administration]. But I did some research. When the car left the Mercedes factory in 1988, it had cost $360,000. I found out that only three of this variety were made and, of those three, only one was white. The factory also told me that three

replacement vehicles were delivered to Iraq in 1998, which corroborated a story told to me by the seller. I figure it's worth it. Plus, it's a great
conversation piece. The car's factory armored. The windows are two to
three inches thick and armored against .50 caliber armor-piercing rounds.
It has a self-sealing fuel tank and run-flat tires. Before it got stripped, it
had this really cool feature, a button on the dash that activated speakers
and microphones hidden in the side mirrors. You could hear people
talking outside the car and talk back to them without ever opening the
windows. I suppose that would have been a bad move. Someone could've
tossed a hand grenade in.

But the neatest feature was these pipes hidden underneath the rocker
panels and connected to a small propane tank like you'd have on a
BernzOmatic torch. There was a switch that the driver could hit so that,
if anybody got too close, you could send out a momentary jet of flames
from under the vehicle. I went online to check these devices out.
They're made in South Africa and they're very popular over there for
use against carjackers.

Later on I came across three pictures of Saddam sitting in a white armored Mercedes just like mine. I have no idea if it's the same white Mercedes, but I know that mine belonged to the Iraqi government at one
point. My wife, by the way, is not too thrilled.

Some things I've said here today the military and the government might
not be too happy about. But all I want is to be quoted accurately. If they
don't like what I say? That's okay, that's my problem. I learned long
ago to speak my mind. And as an NCO, one of the things I teach my
soldiers is, It's better to ask forgiveness than permission. Meaning: Do
what you think is right. If someone else thinks it's wrong, then say, "I'm
sorry."

Let me tell you this one last thing.

The army is overwhelmingly Republican. I'm a registered Republican. But I'd say that the majority of people I worked with over in Iraq
are not voting for the president this coming election[47] because we felt
misled about why we went to war. Here's why:

A couple days after arriving in Baghdad, my unit hired a few Arabic

---

47. The presidential election of November 2004, in which incumbent President George Bush narrowly beat
out his opponent, Senator John Kerry (D-MA).

interpreters, mostly guys who had served as soldiers in the now-defunct Iraqi military. These men overheard us talking about the WMDs [weapons of mass destruction] and they all started to laugh at us. They said, "There are no WMDs, we got rid of them in 1993, and your government knows it." At first we thought they were full of crap. I mean, two or three days before these men had been our enemies and now they were working for us, that's hardly a perfect character reference. Plus we believed what the government told us. We invaded Iraq because the presence of weapons of mass destruction threatened American security. But there were no WMDs. There was not an imminent threat to our security.

So a second justification for the invasion was offered: Saddam was working with al Qaeda. I mentioned before that I'm an antiterrorist instructor. I can tell you flat out that there was no link whatsoever between Iraq and al Qaeda, this even came out in the *9/11 Report.*

Think about it. Saddam was a secular leader. The last thing he wanted was a fundamentalist Islamic organization operating in his country. His population was Shiite by majority. He wasn't about to invite al Qaeda into his country to start trouble. So this second reason for going into Iraq also turned out to be specious. As a result of this kind of deception, a lot of the soldiers I worked with got a bad taste in their mouths.

So why are we there? I can tell you an interesting story that'll probably never be proven. Once I worked with an officer from Texas and he said to me, "You remember back in 1993 when Saddam tried to kill the former President Bush? He tried to kill him at a meeting in Kuwait. Tried to have him assassinated. Down in Texas we don't forget things like that. Plain and simple? The reason we invaded Iraq is because Saddam tried to kill George W. Bush's daddy." This gentleman thought, by the way, that this was a perfectly good reason to invade a country. I don't.

We wouldn't do something like that, would we? I can't find any valid reasons *why* we invaded Iraq and I'd truly hate to think we did it for those reasons. And before you go off yelling that I've got this all wrong, I'll tell you flat out: Saddam was a bastard of the first order. He did terrible things to his own people and deserved to be eliminated. But if the president had come to the American people and stated his case like that, if he'd said, "This man, Saddam, has done so many terrible things. He's tried to assassinate the president of the United States, he's gassed his own people, and shown no regard whatsoever for playing by the rules of the United Nations. Therefore we feel we should go in and remove him from power for our own safety and the betterment of the Iraqi people." . . . If he had stated the case like that, I'll bet the majority of this country would be with him.

But to make up excuses for an invasion? The reason we invaded in March had nothing to do with when the UN inspectors finished up their inspections. It had to do with when the weather was cool enough in Iraq to deploy troops. Everyone who's ever been part of a ground assault knows that.

We're in a quagmire, and I don't see it getting any better. Everything I saw reminded me of my short time in Vietnam and it scares me. It really does. Unfortunately, if we pull out prematurely and Vietnamization is replaced by Iraqization, we'll have a worse mess than if Saddam had stayed in power. It's sort of a Hobson's choice, isn't it?

By the way, here's the kicker: my unit's scheduled to go back again next year.

Ed. Note: By the final editing of this story, Bill von Zehle had been promoted to command sergeant major.

BUILDING THE PERFECT BEAST

Captain Matthew Hancock

U.S. ARMY RESERVE, ATTACHED TO THE REGIMENTAL SUPPORT SQUADRON, 2ND ARMORED CAVALRY REGIMENT

Matthew served four years of active duty with the army after graduating ROTC at West Virginia University. He spent three subsequent years in the Maryland National Guard and two more in the Inactive Ready Reserve. He joined the Active Reserves in response to 9/11. Currently, age 33, he lives in Dallas, where he works as an assistant project manager for Adolfson and Peterson, a construction company.

Captain Hancock is one of the few reservists who volunteered for active duty in Iraq. He left behind his job and his life in Texas because "this is what I trained all my life to do. How could I not contribute something?"

I'm an engineer so I was specifically sent to Iraq to serve as a camp construction expert for the Al Rastimiyah site in southeast Baghdad, directly south of Sadr City. The site used to be the old College of War for the army of Iraq, but we took it over once we stormed Baghdad. It was a fine location for a camp, and there was a certain beautiful irony to the fact that we, the conquering army, were living in the routed Iraqis' War College. Al Rastimiyah was sort of an intimidating name for Westerners, so while I was in Iraq we renamed the facility Camp Muleskinner. After I left, they renamed it again. This time they called it Camp Cuervo after a PFC [private first class] who was killed in an ambush nearby.

Here's how I got deployed. My employers at Adolfson Peterson were closing their Dallas office so I got a job with another company. Between leaving Adolfson Peterson and starting the new job, I went to my two-week annual reservist training. Right after that I got my deployment orders, summer of 2003. Under the circumstances, I have to say that my new bosses were very gracious. Here I'd just signed on with them and, before I'd even settled in, I announced I was leaving for Iraq. It was the ultimate HR *whooopsee*. Obviously, my bosses weren't happy, but they decided to grin and bear it. They said, "Well, we think this is a very patriotic thing you're doing. Thank you for volunteering." They promised to hold my job open while I was overseas. I reciprocated by staying in regular contact and keeping myself up-to-date on certain projects.

For deployment, I went up to El Paso alone to muster, found out I'd been thrown in with a big group of soldiers, about seventy in all, everyone in the same situation: No one'd been assigned to a unit. I met two guys in El Paso who'd been activated involuntarily. Suffice it to say they were not happy campers. Back then, the need for soldiers was running high. The U.S. was still in an early stage of the campaign and a lot of personnel were being handed their first term extensions. Rumsfeld's promises of a six-month campaign were turning out to be a load of crap. A lot of folks figured they'd get home soon, but it was becoming evident that no, they'd be in-country much, much longer than expected. Overall, there was a tense, angry atmosphere.

Half of the seventy soldiers were medical personnel—doctors, dentists, specialists, physicians' assistants, you name it—mostly pulled from individual hospitals. A couple of them gave me that weird look when they found out I'd volunteered. No one questioned it, though. Later on, when car bombs started becoming the norm in Iraq, I noticed people had a different evaluation of my decision. They thought I was out of my mind.

If you've never heard of "camp construction" duty in a war zone, don't worry, you're not alone. I didn't know what it was either until I landed in Baghdad. For my first few days in-country I met with the regimental engineer, Major Bozik. He picked up immediately on the fact that I'm a civilian construction expert, and that was all he needed to hear. Major Bozik brought me up to speed on an ongoing project he'd undertaken with Colonel Marich, engineer for the First Armored Division. Like everyone else, Bozik and Marich had just started figuring out that Iraq wasn't going to be a six- to nine-month rotation. More like a couple of years. Probably much, much longer. That wasn't the problem, there was nothing anyone could do about mission extensions. No, the problem had to do with tents.

At that point, our soldiers were living in tents, hundreds and hundreds of them clustered together into cities. It was a good idea for a short-term op, but you can't sustain an environment like that for long without creating quality-of-life issues. If the U.S. Army was going to stay in Baghdad much longer, we'd need to build barracks and fortifications, structures to protect our troops against incoming mortar fire. The troops needed air conditioning to combat the desert heat, plumbing for restrooms and showers facilities, dining facilities for healthy meals, recreation areas, the works. We needed it all and we needed it fast. But how?

First Armored was laid out chaotically. Its soldiers were bivouacked all over the place, in seized palaces, tents, and classroom buildings. They lived on any plot of ground they could sprawl on and hang a tarp over. Some units had taken it upon themselves to create more permanent accommodations, but there was no unity to the effort and unity is a vital part of military operations. Without unity, the whole system begins to teeter and buckle. Major Bozik said that we had our work cut out for us, but that was an incredible understatement.

First AD created a governing body called the BCCA, the Base Camp Coordination Authority. Essentially this group said, "Hey, why don't we try to put all our construction efforts on the same page? That way we can bring in a set of standards and allocate work more efficiently." BCCA set a goal for itself: after the first troop rotation, no American soldier would be living in a tent. It sounds like a simple, commonsense initiative, but remember, this was life in a war zone where problems, both the known and unforeseen, could make life miserable. If nothing else, this effort set a precedent. First AD was the first division in Baghdad to pony up to the table and get it done.

Now, the rule of thumb for American military presence in a foreign country is this: if our forces occupy a plot of land for any significant length of time, we try to upgrade it so we leave it better off than it was before we arrived. Why do we do this? Two good reasons. First, we have to meet the needs of our own personnel. The U.S. Army doesn't like to have its soldiers living in tents for long periods of time, sleeping on rickety cots in buildings without air-conditioning in the middle of a desert, that sort of thing. We want our troops to have clean and ample drinking water, we want them to feel safe. You get the idea. We upgrade facilities to make life easier for ourselves.

The second reason we do upgrades is to show respect for the foreign nation we've entered. Or at least that's what I thought until I saw the way we conducted business in Iraq.

I'll tell you what I mean. I spent my first couple months living in the War College hospital. It had a roof and walls made from six-inch-thick poured concrete. Grenades and mortars couldn't damage them, so I never felt especially vulnerable there despite the fact that hostilities in Baghdad were running high back then. I thought, *Huh. Here's a possible solution to the housing problem.*

Before the BCCA created their initiative, my team and I upgraded one of the Iraqi post buildings to U.S. military standards. Call it a test run. It went just like I said, a standard construction job: revamp the electrical, install air-conditioning, upgrade the plumbing system. We put in showers, drains, sewage systems, everything. We were able to do it all and keep the building an all-inclusive environment, meaning no annexation. Because God forbid you have somebody running outside to take a shit or a shower in a separate trailer while the enemy's shelling you. That's a good way to lose people. No, house them in a good, solid building like the old army post. Someone lobbing a mortar or grenades might blow out a window, but they wouldn't scratch the superstructure.

We followed all the military construction codes, which are ample. And I'll admit: it's hard to equate materials prices in the Iraqi wartime market to prices in peacetime America—I'll use my best professional judgment when it comes to that. But overall, guess what it cost us to furbish that army post? Anywhere from $100,000 to $300,000! That was it. Just $300,00 to house up to thirty troops in style, safety, and comfort.

When the BCCA set its initiative, I did some walk-arounds with BCCA members. We eyeballed all the places U.S. troops were bunking in, and it became very clear: we could pull similar revamp jobs on structures around the base like the hospital I was staying in. Add electrical, put in some bathrooms, trick out the existing superstructure with fire safety equipment, air-conditioning, and insulation. We'd have a roof over everyone's heads in no time for practically nothing. Plus, the plan featured a bonus: when U.S. troops pulled out, Iraqi citizens would have a brand-new facility to use once their democracy was established. We thought we'd struck gold.

Command nixed the idea right off the bat. If we heard this from them once, we heard it a thousand times: no permanent structures. The unofficial translation being we do not in any way want American forces to appear like an occupying army. I had a very hard time understanding this perspective. After all we'd done to that country, bombing it, starving it with embargos, rolling in troops, instigating governmental change, it seemed silly to me to pull up short all of a sudden and say, "Oh, but wait a minute. Don't get us wrong. We're not really *here*. We're just passing *through*." I wasn't alone in this kind of thinking. The Regimental Support Squadron commander was a man named Lieutenant Colonel Curran. He didn't agree with this set of "logistics," either.

The higher-ups said they had a better plan. They wanted to install white, modular trailers to serve as troop quarters. Each trailer could house two soldiers. They said, "Install as many of these as you can get your hands on." I hated the idea. The economics of it alone made my teeth itch. For a hundred thousand dollars, you could buy two, maybe three trailers. Meaning we'd spend fifteen times the money to create an environment that was less safe, less comfortable, and entirely nonrecyclable for the Iraqi people who'd eventually return to the region. I'd always wondered where all the taxpayer money goes in a war. Now I was finding out. The government went with the trailer idea.

They argued that trailers were easy to set up. They're modular and therefore easy to reconfigure. And when the war's all finished, they said, you can hook them up to vehicles and drive them over the border and out of the country. Voilà! No more American presence. It's like we were never here in the first place. I was thinking, *Yeah, right. Tell that to the citizens of Iraq.* But my biggest question was, What do we do with the trailers once they've crossed the border? Do we ship them back to the U.S.? That would cost us another fortune. Do we leave them in the Middle East? Who would use them? And honestly—how is discarding a bunch of trailers in a foreign country any more logical than fixing up the original buildings?

No one ever gave me an answer on that, no matter how hard I pushed. Being a reservist who served with an active unit, I wasn't part of the normal line of ass-kissing. Any comments I made would never be tied to my evaluation report, so I was always willing to say, "Sir, I think that's wrong. I highly recommend we do this instead." I never had to fear the consequences of being honest. What's the worst the army could do to me? They could either extend my tour or send me home. Either way would have been fine with me. Looking back, I was a little surprised at how "unhonest" some of the conversations were over there.

My second big question was, How on earth are these trailers a good use of taxpayer money? Fulfilling the troop needs would require thousands of trailers. Thousands! Do the math on that. Then somebody please tell me how this makes any sense at all. But that's what the government wanted. So that's what we did. Not at Camp Muleskinner, but practically everywhere else.

Construction on base was handled exclusively by Iraqi contractors. In many ways, I found myself handling them—and my job—the same way I would've handled a project here in the United States. I got three bids for every project we initiated. Each bid had to go through an approval process before we settled on a contractor and awarded the job. Then we'd pay the contracting firm a third of the total job invoice in good faith to get the job rolling.

Colonel Curran made the decision to use Iraqi contractors and I completely agreed with this move, it made perfect sense. Paying local companies to work meant we were stimulating the Iraqi economy; undeniably, this is one of the long-term goals of the American presence in Iraq. Plus using local companies meant that we obtained our materials from local sources, allowing construction to happen quickly. Rather than ordering our supplies from overseas and waiting months for them to arrive, we had the pleasure of watching the Iraqis make things happen in a matter of weeks, if not days.

Naturally, there were some drawbacks. Namely, security. Do you remember the camp bombing from a couple of weeks ago?[48] Well, that's the kind of thing that can happen when you're not very, very careful screening your indigenous workers. We were careful, we installed a lot of security protocols. In fact, I don't think it's any great breach of confi-

48. On December 22, 2004 a twenty-four-year-old Arabic man who'd been working as a mess-tent attendant at an American base in Mosul killed twenty-two people (including thirteen U.S. soldiers) by strapping explosives to his body and detonating them at the height of a lunchtime crowd. At least sixty-nine others were wounded in the attack, including forty-four U.S. soldiers, seven American civilian contractors, five U.S. Defense Department civilians, two Iraqi civilians, and ten civilian workers from other nations. Forensics experts later determined that shot pellets or ball bearings must have been loaded into the bomb to ensure maximum casualties. The attack, obviously well planned, raised alarming questions about security measures at U.S. facilities in Iraq.

dentiality to say that we had one American soldier standing guard over every five Iraqi contractors at all times. Any Iraqi worker found wandering around for whatever reason was immediately detained, searched, and escorted off post. We frisked people routinely, too. Any worker found with a camera, cell phone, or any other type of prohibited equipment was detained, searched, and escorted off post. No exceptions.

The system worked, but it was very manpower intensive. The regiment had already doubled its mission capacity, meaning that our city patrols had to watchdog twice the number of Iraqi civilians we'd originally been tasked to. Plus, no small item, the base was in the middle of a war zone, remember. We had to run round-the-clock surveillance on our own grounds, particularly at our most vulnerable flank, the northern gate. Then to baby-sit 250 contractors on top of all that? It was a lot to ask. We were stretched pretty thin.

Colonel Curran took a very firm stance, though. He'd say, "I have a mission to rebuild this place as well as a mission to defend the people of this base. I can do it. I will do it." It made things a rough ride for everyone, but the colonel was right to take that position. I say that because, in all the time I lived at Camp Muleskinner, we never suffered a single death on post due to enemy action. Not one.

There was so much work going on, we'd typically put in fourteen- to sixteen-hour days, seven days a week. For me, a typical day went something like this: I'd wake up at six-thirty or seven. First stop was always the dining facility [D-Fac], which we got a few months after I arrived. Ours was the second largest D-Fac in Baghdad. Then I'd head to the office, check e-mail, meet with the camp manager and coordinate my agenda for the day. Then I'd walk over to check in at the command post—this would be at around eight-thirty or nine o'clock. I'd meet the contractors' foreman and discuss a few things with him. His laborers would have arrived by seven, so by this point they were hard at work.

The foremen and I would make rounds and review the work being done. I'd give notes: "This is okay. This is excellent. This needs more work. This is subpar." Like I said, this was exactly the same way I did my job here in America. The only real difference was that I spoke to the foreman using a translator. That, and the fact that everyone around me was armed to the teeth and ready to shoot on sight.

Okay, maybe it wasn't *exactly* the same job I'd do here in America. Here in the States you tend to pop into the office, grab a cup of coffee, and spend most of the morning bringing yourself up to speed with co-workers. In Iraq, it was, Get to the post, put your gear on, make sure your weapon was locked and loaded. Screw the coffee. The possibility of getting whacked by a stray AK round or some sort of IED? That's enough of a stimulant for me. No reason to bring yourself up to speed with co-workers, either. I just saw them less than eight hours ago, we spent most of our time together, and anyway, we're all in the same boat, looking over our shoulders and trying to get things done.

We'd walk the job site, then I'd hand the foreman off to someone else, go back to the office, and check bids. That was probably the biggest part of my job, I generally had thirty or forty projects rotating at any given time. Some would be opening up as others closed down, but they were all in some stage of activity. Mostly I checked the bid forms for noticeable discrepancies. The system over there was very corrupt. You'd often get the same company attempting to bid on the same project three different times, using three different names. I was able to catch most of them most of the time. And that was the bulk of my morning.

In the afternoon, I'd meet with the base security chief and check the progress of the security wall. We were building a fourteen-foot-high concrete perimeter around the camp, complete with guard towers. This was a massive undertaking in itself. If everything was going smoothly there, I'd move on and check on everything you'd normally find under a Department of Public Works—the water supply and sewer lines, the port-a-let trucks, the electrical grid. I'd make sure all the filtration systems were being cleaned. My group was also in charge of camp maintenance.

Toward the end of an evening, it was pretty common for me to look around at all this work being done and wonder where the hell it was all going. By that I mean, we were doing all this construction on the northern part of the base because we'd already pledged to give the southern part back to the Iraqis by the end of the year. But we had three whole units living in the southern sector. Where the hell were we going to put them when the time came to move?

We had one soldier get shot. It was the weirdest thing. She was at the salad bar in the dining facility when all of a sudden she just dropped to the ground like someone had clocked her in the head with an invisible baseball bat. She was unconscious by the time she hit the ground. The dining facility was in a tent; unbelievably, a bullet had fallen out of the sky, torn through the tent roof, and smacked her right in the forehead. Imagine. She's a very lucky woman. I guess if she had a thinner skull, the round would have killed her. I could say something here about women having thicker heads than men, but I'd probably piss somebody off.

It was just one of those things that happens over there. Iraqis tend to celebrate special occasions by shooting their AK-47s into the air. You could hear them all the time, the ripping sound of someone burning through a full clip of Soviet-made ammunition. All well and good in the heat of the moment. But there's this little-known law over there called gravity. It pulls bullets out of the sky and, eventually, they have to land somewhere. In this case, one of them hit our camp and smacked that soldier in the head. We know for a fact that the shot was a stray because we did a trajectory analysis. If that round had been fired on purpose in any way, that soldier'd be dead, no question. She lived. Unless God is on the Iraqis' side, and I've reason to believe he is not, the whole thing was just a fluke.

Stuff like that happened all the time over there. I have five bullets that I picked up off the ground while walking around on my site inspections. I still keep them as souvenirs.

You get frazzled pretty quickly working seven days a week. Thankfully the Muslim day of rest, I don't know, what do you call that? A Sabbath? Their holy day was on a Friday and most contractors would take the day off. We encouraged this in a big way. It provided us with necessary downtime, especially for the guys who'd pulled duty all week standing guard over the workers. We gave them the day off, too, and pulled in guys from other units to walk the rounds. Mechanics, cooks, supply guys, it didn't matter. Every Friday you'd see a crew of very unlikely guardsmen standing watch along the base perimeter. It was the only way we could keep up the pace all week.

Sometimes I'd take a half-day off on Sundays. I know I took a half-day off on Thanksgiving. But I want to impress you with this: we worked all the time over there. Our base was special for a number of reasons, not the least of which was the fact that we were positioned right smack dab in the middle of Baghdad. I'm saying there wasn't room for error, you had to be constantly alert. We were very aware—hyperaware, I guess you'd say—that anything at all could happen at any moment. Force protection became one of my biggest initiatives by necessity. My biggest initiative and my biggest headache.

The fourteen-foot-concrete wall we built was part of the force protection initiative. The guard towers, the indirect pits, the bunkers, the fact that fully half the money in my budget went toward building or maintaining structures designed to deflect or deter attack, that was all part of force protection [FP]. FP became a priority at Muleskinner due to command emphasis, meaning that's the way our brass wanted it done. To emphasize this, Colonel Curran brought in a chief warrant officer 5. There's only a handful of them in the entire United States military and we were very lucky to have ours, a guy by the name of Chief Watson. Watson was a OH58 Delta test pilot and he'd worked in the Comanche program, a real heavy hitter. Suffice it to say he'd been around the block a few times, so when he arrived on base the colonel grabbed hold of him and said, "Look, I want you, I *need* you to be head of my security."

That was all she wrote. Watson inaugurated a major construction campaign aimed completely at force protection. As it turned out, he was an incredibly paranoid man, paranoid in a good way. You know how the old saying goes: You're not paranoid if they really *are* out to get you. All you had to do was take a peek over the perimeter wall to know that, yes, there was a whole city of people out there just dying to punch our tickets. That was enough stress to live under without the added tension of thinking that someone on our own side might—for inadvertent, stupid reasons—injure you in some kind of accident. Deaths and injury by friendly fire or mishap were enormously common while I was in Iraq. For a while, we actually logged more casualties inflicted from our own side than we did through contact with the enemy. That's not a particularly proud statistic.

Chief Watson routinely emphasized that no one on our post was going to die for a stupid reason. If someone died, he said, it wouldn't be because we could've done something to stop it and opted not to. It was only going to happen under circumstances completely out of our control and nothing else.

Complicate this huge construction fiasco with the fact that we didn't really have a budget. Or actually, I should say we were given too many budgets. The money we were allocated and the criteria for dispersion fluctuated or utterly mutated practically every day. But regardless of how the budget changed, one thing was always certain: the amount of cash we dealt with over there was staggering.

The way money worked in Iraq, you had two real sources. You had "PR and C" money, which we used for new purchases. No, I don't remember what that acronym stands for. Suffice it to say that PR and C money was supposed to be used for permanent, long-term construction, although, here we go again, the army stayed as far away from the term "permanent" as they could in any and all instances related to construction. PR and C money had to be approved, of course. You'd draw up three bids, write a memorandum saying that you'd like to do this project with such-and-such contractor. Then, depending on the amount required, there were certain hoops you had to jump through at the corps level, which I think was Fifth corps at the time. The approval process could take anywhere from three to eight weeks. We were constantly trying to streamline the process, cut corners, save dollars, and still get the work done. It was practically a hopeless cause and very frustrating. Waiting eight weeks for request approval on a bunker is a really long time when you're living in a war zone.

If the request went through the process and didn't get approved from PR and C, we didn't give up. We'd try to draw funding from the other big pile of money, which was designated for "morale and welfare." Morale/welfare money worked like this: you got the same x amount of dollars for all eligible units, regardless of size. So a battalion might be allotted $20,000 and a platoon would also get $20,000, which didn't make much sense to me. Depending on your classification, there were differences here and there, but that's largely how things went. Morale/welfare funds were supposed to be used for one-time-only, nonrecurring purchases. Like you could buy a TV to keep up the morale of a unit. Or ice that might last for a week.

You weren't supposed to spend morale/welfare money on permanent assets. Technically, even air conditioners should've been bought through PR and C, but you know how it is. When money's scarce, you do what you have to do. Put it this way: I know of at least one base camp in Iraq that was built with money from the wrong fund. Who cares? It got built.

Yes, it was wrong using morale money to build camps, but you have to understand the problems we ran into over there. Case in point: We were living in the desert where the temperature routinely hit over 120 degrees during the cool months. None of our guys had air-conditioning for their quarters, and none of our requests for same went through at PR and C. I've got a hundred soldiers dying of heat prostration and $20,000 of morale money just sitting there, you're telling me I'm *not* supposed to buy air conditioners? Ultimately, you had to make decisions. I'm going to use this money to buy my soldiers air conditioners or pay Iraqis who'll fix my broken generator. Allotment of money from two sources was ridiculous. There's a war going on! In dire-need situations, who gives a red hot damn where the money comes from? It's all coming from the same source, right? Taxpayer money. Taxpayers who probably want their sons and daughters in Iraq to have air-conditioning lest they get heatstroke.

As far as I could see, the system was absurd. If I wanted to use morale/welfare money to buy a pool table, a big-screen TV, or a DVD player, that was cool. But if three of my soldiers had been hospitalized for heat-related ailments and more were wobbling around the camp like drunken sailors, ready to drop at a moment's notice—so sorry. I had to wait up to eight weeks for approval before cash allocations from PR and C came through to buy air conditioners, assuming the request was granted. I'm sure that the rationalization for funding allocations makes much more sense the higher up you go in the chain of command. But down on the level I was at, it looked ridiculous. Not to mention potentially dangerous.

Let me tell you my generator story. Our camp wasn't operating off the Iraqi power system since their grid was undependable. On any given day the Iraqi grid might work for three hours, then shut down for nine, work another six, then shut down for twelve. You can't maintain an invasion army on a system like that. So we used generators, big one-megawatt jobs that cost about $100,000 each. One of those things could power an entire street block in New York City if you kept it filled with diesel fuel.

We'd actually inherited two of these gennys from the old Iraqi Air Force hospital, but we only used one since the other kept breaking all the time. The one that worked was a real lifesaver. Damn thing literally roared along 24 hours a day, 7 days a week, supplying power to the whole camp. But if we ever had to do maintenance on Number One, we had to shut down the whole camp 'til the genny was back on its feet.

Muleskinner'd put in requests for a new generator before I even got to Iraq. The suppliers I talked to said they had to ship units from the United States since every available unit in Europe had been commandeered for service. I could sympathize with the need, everybody needed electrical power in Iraq. But here we were living in the heart of Baghdad. I figured that alone might earmark us as a priority. Nope.

By November, the backup genny was completely dead and Old Faithful was chugging away, looking tired as hell. We'd already shut her down once or twice for maintenance and blown parts. If we kept pushing her at the pace she was going, I figured she'd be ten toes up by Christmas. So my job in November became all about generators, generators, generators. I was on the phone at all hours trying to scrape one up. Nothing. No effect whatsoever. Which is when we moved to buying a genny with morale money since we couldn't get funding through proper channels. I left Iraq in late December. The genny came a week later, in January. The bottom line: at one of the main army bases in downtown Baghdad during the war, it took us five months to get a generator. I don't care how you look at it: that's a pretty ugly situation.

So here's the weirdest thing that happened to me over there, but let me preface it by saying this: at one point, someone parked a trailer in front of the Al Rasheed Hotel.[49] This thing looked like a U-Haul trailer so everyone ignored it. It was actually a rocket battery. One day, the trailer

---

49. The Al Rasheed Hotel became infamous during the first Gulf War when CNN journalists—the only news reporters left in-country to cover the invasion—used the fortresslike building as their base of operations. Used to catering to an international clientele under trying political circumstances, the hotel's once-elaborate now down-at-the-heels decor is augmented by a notorious mosaic of George Bush Sr.'s face set into the lobby floor. Reportedly, the mosaic was commissioned by hotel workers who were angry at Bush Sr. for having invaded Iraq, and whom they blamed for a misguided cruise missile that landed on hotel grounds and exploded in 1993.

opened up, the missiles elevated and *phoooosh*, it fired. You can imagine how many people messed their britches when this happened. Suffice it to say, that's the kind of environment we dealt with over there. Insurgents can be incredibly clever. They have a true knack for devising new and interesting ways to inflict massive casualties on coalition forces.

Like I said, part of my job was to take regular walks and inspect camp. I was frequently accompanied by Colonel Curran and the post's intelligence officer. After rounds, we'd often find ourselves sitting around telling jokes to lighten the mood. I'm a huge smart aleck and these guys could match me toe to toe. One time not long after the U-Haul incident, we got a report saying that insurgents had begun to place bombs in the carcasses of dead donkeys lying by the sides of the roads. Dead donkeys were everywhere in Iraq so I suppose they thought that American troops would see the dead donkey, think nothing of it, drive on past, and *boom*! I don't know if we ever suffered any casualties like this, but the report put us all on edge.

So: typical Army situation. We're in an intelligence briefing. The intel officer clears his throat, checks his notes, and says, "Okay. So. New action point. Be on the look out for DBIDs. Say again: We have now issued a DBID warning." Dead silence. Colonel Curran looks around, but no one wants to be the one to put his foot forward. So he sighs and shakes his head. Says, "Okay. I'll bite. What's a DBID?"

I'll say this for the guy: he tried really hard. Couldn't pull it off though. Impossible to keep a straight face when he said this. "Well, sir. It's a Donkey-Borne Improvised Explosives Device." Which cracked us all up. Everybody in the room starts making *HEE-haw, HEE-haw, BOOM!* noises. Might've been the funniest thing we'd heard in weeks. Wouldn't you know it? Two days later, a donkey bolts toward base and zips past the back gate guard who fairly loses his shit. This donkey runs to the center of camp. It's scared as hell, kicking around all over the post. Its eyes are rolling back into its head from fear and it's going *HEE-haw, HEE-haw, HEE-haw!* which made us laugh hard enough to crack ribs. "That's it!" we howled. "That's the Donkey-Borne IED! We're all gonna die!"

We weren't afraid. It wasn't saddled, it carried no packs to hide explosives in—unless of course someone had gone a long way and crammed a bomb up its ass. Who knew where it came from? It didn't really matter.

The damn donkey was scared enough for all of us. You should have seen how hard it kicked, it was petrified. The Fourth Aviation Squadron got hold of it and calmed it down and adopted the thing as their mascot.

Man, what are the chances on that? Perfect comic timing from a pack animal. Speak of the DBID and it appears.

When I got back to the States, I found out the new firm I'd joined had rotated three different managers into my position. Three of my bosses, the guys who'd hired me in the first place, had left the company. Guess you could say it wasn't the environment I'd signed onto, so I resigned. They kept that job open for me all that time but it wasn't a good fit anymore.

Why did I volunteer to go to Baghdad? My girlfriend asked me that and I guess it's a reasonable question. I told her, I told everybody, I want to come back with a good war story. She yelled at me. Nobody else really accepted it. Some folks called me a few names that I won't repeat in this interview but I kept saying it all the same. I want a war story, I want a war story. Well I got one. I was one of the first responders after the United Nations car bombing. After carrying wounded UN workers and pulling bodies out of the ruble, I stopped talking about war stories. My service as an engineer might not sound heroic to some folks. But it's service. I put in the time. I did what I did and I'm proud of it.

When I came home I was assigned to the 493rd Reserve Engineer Unit. Turned out one of my good friends, Major Otteson, was head of the Base Camp Coordination Authority. He lives nearby my stateside home and we grill together almost every weekend. Jack says that our base camp was the best one in Iraq, meaning it had the best quality of life. We didn't lose soldiers for stupid reasons. Of course that wasn't my doing single-handedly, but I like to think that my civilian construction experience and attitude had some resonance to the inertia of the war zone.

At the time I volunteered, I firmly believed in what we were doing. We had 130,000 soldiers over there and I figured they'd need the kind of help I'd trained all my life to provide. As a soldier, I've been trained to shoot a rifle, but it's not really my greatest strength. The skills I excel at can still save lives, or at least make the quality of life better for our people so *they* can go out and save lives, both Americans and Iraqis. If I went to

Iraq and ended up helping one person, wouldn't that be worth it? Has my attitude changed at all? Yes, it has. I'm not saying I didn't get my opportunity to help. I just wonder what we're doing over there in the first place.

I've since resigned my commission effective September 15, 2005. Thank God I submitted my paperwork in time. The reserve tried to reactivate me in June 2005 for an eighteen-month tour. I suspected my number would come up again since I'd only used six months of a possible two years of mobilization time. Of course the conversations I had over three days when I was supposed to report could be a story in itself. Ask me about it sometime.

A LOVE STORY

✴

Sergeant Natalie Stinson
U.S. ARMY, FIRST CAVALRY DIVISION, 312TH MILITARY
INTELLIGENCE BATTALION, DELTA COMPANY

The army sent Sergeant Stinson to DLI[50] in California where she studied to be a 98 Golf, a Korean cryptolinguist. "Then they sent me to Korea," she says. "I was in Military Intelligence and my job was to listen to the Koreans. I can't tell you anything more than that, though. It's classified."

When the war began, Natalie had already logged the maximum amount of time she could serve in a strategic assignment. "But I still had time left on my contract," she says. "They had to do something with me, so the army shifted me to tactical duty in Baghdad." Natalie deployed for Iraq on March 17, 2004 and was stationed in Baghdad. She returned to the States on March 18, 2005. When her five-year contract with the army came due the following November, Natalie, age 28, left the service.

I felt like a fish out of water in Iraq. No one there speaks Korean, so my skills were completely useless. The army solved that problem by cross-training me to do secretarial work. They set me up in an office at Al Salaam, which had been one of Saddam's palaces before the war. I sat behind a desk and collected the intel reports being gathered on site. Then I'd put the reports into e-mails and send them along to the higher-ups. That's it, that's all I did. It was an easy assignment with very few responsibilities but the hours were long, 12 hours a day, 7 days a week.

I got bored. I guess anybody would when you're sitting behind a desk. Looking back, it's pretty easy to see how things happened the way they did. I fell in love with a married man, a married man who had two beautiful little girls, no less. Yes, I felt horribly guilty about it. Part of me

---

50. Or DLIFLC, Defense Language Institute Foreign Language Center, the world's largest language school and the only government language school with degree-granting authority. Located at the Presidio of Monterey in San Francisco, California, DLIFLC "provides foreign language education, training, evaluation, and sustainment for DoD personnel in order to ensure the success of the Defense Foreign Language Program and enhance the security of the Nation." (mission statement per the DLIFLC Web site.)

doesn't even want to talk to you about it. There's no way to describe what happened that will do it any justice.

Al Salaam palace sat way up on this hilltop overlooking Baghdad. The palace was very tall. One time we dropped a stone off the rooftop and timed how long it took to hit the ground. Using the gravity equation, we calculated that the rooftop was about a hundred and fifty feet in the air. The elevation gave us an incredible view of the city. From the rooftops of Al Salaam, you could see all of Baghdad spread out and stretched away below.

I didn't see as much of the city as I would've liked, but a few things stuck out for me. First of all, I'd expected everyone to be dressed in traditional Islamic garb, but that wasn't the case. A lot of women especially wore traditional clothes, but just as many people were walking around in T-shirts, jeans, and sneakers. Also, the architecture wasn't really modern. Everything was sand-colored, as if the buildings had been made from the desert itself. Visually, the structures would blend in with one another. But there was a lot more vegetation than I'd expected to see in such an arid climate. Our little corner of Baghdad was very green. We had palm trees and rosebushes all over the palace grounds, and one particular type of tree bore a fruit that resembled a tiny orange or a tangerine with spiky skin. These things were falling off the trees all over the place the first month we arrived. I tasted a few. The fruit was definitely citrus, but sour not sweet. I never got the name of them.

Sometimes we'd go up to the top of Al Salaam and watch the war or the insurgency or whatever you want to call it. It went on everyday. Far below us, Baghdad was a constant clatter of small arms fire, mortar fire, and RPG explosions. You'd see distant muzzle bursts and tracer bullets at night, the flash of car bombs detonating, explosions consuming buildings, dust clouds being raised. The daily soundtrack at Al Salaam was the crackle of a war we could never touch from where we were stationed.

We were like shut-ins at Al Salaam. The palace was surrounded by a gated area about two miles in circumference. We shared the camp with a Reserve infantry battalion, and it was very safe, almost like a war wasn't really going on just a short distance away. Our camp was very comfortable. We had an Internet café run by Iraqi nationals, for instance. We could use the café like a general store to buy things we wanted, too. We weren't allowed off base, so the Iraqis who ran the café brought us whatever we asked for. They took orders for TVs, VCRs, DVD players, and brought the goods in when they came to work. We had our own little courier economy. Compared to what other soldiers went through, it was paradise.

Still, I was having problems. I'd just been promoted before we deployed, and in the jump from specialist to sergeant I took on a lot of new responsibilities for which I had no experience. Leadership didn't come easily to me. My platoon was small, maybe fifteen people. I'd met them only eight weeks before we shipped out, so I found it difficult to establish my role with them. I was also having personal difficulties. I'd just broken off a relationship with someone, and I was devastated. With all this going on, I'll admit, I was also a little terrified when I got the order to deploy for Iraq. Who knew what to expect? I wrote out letters to family and friends as a precaution. A lot of soldiers do that. The letters said how much I loved them, how much they'd filled my life, how I hoped they'd never have to read this. When I found out I'd been stationed in what was probably the safest enclave in the whole country, I was relieved.

Very soon my relief turned to frustration. We were safe, but we were holed up in this tiny spot, only allowed to leave the compound on very special occasions, and for that you had to don forty or fifty pounds of protective gear: Kevlar helmets, flak vests with SAPI [small arms protection insert] plates,[51] survival gear, extra ammo, your weapon locked and loaded. Nobody went outside unless they absolutely had to, so we ended up incredibly isolated. And I hadn't made many friends.

Within three months I found myself wondering, What are we doing here? Are we helping the Iraqis at all? Or are we really just helping ourselves? I couldn't see any tangible proof that we weren't. Every day we'd hear the explosions coming up from the city and whenever you heard one, you knew someone had died right there and then. Maybe it was one of us, maybe it was one of them. Either way there was nothing I could do about it, nothing at all.

---

51. Plates made from ceramic, boron carbide, Kevlar, and other reinforced plastic materials used for backing. The plates are capable of fracturing the core of small arms projectiles on impact because a major portion of the incoming round's kinetic energy is absorbed by the tiles and redistributed into the backing.

I found myself wishing I was a soldier fighting in the streets. At least then I'd have some kind of hands on experience to base my trauma on, an experience I could process. What was my experience of Iraq? Twelve hour shifts of glorified secretary work. I answered the phones, sent out the e-mails, and monitored the radio for major events, which never seemed to happen. All to the constant background din of explosions and gunfire.

My days went like this: I'd get off work, take a shower, go to bed. Wake up, go for a run, report for work. Get off work, take a shower, go to bed again. Over and over and over again. Al Salaam palace was vast and lavishly ornamented, but my office was on the top floor in what used to be a storage room. No windows, no natural light. Fluorescent rods hung from the ceiling. Bare, cracked, stone walls. We'd taken ourselves off the Baghdad city power grid because it was unreliable, but the generators that fed us electricity would break down often due to lack of fuel or maintenance.

I was only getting along with two people. One of them was Jen, an Arabic-language specialist. She'd been in the army and gone to DLI. She'd left the service and gone to work for Titan as a contractor. She lived on base with us as if she were part of our unit and we became workout partners. We ran together nearly every day.

My other friend was a man named J.R. He was a Korean linguist, too, although he was additionally certified as an analyst. We'd gotten to know each other shortly before we deployed. The army'd assigned him to the same job as me, a slot that fell far below his ability level. We were counterparts. In the beginning, we worked alternating shifts. We'd drop by and visit while the other person worked. Talking to a friend was good in that place and it didn't affect our job performance at all. Our assignment wasn't mentally taxing.

I'm not really sure how it happened—God knows I didn't want it to. It just did, that's the long and short of it. J.R. and I fell in love.

Our specialties gave us a lot in common. Neither one of us are Korean by ethnic descent, we're just plain old white people whom the army trained to speak Korean. I'd confided in J.R. about my relationship troubles, that was another point of connection, but I can't stress this enough: I didn't confide in him with any kind of ulterior motive. I knew J.R.'s wife and two little girls from social functions back in the States. His wife and I weren't friends; suffice it to say we're very different people. But we were friendly. I respect her.

It's just that, as time went on, J.R. and I became closer. Neither of us got along with the rest of the soldiers in our platoon, so all we had was each other. A few soldiers thought it was odd that a married man spent so much time with another woman, but we weren't doing anything wrong, we just liked talking to each other. Nobody else saw it that way, everyone had strong opinions. They looked at us as if we were bad people and started talking behind our backs. Most would smile in our faces, then run off and gossip. Some were openly hostile. The more they disapproved, the more J.R. and I stuck together. What else could we do? Eventually Command got involved. There was no law against what we were doing, but the higher-ups were protective of J.R.'s marriage. Pretty soon, Command made it very clear that they didn't condone our relationship.

First they verbally ordered us not to speak to one another. J.R. and I felt this was silly. Childish, in fact. Of anyone on that base, we were more aware what lines we had and hadn't crossed. What crime had we committed? Being a friend to the other person? Of course we followed the order, we were in the army, after all. But it began to make things difficult for us personally. By that point we were each other's best friends, and not being able to talk to your best friend is painful. When we were apart, we felt completely alone.

Then J.R. did a very strange thing. He told me that it was true. He really did have feelings for me. He was awfully sorry but he'd been on the phone with his wife and their relationship was pretty shaky right then. During the conversation, he admitted that he and I'd been spending time together. He told his wife that he thought he had feelings for me. He was just being honest with her. Then his wife called our commander and asked him to keep an eye on us.

I was shocked and I didn't know what to do. I ended up ignoring J.R. for about a month. We didn't talk, we just worked to keep up appearances. But that felt even worse than when he told me he had feelings. Now I was really confused. I got angry with him, I wanted to know why he'd told me that and run the risk of ruining our friendship and his marriage all at once. I thought he should've just kept it all to himself and gotten over it. But then I saw that he wasn't getting over it, he was really hurt. And that's when I realized that maybe I had feelings for him, too.

We started sneaking around to be with one another. That probably doesn't reflect very well on either one of us but that's what we did.

J.R., Jen, and running were the only things that kept me sane in Iraq. With everything going on, I worked myself up to thirty miles a week or thereabouts, just running to blow off stress. Thank God Jen was there. I talked to her about my situation with J.R., but I didn't want to just dump my troubles. If she ever thought negatively about me for everything that was happening, she was kind enough to never let on. I'm very appreciative of how she withheld judgment. She was a friend to me when I truly needed one. I think she knew that, deep down, I was ready to go crazy. Neither J.R. nor I were going to let go of each other just because the army said so.

The next warning was more severe. The lieutenant who commanded our platoon called us into his office and had us stand at attention in front of his desk. Our platoon sergeant was present, watching us. The lieutenant said, "Sergeant Walker, Sergeant Stinson. You will not spend any more time with each another outside your official duties. You are not to speak to one another outside whatever you need to say to each other during your official duties as soldiers." We said our Yes sirs, but pretty soon we disobeyed that one as well. All along they'd been putting written counseling into our files. The orders said something like, "You were previously counseled on many occasions not to spend any time with this person." You are never to speak to one another unless it's work-related and in the company of at least two other soldiers," etcetera. They tried to make it hell for us, as if it wasn't hell for us already. Night and day we had to undergo the scrutiny and judgment of our peers.

Nothing physical happened between us until later. J.R. called his wife and told her he thought their marriage was over. Then he went home for two weeks leave in September and talked things over with her. J.R.'s a very private man and he hasn't told me much about what he and his wife said. All he told me was that he was honest with her every step of the way. He said she listened, and it was hard for both of them. But she finally said, "Look. If you're not in love with me anymore, I understand that. We'll get a divorce." He said, "Well, I think that's probably for the best." She said she was okay with that. She was going to take the girls and move out of the house in November. So that's what they did.

Now J.R. and I live together in Texas, and everything's different. We're happy. His little girls come over a couple of days a week and every other weekend. They were just here for dinner this evening and we get along great. A stray dog wandered into the yard today and we took it in. Then we nearly had to evacuate the house because of the brushfires we've been having, but the wind shifted and we were safe. It's a life.

When I look back on the war, I think I'll see it as the beginning of my romance with J.R. I know that's a narrow, selfish perspective, and I have a lot of conflicting feelings about it. Obviously war is a terrible thing. Innocent people die, guilty people get rich, and families get torn apart. But something good came out of it. J.R. and I, at least, came out of it. That's what I'll want to remember looking back. That and the beginning of a brand-new democracy for Iraq.

Like I said, while I was there I wasn't really convinced that what we were doing would make a difference. I didn't think the Iraqi people cared what was happening to their country one way or the other. But did you see the turnout for the elections?[52] I was overwhelmed. People came from everywhere, not like what you see here in the United States. I heard that women outnumbered men at the polls, and I suddenly found myself optimistic all over again. It heartened me that, in this land that had known such terrible oppression, people were finally standing up and taking charge of their future. That's a beautiful thing, maybe even the most important thing.

---

52. Referencing the first-ever national elections in Iraq, held in December 2005.

A DIFFERENT KIND OF CASUALTY

✴

Specialist Gerard Darren Matthew
NEW YORK ARMY NATIONAL GUARD, 719TH TRANSPORTATION COMPANY

After serving a four-year hitch in the Marines Corps, Gerard Matthew en-
listed in the Army National Guard. Service as a guardsman helped pay
for his education in occupational therapy. "They gave me money to get
great training, and all I had to put in was one weekend a month plus two
weeks out of every year," says Specialist Matthew, age 30. "I thought, who
could turn down a deal like that? Things got more complicated when we
declared war on Iraq but I still considered myself lucky."

Gerard believes that during his deployment to the Persian Gulf, he
was exposed to depleted uranium (DU). Depleted uranium, when alloyed,
forms an incredibly dense metal that the U.S. military has used for nearly
two decades in armor-penetrating ballistics and protective plating for ar-
mored vehicles. Depleted uranium is reputedly a toxic substance, however,
capable of producing debilitating symptoms[53] in those exposed to certain
forms. At the close of 2004, media and activist groups began debuting ev-
idence that seemed to indicate how a large number of soldiers sent to the
Persian Gulf since the early '90s have contracted DU poisoning. Some
doctors, journalists, and soldiers have speculated that exposure to DU
might play a key role in the development of so-called Gulf War syndrome,
which the United States government has denied exists.

---

53. According to the Campaign Against Depleted Uranium (CADU): The misnamed "depleted" uranium is
left after enriched uranium is separated from natural uranium in order to produce fuel for nuclear reactors.
During this process, the fissionable isotope uranium 235 is separated from uranium. The remaining uranium, which is 99.8 percent uranium 238 is misleadingly called "depleted uranium." While the term "depleted" implies it isn't particularly dangerous, in fact, this waste product of the nuclear industry is
"conveniently" disposed of by producing deadly weapons. Depleted uranium is chemically toxic. It is an
extremely dense, hard metal, and can cause chemical poisoning to the body in the same way as can lead or
any other heavy metal. However, depleted uranium is also radiologically hazardous as it spontaneously
burns on impact, creating tiny aerosolized glass particles that are small enough to be inhaled. These uranium
oxide particles emit all types of radiation, alpha, beta, and gamma, and can be carried in the air over long
distances. Depleted uranium has a half-life of 4.5 billion years, and the presence of depleted uranium ceramic
aerosols can pose a long-term threat to human health and the environment.

At first I got these chronic, piercing migraines with a complication called aura, where your eyes get as red as ketchup. My face would swell up like a balloon, that's called idiopathic angioedema.[54] This all started when I first landed in the Gulf and nobody knew what to make of it. But let me go back and tell you how it all started.

Being in the National Guard was great for me. During the day, I worked my job as an occupational therapist here in New York City, right? At night, I had another job pulling the graveyard shift forty hours a week at a juvenile counseling facility up in Somers. Then I served one weekend a month and two weeks every year as a guard. I guess you could say I'm a very hard worker. I love what I do.

My unit got called up to serve in the Gulf, so I was OCONUS [outside the continental United States] by the spring of 2003. I wasn't there long when I started getting this weird swelling on my face. I didn't know what to make of it. When I went to shave and I looked in the mirror, I couldn't recognize the guy staring back at me. The skin under my right eye had grown very puffy. Later on, the puffiness spread down my cheekbone. I thought, *Huh. This is odd.* But I didn't do nothin' about it.

See, it was really hot in Kuwait and I'm originally from the Caribbean. I know what extreme heat can do to a person if he doesn't drink enough water. Dehydration causes all sorts of weird things. So I figured, No big deal. Better drink more water. But as time progressed, the symptoms got a lot worse.

In those early days my unit wasn't even considered active yet. We were a transportation company out of Harlem, New York, 169 men strong, but our trucks hadn't arrived yet, they were still being shipped over by boat from North Carolina. When we first arrived, we didn't have anything to do, so command dispersed platoons to other camps in Kuwait. Some went to Camp Doha, some got assigned to Camp Wolf. A few more stayed at a place called Arab John. I drew a station at the Theatre Development Center [TDC] in Camp Doha. We lived in tents in an area called Truckville, a major staging ground for shuttling equipment

54. *Angioedema* is a medical term that means, "swellings which come and go." When doctors can discover no cause for chronic recurring angioedema, they will often note it as "idiopathic," which means "of its own cause." According to Dr. Martin Stern of Asthma and Allergy Information and Research, "Blaming a physical condition like angioedema on your mental state is, quite literally, 'adding insult to injury.' Angioedema is a physical illness with physical treatments and is not due to 'nerves.'"

north across the border, and from there, wherever it needed to go. When you serve in a transportation company, you drive equipment and supplies to different sites throughout the war theater. That's your job.

Well, Truckville was a very busy place. Vehicles rolled through at all hours, all the time. They were loaded with who-knew-what, coming back from who-knew-where. A lot of vehicles returning from combat missions, banged up and needing repairs. I noticed the guys in those vehicles never had a lot to say.

Once our trucks arrived, we started running missions immediately, every day. We made deliveries to sites throughout Kuwait and the southern section of Iraq, I never made it into the north country. Standard procedure, we carried cargos of MREs, water, ammo, you name it. Sometimes, though, we didn't know what we were hauling. They loaded our pallets and flatbeds with wooden crates covered with tarps. Depending on how your orders read, sometimes you'd arrive at your drop site and leave the freight for somebody else to unload. You'd leave the whole system behind, tractor, trailer, and cargo with everything still in the back, hop an empty flatbed, and ride back to base. You never asked questions. As it turns out, I ran a lot of missions on the Highway of Death.[55] You could see the charred remains of blown-up equipment lying on either side of the road, like corpses. Some of the stuff was residue from the Gulf War, fifteen years old. Some of it looked very new to me. I got pictures if you want to see them sometime.

A lot of times I ended up at a place called Cedar Two, this camp that served as a major supply drop. That place was unbelievable. The government had amassed incredible stockpiles of supplies, ammo for every type of gun you've ever seen, food and water, spare parts, fleets of vehicles, all this stuff just lying around out in the open. Thousands of sol-

55. A name given by the press to the road from Mutlaa, Kuwait, to Basra, Iraq. It is a particularly controversial location since it derives its name from a massive attack carried out by U.S. planes supposedly after Saddam Hussein announced a complete troop withdrawal from Kuwait in compliance with UN Resolution 660 to end the Gulf War. U.S. planes disabled the forward and rear vehicles in a column of over two thousand. The incinerated and dismembered bodies of tens of thousands of human beings tell the story of what happened next. Photographic evidence of the corpses suggests that napalm, phosphorous, or other types of incendiaries were used—each of these is a type of antipersonnel weapon outlawed under the 1977 Geneva Protocols. In addition, there is strong evidence to suggest that many of those killed in the attack were Kuwaiti civilians attempting to escape what they believed to be the impending siege of Kuwait City once the Kuwait military returned and took over from U.S. forces. For more information, see the report given by former U.S. Attorney General Ramsey Clark on May 11, 1991, in New York.

diers crawling all over the place. You ever seen a war in action? I mean, up close and personal? It'll blow your mind, man.

At the TDC, we commonly transported retro-equipment, which is any spare part that's been blown up or otherwise broken down into pieces. Things like tank tracks, used tires, cannibalized parts for artillery pieces, Humvee chassis, you name it. I never knew specifically what the stuff was or where it came from. Like I said, though, didn't have to. My job was to transport it all from point A to point B, that's it.

A lot of the stuff was blown up pretty good, though. Looking back, I suppose it's possible I touched something that had residue on it. Dust which I inhaled. Maybe a piece of irradiated metal, who knows? Looking back, I had so many opportunities to come in contact with *something*, it's not even worth thinking about. How it happened doesn't matter anymore. The point is, it happened. We could sit here speculating all day. Something happened.

The swelling on my face started acting weird. Mostly it hit me in the mornings. Some days it wouldn't even show. Then some days it'd spread all over the place and I'd start getting the headaches. At first they weren't such a big deal, but later on it got so bad I'd have to sit down and hold my head. I didn't tell nobody about it first, I'm not the kind of person who likes to go around telling people, "Hey, I've got a problem." I guess I don't like calling attention to myself. Plus I didn't want anybody telling me I was some kind of malingerer who had to be sent home. I wanted to serve. I liked the pay, the job was good. I was a soldier doing my duty.

As it turns out, my wife underwent an emergency appendectomy in July of '03, so I got sent home anyway on an emergency medical leave for fourteen days. My symptoms really started acting up the moment I got stateside. The headaches got worse and the swelling got really bad. Two weeks later, I got back to the Gulf and things stepped up even more. On top of everything, now, I was getting so disoriented that I'd swoon whenever I got up from a prone position.

I finally mentioned my condition to my platoon sergeant, Staff Sergeant Gardiner from the 257th upstate in Buffalo. He said, "Look, go get that checked out." But my attitude was like, "No. Forget it. I gotta stay here. The money's too good." I figured I'd stick it out and see what happened. But one day, later on, I nodded off behind the wheel of a Humvee and nearly killed myself and two other guys. That's when I said, "Okay. Enough. Somebody tell me what's going on."

I went to the PX[56] at Camp Doha with two guys, Sergeant Howard and Specialist Anthony. Howard was the squad leader and had seniority, so he signed out a Hummer and we went. We picked up personal effects, hygiene items, shaving stuff, soap, that sort of thing. I had a craving for root beer, so I bought a case. I was driving on the trip back to Camp Wolf, Howard in the passenger seat; Anthony rode in back. We didn't have far to go, maybe twenty kilometers. There was no traffic on the road. We'd made it all the way to the gates of Wolf when suddenly I got hit with this piercing headache. I held onto the steering wheel so tight, my knuckles were clenching. The pain was so bad that it knotted the muscles in my shoulders and neck. You ever been in so much pain and you're trying to hold onto it so nobody can see the agony you're in? I was doing that, just trying to get through it when—I don't know. I just nodded off. My head started pounding, everything went fuzzy. I blacked out at the wheel.

After that, everything happened fast. Suddenly, I looked up and there were four palm trees right in front of me. The guys were yelling. I spun the wheel and turned the Hummer back on the road. We missed a head-on collision but ended up sideswiping the last tree. In the rearview mirror, I could see that tree disappearing. It was a young tree with a thin trunk. The Hummer had knocked it over. Now it looked like it was growing out of the ground at a forty-five degree angle. If you go over to Kuwait right now, I bet it's probably still there, all bent out of shape.

We drove through the gates of Wolf and the guys were laughing. They said, "What the hell happened? You ran into a tree!" I guess it was pretty funny at the time, but not to me. I felt like things had gotten really out of control.

We signed the Hummer back into the motor pool, Howard and Anthony hit the showers. Staff Sergeant Gardiner's cot was five down from

---

56. Post exchange—a store on a military base that sells goods to military personnel and their families or to authorized civilians.

mine in the barracks, so I went to see him. I said, "Okay, I think I ought to go get checked out." He just nodded, so I went the next day.

First, I went to see an ophthalmologist at Camp Doha because I'd begun seeing everything in double and triple images. Coupled with the headaches, this made it difficult for me to move. The doctor was a female major. My face was all swollen that day and she pointed to it first thing, she said, "What happened here?" That day the swelling was only on the right side of my face. "How long's this been going on?" she said. I told her what'd been happening to me, and she took some notes. Then she had me stand a good distance away and read the letters on the eye chart. I couldn't. My vision went from double to triple and the letters didn't make any sense to me. She took more notes.

When she finished her examination, the doctor told me that my symptoms were not consistent. She said the facial swelling was a condition called ptosis,[57] and said, "You may have just had that when you were born." I told her no, I hadn't been born like that, and I showed her some pictures I had of myself, my driver's license, for instance, and a few family photos. My face didn't have any droop or swelling in the pictures, but she wrote down the condition as ptosis, saying I'd had it since birth. In my opinion? I got the feeling she thought I was trying to bullshit her. She said, "You're good to go, soldier," and sent me back to my unit.

I started going out on missions again but I was in agony. The pain in my head got even worse. Now it felt like someone was pounding a nail through my ear and into my brain with a hammer. The pain would enter my skull and rocket around inside my head for a while, then shoot down my spine and into my legs. Sometimes it got so bad, I'd have to stop whatever I was doing and hold my head like a child. I began to count my headache attacks to get an idea of frequency. I was getting between sixty-five and sixty-seven a month. Some headaches lasted six or seven seconds, but some lasted a whole lot longer. I tried not to make a fuss, tried to deal with it, but finally I relented. I was in agony. I went back to

57. *Ptosis* is the medical term for "drooping eyelids." A person with this condition cannot lift one or both eyelids to uncover the eye completely. The condition gives a person a bulldoggish appearance. Ptosis can be either congenitally contracted or otherwise acquired when the tendons of the levator muscle loosen or detach. The condition is correctable through surgery. If left unattended, ptosis can result in permanent damage to vision, as one or both eyes are forced to work harder in order to compensate for the loss of vision. The result is oracular degeneration.

Sergeant Gardiner and told him what was going on. He said, "Go back. Tell them it's still going on. Get yourself checked out again." So that's what I did.

This time I went to Camp Wolf. The doctor I saw was a neurologist named Captain Hartman, a tall guy in his late thirties, white and skinny but fit, with glasses and crew-cut hair. I mentioned the incident with the trees to him and he seemed to take it in stride. Then I described the rest of my symptoms. I told him that as soon as I got out of bed, I'd get very dizzy, very disoriented. The feeling only lasted a few seconds but this, like everything else, was highly abnormal for me. Dr. Hartman listened to everything and didn't say much.

Then he did the test for the twelve cranial nerves.[58] My vision was so blurry, I couldn't read the eye chart. He had this instrument like a toothpick that he scraped up and down my cheek while my eyes were closed. "Do you feel anything?" he said. "Feel what?" I said. He told me he'd touched my face with that instrument and I thought he was joking. I hadn't felt a thing.

He did the same type of test on the soles of my feet to see if my toes would curl, but I couldn't feel that, either. Then he reached the same conclusion that the ophthalmologist came to: my symptoms weren't consistent with anything, so he had me take a CAT scan.[59] He did this all in the same day because he was getting concerned, and throughout the day he consulted with another doctor, an eye specialist. He was confused, too.

To make a long story short, after a roster of tests, neither one of them could come up with a concrete diagnosis. They were worried about my symptoms. Dr. Hartman postulated that I might have an aneurism or something. Whatever it was, he didn't feel like it was worth playing around with, so the very next day they medevaced me to Landstuhl, Germany, to see another neurologist and undergo further tests.

---

58. The cranial nerves are twelve pairs of nerves that can be seen on the bottom surface of the human brain. Some of these nerves carry sensory information from sensory organs to the brain. Others control different muscle groups. Each nerve can be tested using a series of simple, physical exercises to approximate its capability. For instance, to test the hypoglossal nerve (Nerve XII), a patient should stick out his tongue and move it from side to side.

59. Computed axial tomography. In this scan, computers are used to generate a three-dimensional image from a series of flat (two-dimensional) X-rays. In a CAT scan machine, an X-ray beam is rotated around a patient, taking pictures from hundreds of angles, which are then assembled via computer into the 3-D CAT scan image. An invaluable tool to modern medicine, doctors frequently use CAT scans to diagnose and treat a wide variety of ailments, such as cancer, osteoporosis, and head trauma.

The plane to Germany was a C-130 loaded with disabled soldiers from all over the war. Guys with gunshot wounds were packed into stretcher racks that lined the walls of the fuselage. There was a nurse on the plane assigned to take care of the patients' needs. She'd check in with me every hour or so. The flight lasted about five and a half hours. All that time, I kept drinking water. The doctors had insisted I stay off any medication. Since they didn't know what was wrong with me, they weren't sure how drugs would react to whatever was causing my ailment. I wished they'd given me something for the pain. My head felt excruciating. In the middle of the flight, I got hit with a really nasty attack. Pain seared through my skull, everything went black. Then, suddenly, I woke up again in my flight chair. I'd passed out.

When the nurse came around again I told her what had happened. She wrote it all down in her incident report but there was nothing she could do. "No meds," she said. "Sorry."

In Landstuhl I stayed at a place called the Kleeber House, an outpatient facility where a lot of soldiers from the Gulf go to recuperate from injuries. We slept in barracks, ten men bunking to a room. I got a big surprise at Kleeber. I met a lot of soldiers who were having the same problems I was.

The guy in the bed next to mine, for instance. He was a forty-year-old Latino cop from good old NYC name Ray Ramos, a staff sergeant with the 442nd Military Police unit. The 442nd is based out of Rockland County. For the most part the unit's made up of New York City cops, corrections officers, and firefighters. Ramos and three of his guys had the exact same symptoms as me. Needless to say, we got to be real close.

Ramos told me that his unit had been stationed in an area of Iraq called Samawah, where a lot of heavy tank fighting had taken place. He and his guys had bunked for a while in an abandoned railroad depot. No one had told them this, but apparently Samawah was considered a high-radiation area. Ramos and his men slept in a place that was supposedly full of toxic dust, and he thought that might have something to do with their symptoms.

We were in Germany six or seven days. Most of the time, we sat around taking medication and waiting to be seen by the neurologist,

Major Fleischer, who's supposed to be one of the best in the world. To pass the time, we watched TV and some bootlegged DVDs we'd bought in Kuwait, like *The Hulk* and *The Terminator*. It wasn't a picnic, though. They'd put us on Amatriptaline,[60] a heavy medication that made it hard to concentrate. They also had me on a painkiller called Zomatriptan,[61] which quickly arrested the pain and put me to sleep. Plus a ten-day course of a steroid called prednisone to help the swelling in my face. The prednisone didn't do shit for my face but it made me eat a lot. Seemed like I wanted another meal every single second of the day. I gained a lot of weight fast.

When I was finally called in to see Major Fleischer, he began my examination by running the same tests Captain Hartman had. He checked the sensation in my fingers and toes, and asked me to track the motion of his hand with my eyes as it moved over my head and under my chin, left to right and right to left. He had a vibrating wand-thing that he applied to various points of my body to check my sensations—he touched it to my ankles, my knees, my back, everywhere. When he was all finished, Dr. Fleischer wrote on his report that my status was NONDEPLOYABLE until such time as my headaches decreased to four times a month. Then he told me I was being shipped to Walter Reed Medical Center in Washington, D.C. By that point I didn't care if I was going home or not. I just wanted to find out what was wrong with me.

Walter Reed is a huge hospital crawling with wounded soldiers. I was there for fourteen days in a wing called the Malone House, another outpatient facility. I stayed in a barracks-style room where my roommate, once again, was Sergeant Ray Ramos. I started taking daily walks up and down the hallways of the facility and met a lot more soldiers with my exact same symptoms. A lot of these guys also had major complications, though. It wasn't uncommon, for instance, to meet a soldier whose limbs had been amputated and who was *also* suffering from headaches like Ramos and me. On top of that, some of them had the facial swelling, the vision problems, the headaches, all of it. I looked at some of them and thanked God I'd been lucky, you know? At least my body still had

60. An antidepressant.
61. A painkiller commonly used to combat migraines.

all its original pieces. But that's when I started putting things together, bit by bit. Something was going on that people weren't talking about.

The doctor who examined me at Malone House was a woman named Captain Pazdan. She followed the exact same protocols as Fleischer and Hartman, but something she told me was crazy. She looked at my paperwork and saw I was taking the Zomatriptan. "How many are you taking?" she asked. Like it was a routine question. In Germany, they'd told me to take the medication as needed, so that's the way I used it. I thought about it a moment and said, "Seventeen, eighteen. Maybe nineteen times a week."

Captain Pazdan flipped. "That's crazy!" she said. "That's powerful medication. You should only be taking up to four Zomas a week *maximum!*"

I looked at my paperwork again and there it was written down, "Take the Zomas as needed." I got really upset. First of all, the Zomas were the only medication that had helped me get through all this. Now I was being told I'd been given the wrong instructions? Dr. Pazdan actually said that my headaches could possibly be attributed to taking too much Zoma. I couldn't believe the army could be so screwed up.

Eventually, the doctors at Walter Reed attributed everything wrong with me to my headaches. The headaches, they said, are causing the swelling, the vision problems, all the other issues. Beyond that? "We can't offer an explanation." They told Ramos that his symptoms might be attributable to aging. He asked them how aging explained the blood in his urine or the fact that he couldn't feel the right side of his face and that both his hands were numb. "Can you believe this?" he said to me one night. "They think I'm faking it."

After two weeks, Walter Reed shipped me out to the medical hold at Fort Dix, New Jersey. I was supposed to recuperate there until such time as I could be considered deployable, but the army tried to ship me back to the Gulf immediately. According to them, my headaches and double vision weren't an issue anymore. I'd been given a whole slew of medications and discharged from Walter Reed, so obviously I was good to go. I thought this was insane. I pointed out the warning labels on every bottle of army doctor–prescribed medication I had. They all read: DO NOT TAKE IN EXTREMES OF HEAT. Which, I pointed out to them, ruled out going back to Kuwait or Iraq. They relented. I was told I'd stay at Fort

Dix until my headaches wore off. Then I'd be considered eligible once again for deployment.

That never happened. Remember, according to Dr. Fleischer, deployable meant that my headaches had scaled back to four times a month. I wish.

That whole thing about shipping me back to the Gulf? There was a rumor going around at Fort Dix. The army wanted to keep numbers low in the medical hold. It was getting overpopulated. When I arrived, we had over three hundred soldiers, with more streaming in every day. The magic number we heard was five hundred. As in, never let more than five hundred soldiers stay in the medical hold. Ship anybody who can move back out to the Gulf as quickly as possible.

Some of the guys in the hold needed surgery for noncombat issues. They were lined up in queues awaiting operations on their hands, knees, and rotator cuffs, all injuries sustained in the war, though not necessarily via gunshot or shrapnel. Most were ambulatory though a few guys were in wheelchairs or on crutches. A lot of them had the same symptoms I did, and no one knew what was wrong. I'm talking about a *lot* of guys, here.

Anyone staying in the medical hold who was physically capable was expected to work. I was offered three job options but two of them involved driving. Obviously that wasn't going to work. The third option involved working with the doctors in the ward, and I liked the idea a lot. I'm a trained occupational therapist, so I know some medical lingo. Plus, I wanted to get to know the doctors and let them see my symptoms on a day-to-day basis. Eventually, it got to the point where I called them all by their first names.

I worked as a clerk helping incoming and outgoing soldiers fill out their papers. I got a chance to know a lot of the men. They'd tell me what was happening to them and I'd listen. A lot of soldiers were coming back from OCONUS with weird symptoms, though not so severe as mine. All they wanted to do was go home and see their families, and I didn't blame them for that; who *didn't* want to go home and see their family? But, like me, I felt they weren't getting enough information about their affliction. At this point, the subject of DU testing hadn't come up yet. Boy, was I in for a surprise.

It started when my wife told me she was pregnant. How did it happen? I'd arrived in Germany September 6, 2003; Walter Reed Medical Center on September 11. I was at Fort Dix by September 24. I don't know exactly when I conceived my daughter, but my wife came to visit me at Fort Dix in October, and one time that month I got leave to go home to the Bronx. Either way, we were happy to see one another, and one thing led to another.

Anyway, my wife and I went for an ultrasound to have our child checked. By this point it was March 12 of 2004, the day I found out my daughter had a birth defect. A doctor did the test and saw that she had an anomaly. No fingers on her right hand. This doctor's a well-known person. In last year's *Newsweek* magazine poll, he was rated among the top fifty doctors in the United States—Dr. Michael Devon at Lenox Hill. He was really mind-boggled, though. He stared at the ultrasound pictures and said that he'd never seen anything like it.

Dr. Devon sent my wife and I to a geneticist to see if there was some hereditary reason for my daughter's defect. The geneticist checked our lineage on both sides but couldn't find anything. He pointed out that my wife and I each have children from previous relationships. No problems there. So then there was some discussion that perhaps the umbilical cord was wrapped around the hand and distorting the ultrasound picture. They took more pictures of my wife using a new 3-D imaging machine and eventually ruled that out.

After we'd done all this, we sat back down with Dr. Devon, and the first question he asked me was, "Were you exposed to anything over there? At that time?" I could have sworn up and down that the answer was no. I heard myself going through the same explanation a hundred times. My job was transportation. I just moved things around, back and forth in Kuwait and the southernmost regions of Iraq. Exposed to anything? No. Sorry. Not that I could think of.

I mentioned the headaches, though, and my symptoms, the reason they'd shipped me out of Kuwait in the first place and the whole scenario of being in the medical hold at Fort Dix. Dr. Devon just looked at me. Then he said, "Okay. Well. We'll just have to see." He laid out a few choices for us, one of which was to abort the child. At that time, she was almost five months old. I felt an abortion in that case would have been like killing someone. I told Dr. Devon, "I went to Iraq and I didn't kill anybody. To come home and kill my own child? I can't do that." My wife felt the same way. We decided to have the child.

When I got back to my room at Fort Dix, I was out of it, feeling low. I thought, Now—on top of all my problems—I have a child with a birth defect. Wonderful. I'm an occupational therapist, right? I knew what kind of life my child might have. But it didn't matter. Let me tell you, no matter how informed you are, you never really know what to do when they tell you it's your kid. This was a painful time.

So who checks in one day at the Fort Dix medical hold? You got it. Sergeant Ray Ramos. He walked on in with a few of his men from the 442nd. Man, it was good to see them. By that point we were like family, what with all we had in common. But Ramos and his men had interesting news. They told me an article about them was due to come out in the *New York Daily News*. Juan Gonzalez[62] was coming down to Fort Dix to take some pictures. The *News* had gotten Ramos and his men tested for depleted uranium through a Doctor Durakovic, who'd founded the Uranium Research Medical Centre.[63] I didn't know a damn thing about depleted uranium. Up until that point, uranium was just another word I'd forgotten from high school chemistry class. But here I was lying in a hospital bed, suffering from weird symptoms. My daughter's got a birth defect and now I hear about DU poisoning. Not from the government. Only because Ramos and the guys came back to our room and started talking about it. Ramos and another guy named Hector Vega mentioned my situation to Gonzalez. Juan called me up few days later and we started to talk.

---

62. Juan Gonzalez is a columnist with New York's *Daily News*. He's won the George Polk journalism award and received a lifetime achievement award from the Hispanic Academy of Media Arts and Sciences. Born in Ponce, Puerto Rico, Gonzalez grew up in a New York City housing project and graduated from Columbia University. His work as an activist in New York's Puerto Rican community is notable, as is the fact that he built a very successful career in journalism during a period in American media where Latino correspondents were a rarity. Says Linda Robinson of the *New York Times:* "Juan Gonzalez has made a serious, significant contribution to understanding who the Hispanics of the United States are and where they come from."
63. Dr. Asaf Durakovic, a lieutenant colonel in the U.S. Army Reserve, was awarded an International Peace Prize in October 2004 for his work on the issues of radioactive warfare, depleted uranium, and the medical/environmental effects of nuclear weapons on the human habitat and biosphere. Among Dr. Durakovic's published papers are *"On Depleted Uranium Gulf War and Balkan Syndrome" (Croatian Medical Journal, 2001), "The Quantitative Analysis of Depleted Uranium Isotopes in British, Canadian, and United States Gulf War Veterans"* (with P. Horan and L. Dietz—*Military Medicine*, 2002), and *"Estimate of the Time-zero Lung Burden of Depleted Uranium in Gulf War Veterans by the 24 Hour Urinary Excretion and Exponential Decay Analysis"* (with L. Dietz, P. Horan, and I. Zimmerman, *Military Medicine*, 2003).

DEPLETED URANIUM—A BRIEF SYNOPSIS

Depleted uranium came to the attention of the U.S. military in the 1950s and, for a variety of reasons, seemed ideal for weapons manufacturing. First, DU is an extremely dense material. When used as armor plating, it's incredibly durable against standard ordnance fire. Second, DU is available in massive quantities, as it's considered a by-product of the uranium enrichment process used for reactor fuel by the nuclear power industry. The material therefore costs nothing—the arms industry gets it for free from nuclear power companies who would otherwise bear the burden of disposing of the material through a complex series of environmental regulations.

Currently, over fifteen nations possess weapons made with depleted uranium. These nations include the United Kingdom, Greece, Russia, France, Turkey, Thailand, Taiwan, Israel, Saudi Arabia, Egypt, Kuwait, Iraq, Bahrain, Pakistan and the United States. The United States first used DU in large-scale combat during the Gulf War. Records show that the United States fired off close to a million DU rounds in 1991. This artillery barrage destroyed approximately 1,400 Iraqi tanks whose irradiated wrecks were reportedly crawled over on a routine basis by excited, victorious American soldiers. DU was used again in the 1995 Bosnian campaign and the Balkan war in 1999.

A 120 mm DU "penetrator" round contains about nine pounds of DU that, upon impact, ignites to a temperature of approximately 5,400 degrees. The ignition and impact process turns up to 70 percent of the shell's mass into a toxic cloud of aerosolized uranium oxide fragments and dust which can settle within the immediate area of the explosion or disperse via wind and rain. Either way, the tiny particles in a uranium oxide cloud are easily inhaled or ingested. Solid products made from DU are not harmful, but DU dust is considered extremely toxic, as are shards of uranium oxide shrapnel that enter the human body.

Two memos from U.S. government agencies indicate the Pentagon's concession that DU is a substance toxic to U.S. soldiers. The Los Alamos memo, written by Lieutenant Colonel M. V. Ziehmn on March 1, 1991, states in part: "There has been, and continues to be a concern regarding the impact of DU on the environment. Therefore, if no one makes a case for the effectiveness of DU on the battlefield, DU rounds may become politically unacceptable and thus, be deleted from the arsenal . . . Keep this sensitive issue in mind when action reports are written."

The second memo, written by Lieutenant Colonel Gregory K. Lyle from the Defense Nuclear Agency, reads: "Alpha particles (uranium oxide dust) from expended rounds is a health concern but, Beta particles from fragments and intact rounds is a serious health threat . . ."

In July 2004, the VA disclosed that 16.4 percent of veterans returning from Operation Iraqi Freedom—a total of 27,571 soldiers—reported illness. Of these soldiers, over 8,000 suffered from muscular/skeleton ailments. More than 3,500 reported respiratory problems, and nearly 6,000 possessed "symptoms, signs and ill-defined conditions." The VA claims that these figures are within the totals expected for "young, active, healthcare-seeking populations." Many experts disagree, insisting that these maladies spring from DU exposure.

I told him what had happened with my baby, and Gonzalez filled me in. He told me how DU had impacted the guys from the 442nd. All their tests had come up positive. The *Daily News* article was coming out soon and Gonzalez said, "Hey, maybe you want to get tested, too."

I tried explaining to him, What good would it do? I wasn't in the same area as the 442nd. He said, "You never know. Obviously something's wrong with you. Just think about it." So I talked it over with my primary care doctor at the clinic, Dr. Michael Barnes. Like I said, I was working there as a clerk and I'd gotten to know a lot of doctors pretty well. Dr. Barnes thought it over and said, "You know, maybe you should get tested." I figured, *What the hell? I'll do it. What've I got to lose?*

The *Daily News* article came out about two days after my conversation with Gonzalez.[64] You should have seen how the military kicked into high gear. At that point, Ramos was back at Walter Reed for more examinations. I got this call from him saying that the brass had just shown up in his room and started grilling him and the rest of the guys from the 442nd. Sure enough, pretty soon this woman, Colonel Yun, shows up at Fort Dix. She tells all us guys with symptoms that the military's now offering to test us. She'd been sent to oversee the process and answer any questions we might have. She distributed a questionnaire.

A lot of soldiers opted not to participate in the testing. They felt the whole thing was bullshit. For instance, the questionnaire broke your circumstances down into three categories, Levels One, Two, and Three. You'd be classified as Level One if, while you were stationed in the Gulf, you witnessed a fire from a great distance. Level Two had to do with things like, "Did you experience any smoke from a fire?" Level Three indicated direct exposure. "Were you standing next to a tank when it blew up?" That kind of thing.

I thought the whole notion of this questionnaire was insane because it didn't factor ground truth in the Gulf into the equation. For instance, what if you were in an area where a tank had been blown up and then removed? Sure, the tank's gone. But what about the toxic dust released in the explosion? The questionnaire didn't address that kind of scenario. It didn't have any criteria for the vehicles I'd seen coming in and out of Truckville. Given all that, who the hell knew what I was exposed to?

I ended up taking the DU test in early April of 2004. It was easy. You peed in a specimen bottle every time you had to use the bathroom over a 24-hour period. You had to keep your samples in the refrigerator to keep them cold. I followed the procedure, went through the cycle, and turned in my collections. But I took the test through both the military and the *Daily News*. I was filling two specimen bottles every time I went to take a piss, once for the army and once for the *News*. By that point I didn't

64. "Poisoned? Shocking Report Reveals Local Troops May Be Victims of America's High-tech Weapons" *New York Daily News*, April 3, 2004—Special Investigation by Juan Gonzalez.

know who to trust. The way I saw it, I was playing it safe. The army didn't know I was preparing samples for the *News*. If two different testers got two different results from the same urine, wouldn't that be interesting?

A follow-up article appeared in the *Daily News* in May.[65] It pretty much lambasted Lieutenant Colonel Mark Melanson from the army's Center for Health Promotion and Preventative Medicine. This guy said that the Pentagon had tested a bunch of New York National Guard soldiers returning from Iraq and none of them had "measurable amounts" of DU in their systems. Durakovic said this was a load of bull, that the army hadn't used proper testing procedures. First of all, their equipment wasn't calibrated to measure uranium isotopes like the ones found in DU—they only checked for cold uranium. In other words, the parameters for the military's tests were too crude. Also, the tests assumed that radiation spreads out evenly over the whole body, which isn't the case when DU dust enters a human body through inhalation.

Durakovic said that the army tested only for DU's radioactive presence and completely ignored the fact that DU is a chemical toxin as well. That's like running a high-level, extremely expensive diagnostic test on a machine gun bullet and declaring it harmless to humans. Well, of course it is, until you load it into a gun and fire it. It's all a question of context. Another scientist concurred with Durakovic's findings.[66] To the best of my knowledge, the army has yet to respond to those accusations except to say, "We're right, everybody else is wrong."

Time passed. I left Fort Dix in mid-April of 2004 since my active duty status was up on May 5. I guess the army figured, why keep me around three more weeks? As it happened, my time with the National Guard expired the following September 7. After that, my military obligations officially ended. I was still getting sick. I'd begun to notice a urine dribbling out of my penis every time I went to use the bathroom, but it hadn't turned into incontinence yet; that happened later on. I'd begun to see an allergist from outside the military. I was hoping to find the reasons for my facial swelling. The first question she asked was, "Were you ever exposed to anything over there?" As if I wasn't already starting to get the hint.

65. "Murky Facts on Sick GIs" *New York Daily News*, May 6, 2004, by Juan Gonzalez.
66. Richard Legget, a senior researcher at Oak Ridge National Laboratory and a member of the National Council on Radiation Protection and Measurements.

Sgt. MacEwen: "While driving back to Camp Victory we encountered a roadside IED device. It went off before we came across this road area. Thankfully, no one was hurt." *(courtesy Justin MacEwan)*

❖

Camp Victory at nighttime. Sgt. MacEwen: "It was amazing. Even with all these lights, the insurgents could never hit this building. They dropped rounds all around that splashed in the water, but no hits were made on the structure." *(courtesy Justin MacEwan)*

Sgt. MacEwen and his translator in downtown Baghdad, in the so-called "Green Zone." *(courtesy Justin MacEwan)*

The aftereffects of a mortar attack on LSA Anaconda (right across from Camp Victory). This commercial truck was hit when the mortar rounds hit the POL (petroleum, oil, and lubrication) storage site. *(courtesy Justin MacEwan)*

This Mitsibushi Montero (aka Pajero in the Middle East) was hit
by fragments from an Iraqi-made 127mm rocket artillery shell.
Sgt. MacEwen: "No one was injured, but the round came over
our tent like a freight train." *(courtesy Justin MacEwan)*

❖

A checkpoint at the entrance for the then-CPA (Green Zone).
(courtesy Justin MacEwan)

No better way to fly than Iraqi Airways. Sgt. MacEwen: "During an operation, I made my way onto one of these old passenger jets and was going to make a picture as if I was the pilot with an AK-47." *(courtesy Justin MacEwan)*

❖

Sgt. MacEwen and a buddy sit in a "Ghetto Tent" while under enemy fire. Sgt. MacEwen: "Even with the shelling, we wanted to watch season two of *Alias* with Jennifer Garner." *(courtesy Justin MacEwan)*

Sgt. MacEwen in the big Saddam Chair at the "Victory Palace."
Sgt. MacEwen: "There must be thousands of pictures of this chair
roaming around the U.S. Everyone sat in it and got their picture taken.
Like a department store Santa Claus." *(courtesy Justin MacEwan)*

❖

Victory Palace on Camp Victory, Baghdad. *(courtesy Justin MacEwan)*

The only Burger King that will never get robbed. This Burger King was located at BIAP (Baghdad International Airport) right next to the large post exchange. *(courtesy Justin MacEwan)*

❖

The original Ghetto Tent, a U.S. Army issue GP (general purpose) large tent. The large rip on the top piece is where a shell fragment went through during a mortar attack in April 2004. *(courtesy Justin MacEwan)*

A view of the 14-foot concrete wall and guard towers being built by
Captain Matthew Hancock's construction team. *(courtesy Matthew Hancock)*

❖

Iraqi contractors roofing renovated barracks. *(courtesy Matthew Hancock)*

Iraqi contractors pouring concrete. Note the soldiers keeping watch in the background. *(courtesy Matthew Hancock)*

❖

"The Sheriff"—Captain Hancock inspects the post's water purification plant. Also shown: a KBR employee. *(courtesy Matthew Hancock)*

Captain Hancock's contracting office/bedroom. The laptop was his
personal unit since the Army didn't have enough to go around.
(courtesy Matthew Hancock)

❖

Captain DeKever: "As we crossed the Kuwaiti border into Iraq, I put my
future wife's picture in front of me so it would seem like she was with
me." *(courtesy Andrew DeKever)*

"SCUD!" DeKever in a gas mask during a SCUD alert.
(courtesy Andrew DeKever)

❖

DeKever standing on an Iraqi jet at Balad Airbase (LSA Anaconda).
(courtesy Andrew DeKever)

A child waves an American flag at passing convoys crossing through southern Iraq. *(courtesy Andrew DeKever)*

This monument to Saddam was toppled at Balad after Allied troops liberated the airfield. *(courtesy Andrew DeKever)*

".50 cal." Chad Vance perched atop a gun truck in Kuwait, waiting to deploy for Iraq. *(courtesy Chad Vance)*

❖

Taken near Camp Cedar I in south central Iraq. Vance: "We stayed at Camp Cedar about three weeks when we first got to Iraq, before moving to Camp Dogwood, 30 miles south of Baghdad in May. The sand blew like hell while we loaded our PLSs. *(courtesy Chad Vance)*

A wretch gets ready to put a Connex on the back of a truck. Also taken at Camp Cedar. *(courtesy Chad Vance)*

❖

Convoy trucks head out from Camp Dogwood one morning, loaded with connexes. Note the two gun trucks on the left side of the picture. *(courtesy Chad Vance)*

Camp Victory in Kuwait. Vance: "We stopped for the night on a mission and lined up our trucks as shown in the picture. Then the bottles of whiskey would come out and we'd start the relaxation process." *(courtesy Chad Vance)*

❖

Sgt. Adamiec gets a bird's-eye view of a Muslim protest in the streets of Qualaza. *(courtesy Jason Adamiec)*

Coming home after a long patrol. *(courtesy Jason Adamiec)*

❖

This is what a Squad Automatic Weapon looks like from the wrong end. *(courtesy Jason Adamiec)*

Roadsigns. Halfway between nothing and nowhere.
(courtesy Jason Adamiec)

Specialist Stephen LoPinto, the
photographer, getting ready to go
out on patrol in the city of Mosul.
(courtesy Stephen LoPinto)

The allergist did a patch test on me, exposing my skin to different samples of material to verify what I'm allergic to. The only substance my skin reacted to was thimerosal,[67] which you find a lot in shaving cream. I checked the shaving cream I used in the Gulf. No thimerosal. Despite the fact that this was an interesting find, it wasn't helpful diagnostically.

I'd maintained contact with Juan Gonzalez between April and September. I wanted to know how the tests had turned out. He said they were waiting for other soldiers to get tested and they'd rather release the findings as a group. Then he called me on September 17 or 18. I'd been out of the military just over a week. He said, "Gerard, I have the results of your test." I remember getting really tense.

I said, "What does it say?"

"You've been exposed to DU."

I was like, *What?!* Even after everything that had happened, I was stunned. I said, "What are you talking about? Fax a copy of that right over to me, will you? I want to see it for myself."

Juan faxed the results while we were talking and explained some of the details to me. I'd been exposed to levels of DU four to eight times greater than the two other soldiers who were tested with me. The labs had labeled the test samples A, B, and C so that whoever performed the tests wouldn't know they were handling soldiers' specimens. I was Subject A, the other two people were B and C. Juan said that the lab was so shocked at my results that they ran the experiment twice just to make sure. Both times, it was very clear: my levels were very, very high.

I decided to call Fort Dix. I hadn't heard anything from them regarding the military's DU test. I hoped that the doctors I'd worked with in the medical hold would be willing to help me. They were very kind and gave me phone numbers to call at Walter Reed in order to track down my test results. But when I called Walter Reed, they made me speak to a lady who apparently worked for deployment soldiers. She said they'd looked all over for the specimens I'd turned in. They'd checked Walter

---

67. Thimerosal is a preservative used in vaccines since the 1930s. It is 49.6 percent mercury by weight, and metabolizes or degrades into ethylmercury and thiosalicylate. At concentrations found in vaccines, it meets the requirements for a preservative as set forth by the *United States Pharmacopeia*. This means it kills the specified challenge organisms while preventing growth of challenge fungi. Prior to its introduction in the 1930s, data were available in several animal species and humans providing evidence for thimerosal's safety and effectiveness as a preservative. Since then, thimerosal has a long record of safe and effective use preventing bacterial and fungal contamination of certain vaccines. No ill effects have been established other than minor local reactions at the site of injection.

Reed and Fort Dix. Nothing. They couldn't find it. Apparently my specimens and any test results linked to them had just disappeared.

I was very angry. I asked if I could take the test over. And I didn't mention anything at all about the test results through the *Daily News*.

I'll say this for the army: they hate to be caught with their pants down. Within forty-eight hours of my call, they had two sets of new specimen bottles at my place in the Bronx. I thought that was pretty good considering I wasn't active in the military anymore. They said they'd send an envoy to pick up the bottles once I'd filled them. In other words, they wanted to make sure that—this time—everything got where it was supposed to go. Included with the specimen bottles that arrived was a letter dated September 17. The letter bore a disclaimer, "DU exposure does not cause birth defects." The army had finally assumed an official stance on matters that directly affected my family and me. Regardless of whether or not I tested positively for DU, in their eyes what happened to my daughter, Victoria, was my problem, not theirs.

It was mind-boggling to me. I'd never received a single notification by mail, word of mouth, direct order, nothing that said soldiers in service overseas might be exposed to radioactive substances. Yet here was the army providing written copy saying in effect, "Oh, by the way. We're not responsible for anything related to depleted uranium poisoning. Have a nice day."

If they knew that stuff was over there, why didn't they tell us in the first place? Why didn't they give us instructions like, "If you're handling such-and-such pieces of equipment you should follow these procedures to make sure you stay healthy." We didn't receive any foreknowledge, no training in how to properly handle radioactive substances or what those radioactive substances might be. But we sure as hell received the kiss-off in writing. The way I see it, the government of the United States is concealing a lot from its soldiers and the American people. The way I see it, we were sacrificed, plain and simple.

A couple of days passed and a Colonel Washington, a chief from the Department of Preventative Medicine at Walter Reed called. She said, "There's been a change of plans. We'd like you to take the specimens to

West Point." That's only about fifty miles north of New York City if you follow the Hudson River, so I said, "Not a problem." I wrote down the names of the people she wanted me to give the samples to, but I got really busy that day and couldn't find time to make the drive. It's tough enough when you're working full time to haul specimen bottles around with you and pee in them all the time, especially when you pee as frequently as I do these days. Tougher still to find a place that will refrigerate them for you. To make a drive up to West Point? Forget about it. Colonel Washington called me up the very next day and said, "Did you turn in your specimens?"

I said, "No, I didn't. I need more time."

Then she asked if I could provide her with a copy of the *Daily News* test results. I said, "Sure," and I hung up the phone. But the more I started thinking about it, why would the army want a copy of a test conducted by an independent expert *before* they'd conducted their own? Why not ask for the *News*'s results *after* they'd performed their test? That way they could use them as a true verification to confirm or refute their own findings. The whole thing smelled real fishy to me. I decided not to take the military's test. Up until that point, they'd been evasive, deceptive, and dismissive of my issues. Frankly, I didn't trust them. The independent experts hired by the *News* had no reason to lie to me. Hell, they didn't even know I was a soldier.

The army called one more time. I told them, "I'm not taking it. Good-bye." And I hung up the phone. That was that as far as the army was concerned. For me and my family, though, it was just the beginning.

I've been stateside for a year now. My syndrome's begun to progress. Now I get purple lesions on my skin. I have erectile dysfunction. When I urinate, my urinary sphincter won't close fully. So I'll go to use the toilet like any normal person, do my business, and think that I'm finished. But when I sit back down, my pants are all wet. It's embarrassing. I get numbness in my hands and feet, too—that's new. And sometimes I get so fatigued in the morning that I can't get out of bed. But the worst part is my daughter. Victoria Claudine Matthew. She was born June 28 of 2004. She's the love of my life and she doesn't have any fingers on her right hand.

Victoria goes to therapy twice a week, but it's tough for me to afford, you know? Because of my condition, I lost the job that paid my medical insurance. And the government says they had nothing to do with it.

Now I go to the Bronx VA hospital a lot over in Kingsbridge. They're real nice there, really helpful, especially after my article came out in the *Daily News*.[68] But when you boil everything down, all anyone knows for sure is that my symptoms have gotten worse and new symptoms have risen. I've turned into a walking pharmacy. Name a drug and I'm on it for something. Gabapentin, which is Neurontin[69]—400 milligrams three times a day for the headaches. Amatriptilene, too—150 milligrams three times a day because a psychiatrist at the VA told me I have depression secondary to my illness. Still taking the Zomas as needed, that's the only thing that seems to do any good. After hearing what Doctor Pazdan said about overdosing, I've scaled the Zomas back to four times a week, 300 milligrams taken alongside Tylenol with codeine. I don't like being dependent on meds. I don't really have a choice. I have a series of appointments starting this December with an endocrinologist, a urologist; name a specialist, I'm going to see them. Some of their specialties, I can't even pronounce. I doubt they'll tell me anything I don't know already.

To this day, I still see double and triple when I look at anything directly. I have to use my peripheral vision. I've tried wearing these special glasses they made for me, but that only makes the headaches worse. According to the military's official medical diagnosis, I have two issues: migraines with aura, and idiopathic angioedema. For everything else I'm experiencing, they have no comment. Nobody wants to entertain any speculation whatsoever on my possible exposure to toxic or radioactive substances.

At one point, a caseworker at the Bronx VA suggested that my incontinence might be cured if my urinary sphincter got a little more exercise. He told me to masturbate. I laughed in his face. After all I'd been through, this guy was so far out in left field it was—I don't know. It was funny. But later on I got really mad. Who the hell is that guy to tell me bullshit like that? I suppose he was just looking out for my best interests.

---

68. See *New York Daily News* article: *"The War's Littlest Victim (Daily News Exclusive): He was Exposed to Depleted Uranium. His Daughter may be Paying the Price."* September 29, 2004, by Juan Gonzalez. A picture of Specialist Matthew holding baby Victoria appeared on the front page of that issue.

69. Gabapentin (Neurontin) is an anticonvulsant which has also been successful in controlling rapid cycling, mixed bipolar states in patients who have not found relief through other medications.

I mean, my psychiatrist told me I could use Viagra to aid my erectile performance. He noted I was a thirty-year-old male with what you call high prolactin levels—fluctuating testosterone. One day my testosterone is way up high, the next day it drops out for no good reason. But what he doesn't know is that there's no possibility this was a condition preexisting my time in the Gulf. They first noticed it in my blood work in the medical hold at Fort Dix. None of my previous physicals from the marines or the guard picked up on it, and yes, it's a routine parameter for examination every time you have blood work done. It's the DU all over again.

I feel like I'm living my life one bad moment to the next. I wake up every morning and have to see Victoria like that, deal with her problem, I just want to explode. But who do you blame? The situation's created problems between my spouse and me. There's tension between us, and I know the trajectory of it. I blame myself for what happened to Victoria, then I go home and take it out on my wife when, obviously, it's not her fault. It's just a very difficult situation, that's all. A very difficult situation.

A few occasions I've had to stay at my mother's place, you know? But my wife and I are working through it. Our relationship has started getting better since I've started taking her along on some of my medical appointments. Now she sees what I have to go through. She's beginning to understand. I haven't taken Victoria, though. Like I said, the government won't acknowledge any connection whatsoever between my condition and hers. The VA says that the only way they'll take care of my child is if I become 100 percent disabled. I've questioned them directly about how DU exposure contributed to her birth defect. Nobody wants to talk about it. They either pass the buck off to someone else or shut down on you entirely.

Recently, some people in Boston, Massachusetts, invited me to come speak about soldiers being exposed to DU. I accepted the invitation because I thought it would be therapeutic for me to talk about my experiences. Believe me, I had reservations. But I feel that word has to get out about this. And frankly? What more can the army do to me? I've been honorably discharged, let them come after me as a private citizen. It can't make matters worse than they already are.

A lot of media I've talked to won't air the issue. The only ones who really listened were UPN 9 news, the Spanish networks, and the Japanese networks. Japan knows something of the lingering effects of radiation poisoning. Fujitsu TV did a documentary in January of '05. I was also featured in an updated documentary for PVN [Penn Video Network] called "Medal of Dishonor." Sergeant Ramos and I went on Democracy NOW and did a twenty-five-minute show together, and *Vanity Fair* just did a great article that was very informative.[70]

See, I'm worried about my family life, but I'm also worried about soldiers coming back from the Gulf right now, eighteen, nineteen, twenty years old, who might have the same problem without experiencing the same symptoms. What will become of their children? What's going to happen to these soldiers when they start losing their jobs and their job benefits because their syndromes, like mine, render them incapable of working? How will they provide for their families? I don't have medical insurance anymore, not for me, not for my family. I had it through my night job, but I had to quit the job because of the headaches. I found I couldn't drive at night anymore. In the dark, oncoming lights screw my eyes up and I can't see a thing.

I think the military should at least take care of my daughter and me. You give and you give and you give to them, then they pull something like this. It's incomprehensible to me. I'm angry. You bet I'm angry. This keeps me up at night: what if my wife and I want to have another kid? Will it happen again? Dear God.

One bit of good news: Last week[71] the Devone family from Long Island apparently read my story on the computer and called up Juan Gonzalez. Juan gave them my e-mail address, and we struck up a correspondence. After a couple of days, this man, Mr. Devone said, "Could I come to your house and see your child?"

I was a little taken aback by that. It seemed an odd request. But since it came through Juan, I figured everything was on the level. Juan's a prince. Mr. Devone said, "I'm coming into the city in a few days, and I figured—well, I'd love to meet your daughter." I said, "Fine. Okay. You're welcome to drop in." And I gave him the address. This man showed up at my place with a member of his family and a very close fam-

---

70. *"Weapons of Self-Destruction: Is Gulf War Syndrome—Possibly Caused by Pentagon Ammunition— Taking Its Toll on Soldiers?"* by David Rose, *Vanity Fair*, November 19, 2004.
71. Early December 2004.

ily friend. We spoke a while and I showed him some pictures. We talked about the war and how I felt about what had happened to me. They were very nice people.

When it came time to go, Mr. Devone took out an envelope and set it in my daughter's crib, right behind her pillow. He said, "We'd like to help a soldier for Christmas. This is for you, sweetheart." I walked them downstairs to their car and thanked them for coming. When I went back upstairs, Victoria was fast asleep. I moved the envelope to one side. I knew it was cash, fifty bucks maybe, that's what I thought. A nice gesture, you know? I went to the kitchen and made myself a cup of hot chocolate. Later on, I figured I should write those people a thank-you note, so I opened the envelope. There were ten hundred-dollar bills inside. All of a sudden, I didn't know what to do. How do you say thank you to something like that?

The army gives you a medal when you return home from this war. The medal comes in a case with a little card on the cover that says, "From President George W. Bush," and it has his picture on it. I sent the medal to the Devone family. It was the only appropriate thank you I could think of. I don't know those people at all, you know? They're complete strangers. But they did more for me and my family than the government I served in time of war. Imagine that.

A RAID IN NASIRIYAH

✳

Corporal Bradley Becker

U.S. MARINE CORPS, GOLF COMPANY, 2ND BATTALION,

2ND MARINES

Corporal Becker enlisted in the marines because he grew up in a small town, Finlayson, Minnesota—population: 210. Bradley wanted to see the world, and the corps accommodated him. They sent him to boot camp at San Diego, California's Camp Pendleton. From there, he hopped to Camp Lejeune in North Carolina, but this was only the beginning. By the time Corporal Becker got out of the corps, he'd seen stranger places than he'd ever imagined, including one particularly tough spot in Nasiriyah, Iraq.

Bradley, age 25, says that the physical demands of being a marine never really affected him. "I was nineteen when I joined the corps," he says. "The toughest part, I guess, was having some drill instructor in your face shouting at you all the time. But it's what they do. They're showing you that you can do anything you put your mind to—even under the worst conditions."

I was a fire-team leader, which meant I was in charge of three other marines. Fire-team leaders are part of the chain of command, they micromanage an infantry assault. A fire-team leader reports to a squad leader, usually a corporal or sergeant with three fire teams in his billet. The squad leaders report to the platoon sergeant who reports to the platoon commander, and they keep moving on up the food chain.

Urban warfare is the fire-team leader's game. The squad leader tells you which general direction to head in, but the fire-team leader calls all the shots. When you're mounting an offensive assault down a narrow street, it's the fire-team leader who says, "Go through this door. Halt. Post here. Check that window. Sweep left." You're the guy directing traffic and establishing the line of fire.

I remember how the platoon leaders would shout orders to the squad leaders on the training course. Then the squad leaders shouted

118

orders to their fire-team leaders, and we'd all shift our guys around to wherever they had to be, perfect rhythm, total precision, like one big well-oiled machine. You make sure your men are dug in when and where they're supposed to be, make sure they're staying awake. Because when the whole thing works right, it's beautiful, just beautiful. When it doesn't work right, you or somebody you know could get killed.

We got our second overseas deployment after September 11th so we knew it wasn't going to be another party in Europe. Our first assignment landed us in Kosovo, hunting Albanian smugglers bringing bootlegged goods into the region. We set up observation posts, watched the border, and stopped anybody trying to come through. We focused on locating kidnapped prostitutes and weapons, and ended up capturing about twenty-five Albanian smugglers in the month and a half we were there. That posting didn't seem all that difficult or severe, but it definitely made us feel like we were contributing.

After that we pulled three and a half months in Djibouti, which is pretty much the armpit of the world.[72] To give you an idea, in the month of February the temperature rose to over 120 degrees. We worked with another government agency—I believe it was the CIA—to guard two Predator[73] airplanes that were being sent to attack al Qaeda generals hiding in Albania. The planes would fly up into the air and disappear from sight. The guys on the ground would radio Central Command in the U.S., who'd take over the planes' controls in midair by satellite link. Later on, they'd come back and land back on our base in Djibouti. No one on the ground knew where the aircraft had gone. We'd guard [the planes] from possible terrorist attacks until they were ready to fly again.

After that, we went to Kenya for about a month, where we trained

---

72. Djibouti is a small country in northeast Africa. The capital city, also called Djibouti, is a major port on the Gulf of Aden. Its proximity to the Suez Canal makes it a position of strategic importance for powerful nations wishing to control the passage of vessels between the Indian Ocean and the Mediterranean Sea. Djibouti is an extremely poor country with no natural resources. In 1977 it gained independence from France, which had ruled the area since the late 1800s.

73. Predator aircraft are remotely operated aircraft (ROA) designed for the Department of Defense by General Atomics Aeronautical Systems, Inc., based in San Diego, California. Each aircraft is operated by a pilot and a payload operator who are located in a ground control station (GCS). The Predator was designed in the Department of Defense's Advanced Concept Technology Demonstration program (ACTD, 1994–1996). Its specific intent is to provide reconnaissance, surveillance, and targeting acquisition intelligence over areas of interest, though some Predators also carry and fire Hellfire laser-guided antitank missiles, which makes it the first U.S. unmanned system to employ live weapons.

Iraqi freedom fighters. Don't ask me what Iraqi freedom fighters were doing in Kenya, I was too low in the ranks to hear the rationale for things like that. We assumed it was so Baath Party[74] members wouldn't be able to find these individuals and seek reprisals against them or their families while they were training. In all we trained about one hundred men in basic infantry skills—how to clear rooms and so forth. Obviously, we didn't take their tactical training too far; that would have been like giving away American military secrets. Call it a watered-down version of infantry training. We didn't supply weapons, either; the Iraqis worked with their own AK-47s and SKSs.[75] When the training in Kenya was finished, we got two days off in the Seychelle Islands, which, according to the Bible, is where the Garden of Eden used to be. It was a really nice place.

When we first set out on that cruise,[76] we were told it'd be a five-and-a-half-month gig. By this point, though, we'd already been extended. For myself and the other NCOs, five and a half months ended up being eleven. We were told we were needed in the region. By the time we got done in Djibouti, the Iraq war had just begun. We were a forward-deployed unit that hadn't been relieved of command. No one was sure whether we'd be needed or not, so the higher-ups decided to keep us around. Better safe than sorry. As it turns out, we shipped into Boseria, Kuwait, two or three days after the war started, and from there we flew into Iraq.

As we flew in-country, there was a firefight going on near the southeast side of our landing strip. We got warning to have our gas masks on before we touched ground. We were at MOPP Level 4 [see sidebar], where you've got your nuclear, biological, and chemical suit donned; the jackets, the bibs, the whole heavy suit, which is weird to move around in. My pack weighed more than I did—185 pounds. I was carrying an

74. Formally the Baath Arab Socialist Party a.k.a. the Ba'ath Party, an influential political party among Arabic communities, especially in Syria and Iraq. From its earliest development, a key tenet of the Baath Party was the reassertion of Arabic values in the face of foreign domination. The word *baath* means "resurrection" or "renaissance" in Arabic. The Baath Party came to power in Iraq in February 1963 and—one month later—in Syria, on March 8, as part of the so-called March Revolution.

75. SKS M-45 7.62 carbine (Samozariadnyia Karabina Simonova), the *Simonov system self-loading carbine.* This rifle was adopted by Soviet forces in 1946 to replace the Tokarev semiautomatic and Mosin-Nagant bolt-action-style rifles. The Chinese, Romanians, Albanians, and Yugoslavs eventually created their own versions of the SKS, but differences between each make are negligible. The SKS was eventually replaced in the Russian military by the AK-47.

76. Marine slang for "deployment."

ungodly amount of 203 rounds[77] plus an extra machine gunner's drum, three or four mortars, my grenades, and about 790 rounds for my rifle. We carried everything we thought we might need to sustain us for two or three weeks under the worst conditions.

THE FIVE LEVELS OF MOPP
(MISSION-ORIENTED PROTECTIVE POSTURE)

MOPP LEVEL 0—Have your IPE and field gear available for immediate donning. Your protective mask's filter and hood should be installed.

MOPP LEVEL 1—Don your overgarment and field gear. Carry your footwear covers, mask, and gloves. MOPP 1 is generally used when a chemical and/or biological attack in the theater is possible.

MOPP LEVEL 2—Don your footwear covers. You are now carrying your mask and gloves. MOPP 2 is generally used when a chemical and/or biological attack in the theater is likely.

MOPP LEVEL 3—Don your mask and hood. You're now carrying your gloves. MOPP 3 is generally used in areas with no contact hazard or any operationally significant hazard of percutaneous vapor.

MOPP LEVEL 4—Don everything. MOPP 4 is used when the highest degree of chemical/biological protection is required, such as during an attack. MOPP 4 may also be called when the actual hazard has not been determined.

---

77. The M-203 40 mm single-shot grenade launcher (a version of the M-79) mounts neatly beneath the barrel of an M-16 automatic rifle and provides additional infantry fire support without burdening a soldier with carrying more weapons. The M-203 can provide illumination and ballistics by delivering high explosives, parachute flares, and canister rounds. The high explosives can be shot to a maximum range of 400 meters, with a casualty radius of 5 meters.

Turns out there was a unit already on the ground that took care of the gunfight, but we set up in our 180, just in case anything happened.

Then we went to Nasiriyah, and for the first couple of days we set up roadblocks. We caught thirty-two Iraqi troops hiding in the back of a dump truck that they'd camouflaged with mud. Later on, we found a bunch of their SKSs and AK-47s on the side of the road about five hundred meters before the blockade. Looked like they'd seen what they were about to get themselves into and thrown their weapons out before they reached us. We found either the nine or the jack of spades in that dump truck, too, I forget.[78]

While we maintained the roadblock, our sister company launched its first mission, going into Nasiriyah to extract a U.S. marine who'd been taken by Iraqis. Somehow the soldier'd gotten separated from his group, I don't know how; maybe he fell out of the back of his convoy truck. The Iraqis caught him, beat him, and dragged him through the streets. Then they strung him up on a telephone pole. Later on, they threw his remains in a trash Dumpster and mutilated it. Our sister company retrieved the body from a shallow grave behind some buildings.

After the roadblock detail, we were assigned to run routine patrols through town checking for Baath Party activities. We holed up in an elementary school and made it our headquarters. We found a cache of RPGs and some AK-47s hidden in a sewer system beneath the school. It was another example of culture shock: guns being stored in schools.

Understand, we were in a major Iraqi city but the people all around us lived the way Jesus did two thousand years ago. The good buildings we saw had one electrical cord running throughout for lights. Some buildings had no electricity. The school we occupied had a couple of outlets, but aside from that, the windows were open to the outside world, shutters but no glass. Everything we saw was rundown. Third-world living standards.

When we first got to the school, there was a huge bunch of kids sur-

---

78. According to the American Forces Press Service in April 2003, coalition forces in Iraq used specially created decks of playing cards to identify the fifty-five "most wanted" members of Saddam Hussein's regime. The cards were designed by command officials. Each deck contained two Jokers—one listed a primer on Iraqi military ranks, the other listed Iraqi tribal titles. Saddam Hussein al-Tikriti's card was the ace of spades. The nine of spades was Rukan Razuki Abd al-Ghafar Sulayman al Majid al-Tikriti, the Head of the Tribal Affairs Office. The jack of spades was Ibrahim Ahmad Abd al-Sattar Muhammad al-Tikriti, the Iraqi Armed Forces' Chief of Staff.

rounding it. We never allowed them to come closer than five or ten feet
for fear that they had bombs strapped to their bodies, but it became
clear to us that 98 percent of the population seemed extremely happy to
see us. Still, we were wary. The crowd that had dragged that marine
through the streets must've looked just like this one. That's one of the
things that constantly threw me off in Iraq: the people we were fighting,
the people who had it in for us, formed such a tiny minority. Basically,
the bad ones were Saddam's henchmen, but how could you tell? They
didn't dressed in any sort of uniform and mingled with the rest of the
population, trying to wreak as much havoc as they could.

We were a company of 126 working to protect a town of about ninety
thousand people. Thirty-six guys at a time patrolled the streets. At first
we had no idea which areas were hostile toward us and which weren't.
We learned quickly to look for certain key indicators, like Iraqi men who
appeared to be counting our troops or the men who sat in the background and grabbed little kids as if they were watching over their children. If the kids struggled, the guy holding them wasn't their father. He
was just some guy trying to appear normal while he did reconnaissance
on us. Or maybe he was a guy who knew something was about to happen, like an attack, and he didn't want his kids near U.S. troops.

A lot of times we used the kids as a barometer. Normally, there were
thousands of them running around the streets. If we moved into an area
where the kids started thinning out, we knew we'd hit a bad part of
town. See, the Baath Party was trying to build relations among the people, same as we were. They couldn't win favor if they got a reputation for
killing Iraqi children. When the number of kids diminished to fifteen or
twenty, we got extra careful.

We knew two Iraqi kids who'd lived in New York and spoke really
good English. They talked to us all the time, giving us hints on where to
look for insurgents. As soon as any Baath Party members came around,
these kids would suddenly forget how to speak English. That was one of
their clues to us that someone dangerous was nearby. Any way you cut it,
though, it was hard to tell who was friendly and who wasn't.

We ended up getting to know a professor who'd worked in the
schoolhouse. He'd come through the lines to talk to our lieutenants and
give them ideas about which streets we should patrol to check for Baath

Party activity. The professor's daughter was seven years old and she would follow our patrols around like a shadow for five or six miles at a shot.

Let me tell you about the closest call I had in Iraq. We moved on to Al Hai, a town just north of Nasiriyah. We'd received intel that the Baath Party had cached arms there. Our job was to go in and seize the weapons. We planned a company assault to take down three sites at once. The site I got assigned to was the biggest in the raid. According to intel, it was an old one-room-style schoolhouse, like an empty warehouse. Well, intel turned out to be pretty lousy.

We mounted the assault early in the morning. I was on point for the whole platoon. My group and I approached our building and saw that a brick privacy wall five and a half feet high surrounded it. We hadn't been told anything about that. It was the sort of wall you could hop over with the help of another marine, so that's what we did; we made quick work of it. We were trained to adjust to whatever we encountered and to do so fast.

When you mount an assault on a building, it's always preferable, tactically speaking, to blow your own hole in the wall. Barring that, you use the least-expected entryway. The idea is to avoid whatever booby traps have been laid for intruders. We headed for a door on one side of the building and found it bolt-locked, so I ordered my shot gunner up.

He leveled his Benelli 12-gauge pump at the mechanism and fired. The first blast didn't do the job. He fired again. Nothing. Let me tell you, when you're standing in a wide open space in the middle of an assault and it's dark out? Any pause in the action makes your back feel five miles wide. You can't see your hand in front of your face because your NVGs [night-vision goggles] aren't working that great. The whole world is a bunch of shadowy contour lines moving all around you. After the third shotgun blast, I kicked the door in and entered the building. I was the first man through.

First thing I heard was the sound of *pitter-patter, pitter-patter*, some guy running away from me. I never got a good look at him, he ran down the hall and ducked around a corner. I was about to pursue him when I looked to my right and saw what appeared to be a bomb, a lit fuse attached to a large canister. I didn't stop, made a short entry into a room immediately to my left. Turned out the place wasn't a single-room schoolhouse, it was a multiroom building, much more dangerous. It was some kind of youth center or something. I yelled out as I moved, "Multiple rooms! Multiple rooms!" Then I shouted out for the bomb techs to come forward and disarm the explosive.

Everything that happened next was fluid motion, no stopping. My fire team and I pushed forward and found ourselves in this huge auditorium with a stage and balconies and multiple entries. It was an assault team's nightmare, no cover whatsoever. Just me and my three guys, open as a turkey shoot. I think that was the scariest feeling I've ever had in my life. Every second that passed seemed three or four minutes long. The rest of the platoon started flowing in behind us and we swept the bottom floor, clearing room by room. Then we did the top floor, even though there wasn't supposed to be a top floor. Intel got that wrong, too. We heard someone call out. They'd caught the guy I'd heard running away as he tried to climb out a back window. But then we heard the sound of running feet again, this time up on the roof.

I called out, "Man on the roof! Man on the roof!" My squad leader said, "Let's get him." So me, my friends Blanco, Fierro, and my squad leader headed up to cut him off.

This building turned out to be the kind with an interior garden. When we got to the roof we found a ledge running around the interior overlooking the courtyard below. On the other side of the roof, an Iraqi man was out on the ledge and we started yelling to him, "*Keef! Tamay dad!*" Which is, "Stop! Get down!" in Arabic. We kept yelling this, but the guy was acting funny. Members of my team dropped to their knees in firing positions. Some of them put their hands on their heads to demonstrate that we wanted him to surrender, but he kept inching toward us; it was crazy. We'd spent the past two days passing out brochures to the Iraqis explaining what to do in situations like this. We were trying like hell to avoid conflict and here's this guy completely ignoring us, advancing on us, which is not good.

He kept inching forward and I yelled out again, "*Keef! Tamay dad!*" Nothing. He kept coming. I was in the middle of telling my guys, "We're going to have to take action, we're going to have to do something," when the man closed to within twenty feet and my buddy Blanco shot him twice in the chest.

It was a time of war. There was no fucking around. If an enemy doesn't do exactly what you say in a combat situation, you have to make a call. We went to check the body and make sure he wasn't carrying any bombs waiting to detonate. What did we find sitting by his feet? An AK-47. He'd been inching toward it. Later on we found a machine gun bunker on the roof with the man's SKS in it. The machine gun was sited on the exact point where my fire team and I had entered the building, but the weapon had injected two rounds into the chamber and jammed severely. Lucky for us. I guess the Iraqi hadn't been able to get it unstuck, so he ran for the AK.

A more thorough check of the building turned up an antiaircraft gun on the roof with multiple RPGs. We also found three canisters that looked like they could be fired from mortar tubes, the type of canister that contains deadly gases. None of us could understand the markings, but the cans were intact and suspicious-looking enough that we handled them carefully. We later heard through the lance corporal underground that they'd contained sarin gas.[79]

And I wasn't imagining things, I had seen a bomb when we first entered the building. The EOD techs told me later on that it was a really bad rig, a primitive time bomb. A small candle like you'd find on a birthday cake was positioned to burn down and touch off a wick. Basically the birthday candle gave the guy who'd rigged the bomb enough time to get away from the seven-and-a-half-gallon gasoline can that was about to explode. When I'd dodged into the building and looked right, the light from the burning birthday candle got picked up by my NVGs. Three lucky strikes in a row—the bomb, the theater, the gunner. That's more than enough for me.

I've told you a story that's guts and glory, but that's not what the war was for me. We were encouraged to talk to the Iraqi people and get to know

---

79. A colorless, odorless gas that carries a lethal dosage at .05 milligrams for an adult. Sarin gas is twenty-six times more lethal than cyanide gas and twenty times more lethal than potassium cyanide. The vapor from sarin gas is slightly heavier than air and will hover close to the ground. Under wet, humid weather the gas's potency deteriorates quickly, but higher temperatures may increase the gas's potency despite the humidity. The gas can be delivered by various means, including mortar fire.

them. The moment I did that, I started to understand why this war is important. See, I don't care if the war was over oil or weapons of mass destruction or any of that. The people I met really needed our help. The health care in Iraq was abominable, the system of government tyrannous. Give you an example: We found lots of books in the schoolhouse we occupied, flipped through them, and found Saddam's picture on the front page, in the middle, all throughout. There were pictures of him hanging on every wall. It was total propaganda, a constant fear factor installed in the Iraqi people from the time that they were children.

Saddam had the Baath Party installed in every village, ready to keep order. How did they do it? I saw two little girls during my tour; I'll never forget them. One had her face half-burnt off and the other had her nose cut off. Both injuries to shame the girls' families for some transgression against the government. How could I ever forget that? Regardless of everything they debate on the news, I still believe we were right to go into Iraq. Talk to any marine who went into that country. They'll all tell you the same thing.

RADIO BAGHDAD

✦

Specialist Jonah Casaubon
CHARLIE COMPANY, 17TH SIGNAL BATTALION, 22ND
SIGNAL BRIGADE, 5TH CORPS

Jonah, age 20, was born and raised in Maine. All throughout school, his grades suffered from what he calls "a lack of discipline." When it was time to go to college, Jonah joined the army instead. The way he saw it, the army would give him a job where he could earn money for college while teaching him the focus he'd need to excel at his studies. As a serviceman, he could travel the world and help defend his nation in the post-9/11 world. He upped for four years. His signal unit was stationed in Germany when it got the call to deploy to Kuwait in February 2003.

The biggest thing they teach you in a danger zone like Kuwait or Iraq is keep your rifle with you at all times, either in your hand or within easy reach. Never let anyone get between you and your rifle. At night, when you sleep, your rifle should lay beside your bed. It should be *in* your bed, if possible. This might seem fanatical, but the army has its reasons. In a war zone, your weapon is your life. It can keep you alive against the enemy. Lay down your rifle, you lay down your life. Sergeants keep an eye out for soldiers who lay down their weapons and walk even a few yards from them. They punish you if they catch you doing this.

One afternoon while my unit was in Kuwait, I set my rifle down while I was working and walked maybe thirty-five feet away. A sergeant came along, picked up the rifle, brought it over to me, and that was that. I was made to perform extra physical fitness in full battle armor. This meant I had to march up and down a crate, as if it were a stair machine in a gym, while holding my weapon over my head. When the sergeant said so, I put the weapon down in front of me. When the sergeant said so, I picked the rifle up, held it over my head again and continued climbing. Up and down, up and down, up and down. With all the extra weight, in the desert heat, I got tired pretty quickly. The army's smart, though. The sergeant provided me with plenty of water throughout.

Did I resent that kind of treatment? No, I didn't. The NCO was making a point. It was a good lesson. Once we got to Iraq, I never let that rifle out of my sight.

My deployment happened so suddenly. I finished my basic and advanced training on December 19, 2002 and was granted two weeks' leave, so I returned home to my family in Maine. When I returned to Germany on January 5, I found out our unit had received instructions that said, "You're going to Kuwait where you will provide signal resources." How did I feel about heading into the Middle East? Nervous, certainly. Frightened. But also excited and intrigued. Predominantly, I was very conscious of the fact that I had no idea what to expect. We arrived in Kuwait on the ninth of February, 2003. At that point, it felt like a fairly safe part of the world, but everyone felt the undercurrent of tension running throughout the region.

No one at my level had any knowledge we were going to war. We carried our NBC (nuclear/biological/chemical) equipment around because it was policy, we never felt we'd have to use it. All that changed once the army crossed the berm[80] in late March or early April. Once we declared war, that's when I felt the fear hit. We started getting warnings that Iraqi missiles had launched, we'd hear the alarms telling us to don our full MOPP suits. Then we'd climb into a bunker and sit there thinking, *Where's the damned thing going to hit?* You never knew, so you just sat and wondered. A couple weeks after the front line invaded Iraq, my unit was ordered to cross the berm and follow them.

I remember the convoy into Iraq. We'd heard a lot of stories about what RPG attacks and recoilless rifle shots could do to unarmored vehicles, and here we were riding in a long train of about seventy-five canvas-backed trucks, soft targets heading north across four hundred miles of open desert. We weren't accompanied by an MP escort with .50 caliber

---

80. The berm [shoulder or ridge] referred to here is the Kuwait/Iraq separation barrier, a 120-mile line of electrified fencing and concertina wire extending the entire length of the Kuwait/Iraq border from Saudi Arabia to the Persian Gulf. The fence line is buttressed by a fifteen-foot-deep, fifteen-foot-wide trench, complete with a ten-foot-high dirt berm guarded by hundreds of soldiers at a time, plus patrol boats and helicopters. The barrier was constructed in 1991 by the United Nations Security Council with the stated purpose of preventing Iraq's reinvasion of Kuwait. In 1991, construction of the berm was estimated to cost $28 billion. During the Hussein regime, Iraq viewed Kuwait as a part of Iraq. To the Iraqi perspective, the barrier was considered an illegal seizure of Iraqi national territory. "Crossing the berm" refers to the U.S. invasion of Iraq.

machine guns and M-19 automatic grenade launchers.[81] We had no protection but our own weapons: a few AT-4s[82]; an M-249—which is the automatic version of the M-16; and the weapon-type I carried, an M-203 grenade launcher/M-16 combo rifle. Small arms mean small arms fire return. Sum it up, I felt pretty vulnerable.

ACCORDING TO THE ARMY STUDY GUIDE . . .

How may Chemical Agents be deployed?
Mines, rockets, arterial spray, artillery bombs, or through individuals (water pollution, food supplies)

What are the most effective times to use Chemical Agents?
In the early morning and during the evening, when the lack of wind and sun will allow the Chemical Agents to persist.

The U.S. classifies Chemical Agents into three categories, which are:
  1. Persistent
  2. Non-persistent
  3. Dusty

What are the four types of Chemical Agents?
  1. Nerve
  2. Blister
  3. Blood
  4. Choking

---

81. Probably referring to the MK-19 40 mm machine gun.
82. The M-136 AT4 is the U.S. Army's primary light antitank weapon, a shoulder-mounted recoilless rifle used by infantry to deliver an 84 mm high-explosive antitank warhead in a free-flight, fin-stabilized rocket in a disposable, one-piece, fiberglass-wrapped tube. The system weighs fifteen pounds, has a tactical engagement range of 250 meters, and can be utilized effectively with minimal training.

Along with the trucks, our convoy also had a wrecker bringing up the rear, a necessary item. It's a reality that vehicles break down when you push them long distances in extreme climates. We arrived without incident at Baghdad International Airport [BIAP], which you've probably seen on the news. BIAP's a main operations base for the U.S. Army, and my unit was assigned to a separate enclave within the airport compound known as Camp Strike. You could hop in a Humvee at Camp Strike and be at the airport in less than two minutes. I went there often; one time I saw a USO show. There was a lot of army traffic going in and out of BIAP but very few Iraqis. The airport lies outside the city limits of Baghdad and our troops had already taken it over, establishing a safe zone which few nationals were allowed to enter.

One of Saddam Hussein's presidential palaces sat in a huge compound on a ridge overlooking the airport. You could see that it had once been glorious, absolutely beautiful, in fact. But by the time we arrived, everything of value had been looted from it. The buildings stood like empty shells. My unit moved in and co-opted the place as our headquarters. We lived in what had once been a servant's quarter in a northern part of the facility and bunked in a cramped room, eight guys sleeping in a twenty by twenty-foot space.

Compared to the desert, this part of Iraq was paradise, nothing at all like the wastelands we'd driven across or the Kuwaiti desert. Vegetation grew all over the place, palm trees and forests, mostly. We were right in the heart of the Fertile Crescent,[83] near the lush Tigris-Euphrates river valley. There was a pond with some reeds around it in our compound. We weren't allowed to swim in it, but someone had left a little boat tied up there, sort of like a canoe, and during our off-times, we were often granted permission to take the boat out on the water, do a little fishing. Someone had stocked the pond with carp.

At one point there'd even been a zoo in the compound, too. By the time we moved in, all the animals had escaped. We'd hear exotic animal

83. The Fertile Crescent is a section of the Middle East where civilization began to develop thanks to the presence of rich, food-growing areas in an otherwise arid environment resistant to farming. The Fertile Crescent—as its name implies—is a crescent-shaped region extending from the eastern shore of the Mediterranean Sea to the Persian Gulf. Some of the best farmland found in the Fertile Crescent lies in the Tigris-Euphrates river valley, what anthropologists call the Cradle of Civilization and the Greeks called Mesopotamia, a word that literally meant "between two rivers." The ancient Assyrians, Sumerians, and Babylonians all developed their civilizations in this region, which is, in modern-day terms, the country of Iraq.

calls hooting at us in the middle of the night, birds and coyotes, wolves and wild dogs. There were even a few lions and tigers lurking around. The army had to call in special forces guys to trap them. And one time we were sitting outdoors eating a meal when this gazelle-type thing came bounding across camp from out of nowhere. One of my buddies jumped up and chased after it. We started laughing so hard we nearly fell over. The whole predicament was kind of nuts.

A military invasion requires lots of communication and that's where a signal battalion comes in. We provided a variety of services. Video tele-conferencing so generals and colonels could see what was going on at the battlefront and send orders. Data signals and online access for command communications. Satellite links so servicemen could talk to their families. Anything that talked or squawked in the war theater probably went through the army communications net at one point. If you care to think of it this way, our net very closely resembled the Internet in that it was a quilt where lines of electronic communication cross at intersections or junctures like threads—in Internet-speak: hubs. Only the hubs for the army communications network were called node centers, a node being any point where data can enter, process, and reemit to other branches of the net.

The system was created so components could be added or deleted at any time. If you wanted to expand the network, it's no problem whatsoever, just add a few node centers. If you wanted to collapse the network, remove a few nodes and consolidate signals—again, no problem. The Iraq communications network actually changed all the time as troops moved about the countryside and took up different positions. Easy to compensate for. Node centers are mobile entities built on the backs of Humvees. We just broke down the center, drove to a new location, and set it up again.

What did a center look like? Picture a series of Humvees with specialized shelters built on their backs. The shelters look exactly like those tiny mobile homes from the late '70s that sat in the backs of pickup trucks and jutted out over the cabs. You had two types of shelters: V3s, and Foxes. Basically, V3s housed the radio equipment while Foxes housed the decoders and signal switchers. For this reason, a signal company is broken down into two types of personnel: V3s to monitor the radios and Foxes to run the switches.

I worked in a V3 shelter. It housed a lot of radio equipment, all kinds of radios. Inside the shelter compartment you'd find huge instrument arrays. For operational security reasons, I can't go into detail about the instruments. Suffice it say that the equipment we used could both receive and transmit signal.

Within a V3 organization, soldiers are broken down into shelter teams. Preferably, you'd have three soldiers per team, but sometimes you made do with two. I remember a lot of times it was just me and my sergeant working together; each shelter team was usually led by a sergeant. In a single node center compound, four V3 shelters would connect to the Fox shelters via cable. The V3s received data and shuttled it off to the Foxes' main switchers, which decoded the data, interpreted it, and pushed it back out to the V3s for transmission. It sounds like a lengthy process, but this could all happen instantaneously, thanks to modern technology.

Power for the center came from diesel generators towed behind each shelter. You could unhook them quickly and get right down to business, or tow them away for refueling and repairs. I think the machines we used had a five kilowatt output. They ran 24 hours a day for the entire six months we were stationed in Iraq, and we had to contend with a lot of sand that blew in and clogged up their air filters. It became a ritual for us to blow the filters clean with compressors nearly every day. Those generators took a beating but they were army-manufactured equipment, built to stand up under almost any conditions.

You can't send signal without antennae, so we erected those, too, atop two different-size poles, fifteen meters and thirty meters. Each pole could be telescoped out using a hand crank and stabilized with guide wires. We primarily used the fifteen-meter pole, and I want to make sure you can imagine what that looks like, that's a fifty-foot-high extension. One antenna fit atop a fifteen-meter pole, but the thirty-meter poles could accommodate up to three antennae at once. These were what we called line-of-sight antennae, which means that their signal beam wasn't terribly wide, comparatively speaking. Cell phone towers, for instance, use microwaves and project omnidirectionally, but line-of-sight towers have to be pointed directly at another antenna which, in the case of the army net in Iraq, was commonly twenty-five to thirty miles away. A big part of my job was coordinating antennae reception with another node center using directional azimuths[84] handed down to my unit by the higher-ups.

We'd get instructions, for instance, saying, "Alter signal, connect with another node center twenty-five degrees north from your position." You'd begin the linkup procedure by calculating the back-azimuth from the other node center's location in order to establish a clear line of fire. Then, standing at the base of your antennae poles, you'd use a compass to point your array in the direction indicated and shoot a signal toward the contact node. The opposite node would, of course, be trying to find your signal at the same time. Once you made contact, the nodes would talk to each other, usually via coded FM radio, which was a bit dangerous since it's an easily detectable signal. You'd work the shot in by finagling the antennae and reading codes to one another over the radios in order to conquer any signal flow problems. Then you'd troubleshoot the link and hone in on the most powerful RF [radio frequency] signal vector possible. Signal strength was an important issue because the stronger the link, the more data you could send faster and more reliably.

We commonly erected nine to eleven of the fifteen meter poles, each with its own antennae on top. Each antenna controlled its own communication link, so picture a node as the core of a spider web with nine to eleven strands of signal thread spinning out to various points around the countryside. The orchestration of all these signals was masterfully plotted by Command. I say "masterfully plotted" because there was a lot of signal in Iraq while I was working there. You had to keep extremely precise track of it all since, if you ever crossed signal paths, the links would get interrupted. One of the reasons we used line-of-sight antennae in the first place is that, despite how delicate they are, they're almost impossible to tap into unless you know exactly where the signal beam is. Of course, even if the enemy did end up wandering across a signal feed and

84. An azimuth is the direction of a celestial object, measured clockwise around the observer's horizon to the north. That is, an object due north from the observer's position has an azimuth of 0°. An object due east bears an azimuth of 90°; due south equals 180°; due west equals 270°. Sometimes coordinating systems list south as the 0° point for azimuth angles. Compass directions are generally given along with degree measurements to clarify azimuth angles. For example, azimuth coordinates may be listed as N (0°), NNE (25°), W (270°), SSW (202.5°), and so on.

tapping it, they'd still have to decode it. As you can imagine, the army's coding is crazy good.

Data, video, and voice communications flowed over these signal threads in a constant, humming stream. If anything ever happened to that stream—well, just imagine trying to conduct a war without being able to talk to your soldiers in the field. Sometimes we'd double-line our communications to prevent any problems. This basically meant we'd connect to the same node center that another node center was connected to, purely for the sake of redundancy. If anything happened to part of the system, we wouldn't experience collapse. Another part of the net would kick in instantaneously and take over the effort.

A good node center team could set up and tear down a complete node in less than an hour. That was part of our training before we ever got to Iraq: we ran time trials called Switch-Exs [switching exercises] where the clock would start, the team moved in, and we'd assemble a communication center from scratch. Once we'd set up, we ran work shifts just like you'd do at any other job. Sometimes our shifts lasted twelve hours and sometimes they ran for eight; it all depended on how we were staffed. We eventually perfected a system where we set up four V3 shelters close together in two by two formation. This system only required two to three men to run all the shelters at a time. Since we had a crew of twelve, we were able to pare down our shifts to just six hours each, which was good. Remember that a shift meant sitting in your shelter for the full time you were allotted, with no air conditioning even though it was 140 degrees outside and the shelters were already hot from the constant hum of the radio transistors.

For a V3 like me, the job boiled down to watching the radios and making sure they stayed operational at all times. The equipment displayed signal strength in lit bars, just like you'd have on a cell phone. The more bars lit up, the stronger your signal. You had to maintain a bar minimum, just a few bars, for voice transmissions—voice signal is the simplest form of transmission. Data and video required a lot more strength. I was also responsible for minding the antennae and the trucks, making sure that the generators were fueled and running efficiently. If anything happened to the radios in my shelter, it was on my head. The equipment in those shelters was worth quite a bit of money, and every piece of equipment was additionally valuable in that it lent a great deal to the overall operational security in Iraq.

Meanwhile, the Foxes were squatting in their shelters nearby, monitoring the actual transmissions, making sure that the links ran smoothly through the computer systems. All in all, it got to be so routine that I could read a book on the job. But when the signal bars went down or disappeared altogether, that was a different situation entirely. You started troubleshooting immediately, pressing buttons and trying to figure out what went wrong with the link. Was it something wrong at your shelter? Was it something wrong at the other end? Was it something wrong within your node center itself? A power problem? A cable problem? A coding problem? If things didn't fix themselves quickly, you called for help. But regardless of the reason that the link went down, you were responsible for fixing it, and fixing it fast.

Sometimes the wind would blow a cable off an antenna. Or sometimes a truck rolled over a ground cable and broke the wires inside the casing. Luckily, the radio systems were sophisticated enough to troubleshoot themselves. They constantly monitored the links and, if you knew how to read the codes, the machines could tell you in precise terms where breaks in the link were coming from, the switching side, the line side, the radio side, wherever. The radio could pinpoint furthermore if the problem was with the RF signal, the power feed, or both. By following the computer's suggestions, most problems could be handled easily. A few incidents, however, had us completely baffled.

We had one link that went out on us every day at exactly the same time, like clockwork. The link wasn't hugely important, it connected some phones that weren't used too often. But it set a strange precedent. When it first started happening, we'd scramble to fix it, checking every connection we could think of, trying to trace where the breach had occurred. No dice. Then, just when we started to get really aggravated, maybe fifteen, twenty minutes later, the link worked itself back in and clicked on with no explanation. "No explanation" is a troubleshooter's nightmare.

We never figured out exactly what was going on with that link. Since we were located right next to Baghdad Airport, the environment was ripe with signal and we figured that might've had something to do with it. A few guys in my unit even swore it must've had something to do with earth's rotation. I'm not sure what they based that on, but they were dead set in their opinion. Eventually we had to concede that, whatever was causing it, it was something completely beyond our control.

We had other tasks to do when we weren't working shifts at the node. The army always had something to keep busy. We'd pull assignments to set up security fencing around the shelters or set up places to eat, sleep, and wash. This stuff happened when we first arrived at Camp Strike, and it was all part of breaking in the palace buildings to serve our unit's needs. The process of fixing the place up became a sort of ritual for us, partly because we had so much time on our hands and partly because you always want your quarters to be a little better than they already are. A lot of times, we pulled guard duty at an entrance to Camp Strike. We rotated guard duty with other units in the camp so, at our busiest time, I guess I stood watch once every three days or so. Camp Strike was technically within the Baghdad International Airport perimeter so this wasn't hazardous duty. In fact, I felt quite blessed because I know a lot of other soldiers in Iraq didn't have things so lucky.

Other day-to-day rituals weren't so savory. There was a detail that handled waste burning every day; not fun, but necessary. All the garbage and crap we produced went up in a cloud of very bad-smelling smoke. When we didn't have cooks available, we'd get assigned to go on food runs to the mobile PX. When the cooks were around, we'd pull KP duty [literally, "kitchen police—mess assistance] to help them with their chores. A lot of times we ended up eating MREs out of the bags they came in.

We also maintained our PT [physical training]. The army never stops doing PT. It's easy to get out of shape when you're sitting in a shelter all the time watching the bar graphs rise and fall, so each morning or evening, depending on which shelter shift you worked, we'd dress in our PT uniforms and go for a run. Then we did sit-ups, push-ups, leg and upper-body exercises. This generally lasted for an hour and a half.

We had some free time to ourselves, that we could spend however we wanted. In my spare time, I watched a lot of DVD movies on my laptop—movies pretty much saved my life as far as diversions were concerned. I played a lot of computer games, read a lot of books. I talked to my family whenever I could, wrote letters, and looked forward to packages in the mail. To be honest with you, the whole thing got to be pretty boring. Despite all the chores we had lined up, there never seemed enough to do, especially with my job.

Pay was handled differently in Iraq. You got your base salary, but several things were added to it or adjusted. For instance, all soldiers entering combat, meaning any soldier serving in a danger zone, get paid tax-free, that's an army rule. State and federal taxes get waived, but you still have a Social Security deduction, no big deal; it doesn't amount to much. But those tax-free earnings can add up to a nice extra sum of money. I pulled in an extra 240 dollars a month. On top of that we got "danger pay," something like 250 or 300 a month for someone at my level. We also got a small amount of per diem money called "travel duty pay," something like three dollars a day, or ninety dollars a month. TDP's considered extra money for working away from your base of operations. Then we got another 260 supplemental dollars because we weren't eating at a D-Fac.

You get paid every two weeks in the army, and all these additions and subtractions show up on a form called an LES.[85] When I first got my check statements in Iraq, I was pretty surprised. As an E-2, I was pulling in a little over two grand a month. Now, as an E-4, I should pull closer to three grand a month. I don't expect to get promoted again, though. Going from specialist to sergeant is the biggest promotion jump in the army.

From E-1 to E-4, promotions are based on standards such as time in, work performance, conduct, etcetera. I received most of these promotions fairly quickly, I've won them all in two years. But to make the rank of sergeant, you have to stand before a promotions board of sergeant majors and first sergeants who ask questions based on your knowledge of military common tasks and training, tasks specific to your job, and so forth. From what I understand, your job is to remain calm and composed the whole time. Your uniform must be highly pressed and your boots should be shined like a laser beam. Your hair cut and shave should be fresh and clean—you'll be judged on all these things. Being an NCO for the United States Army is a big obligation that no one takes lightly.

85. Defense Finance and Accounting Service Leave and Earnings Statement, DFAS Form 702.

Then, based on all the criteria I've listed, the promotions board assigns you up to 150 points. Your commander can add another 150 to this total. The number of points he bestows reflects your performance under his command. More points can be attained based on awards you've earned, your rifle marksmanship, your PT score, and so forth. It takes a certain number of points to get to sergeant, and the number of points varies according to each job. To make sergeant in my Signal Corps unit, you used to need 350 points. That's quite low. Actually, it's about the lowest threshold to attain a sergeant's rank I'd ever heard of. But a number of people took advantage of the low requirement and made sergeant, so now the point threshold's raised to the highest it can be, which is 798.

If I stood before the board right now, I bet I don't have more than 400 points. That's just not going to cut it. Maybe that would have worked four or five months ago, but not anymore. The threshold might come down again, but I'll bet it won't happen while I'm still in the army. If it does, I'll try for sergeant, but it looks like I'll be an E-4 for a while. It's not such a bad position to be in. As a specialist, you're just a step below sergeant, so I'm the senior operator in my group. My team chief runs the team, but I'm in charge of handling the privates who come to our group fresh out of training. You don't learn everything you need to do your job in training. A lot of knowledge comes learn-as-you-go, from hands-on kind of work. I'm good at helping people through that.

My unit and I were very lucky. We left Iraq because the army needed us back in Germany. They brought us out of the theater a lot earlier than most units and, no, I don't understand the logistics of it all. I was grateful to leave the desert after only six months. I'm scheduled to go back to Iraq again in January of 2005.[86] This time, I'll be stationed there a full year. How does that sit with me? That's a very good question. I've actually been trying to decide that for myself. I remember when I came back the first time the only thought in my head was, Wow, I don't ever want to do that again. In fact, I told myself that, if they told me I *had* to go back, I'd do anything I could to keep that from happening.

When I found out I'd have to return, though, this dull sort of accep-

---

86. One month from the date of this interview.

tance came over me. It was that feeling of, Well, that's my job. Now I have to go do it. I don't feel particularly bad about returning. I guess I don't feel anything at all. But this time I have a plan. I'll go, put in my time, and make a good chunk of money for college. When I leave Iraq this time I'll pretty much be finished with the army, three or four months left before I get discharged. Maybe I'll travel Europe for a month. Then I'll come home and get on with my life.

I look back now and it's very clear to me: if I'd had the money, the grades, and the gumption when I got out of high school, I'd have gone to college rather than join the army. But I needed the army at that point in my life to give me those things, and they have. I feel very well prepared now to excel in college. So just to be clear, I'm very happy with my military experience; it's been a great stepping-stone in my life. I just won't continue with the army once my four years are up.

ROLLING THUNDER

✷

Captain Steve Barry
U.S. ARMY, COMMANDER OF CHARLIE COMPANY
(NICKNAMED THE "CYCLONES"),TANK BATTALION 4-64AR,[87]
2ND BRIGADE, 3RD INFANTRY DIVISION

Captain Barry, age 30, grew up in central New Jersey and graduated West Point in 1996. He says, "I wouldn't trade my education for anything. Most of the instructors at the Point are active-duty officers with incredible experiences to share. Most of the men who taught me were Gulf War veterans, for instance; their mentorship was superb. And that's my next assignment. Currently, I'm attending Ohio State University to complete a graduate degree in military history. After that, I'll be an instructor at West Point."

Captain Barry's tank unit was part of the initial strike into Baghdad.

Armored warfare is a hands-on style of combat. Tank commanders don't sit in a bunker somewhere like armchair quarterbacks watching the game on TV, hatching schemes. You're right up at the battlefront, riding along in the hatch of your own vehicle, hearing reports coming in over the radio in real time. You have to be able to see the ground and the enemy from the perspective of your own vehicles if you have any hope of fighting effectively.

There are fourteen tanks to an armored company. Twelve of them are broken up into three platoons of four. The last two tanks in the company belong to the executive officer[88] and commander, respectively. With all of our attachment personnel included, Charlie Company came to a force of about eighty men. No females in a tank company.

As company commander, I was in charge of fighting my own tank while coordinating the movements and firing patterns of the other thirteen. Trust me, it's tough work. It takes a tremendous amount of organi-

---

87. 4th Battalion, 64th Armored Regiment.
88. Second in charge, who serves as the company commander's assistant for command and control on the battlefield.

zation and focus. You've got three radio systems transmitting information to you at once: the company net which links me to all the tanks in my command; the battalion net, or command net, which generates a lot of traffic as orders change and positions are confirmed; finally, there's my own tank's intercom system, which puts me in touch with my vehicle's team members. I'm on that last system a lot, telling my driver what to do, telling the gunner what targets to shoot at and when. It gets pretty complicated but you get used to it, just like anything else.

We drove M1A1 Abrams tanks, which are designed for a crew of four: a driver, a gunner, a loader, and the tank commander. Each tank weighs about sixty-eight tons with a 1,500 horsepower turbine engine powerful enough to run the vehicle flat out at fifty-five miles per hour on good roads. The vehicle's toughest armor is situated on the tank's front slope. The steel of the front turret contains depleted uranium, which strengthens it to the point where it can withstand armor-piercing rounds. Despite how bulky they might look, the Abrams are very maneuverable machines, heavy and survivable.

They carry four weapons systems each. The primary weapon is the 120 mm smooth-bore cannon, which fires three different types of rounds: a sabot round for destroying armored vehicles, such as other tanks; the HEAT round—HEAT stands for high-explosive antitank; and the MPAT, multipurpose antitank round, which is used to destroy bunkers and lighter-skinned vehicles. Then you've got a 7.62 mm coaxial[89] machine gun mounted on the turret beside the cannon. There's also a .50 caliber machine gun mounted in front of the commander's hatch and another 7.62 machine gun situated by the loader's station.

Basically, an Abrams is built to be an invulnerable, mobilized onslaught. It can carry enormous amounts of ammunition. The Abrams manual recommends a load of 11,800 rounds for the 7.62 machine guns alone, but we frequently carried more than that during the war. A lot more.

A tank battalion consists of three tank companies plus a headquarters company, which provides logistical support as well as command and

---

89. The term *coaxial* describes how the machine gun pivots on the same axis—the turret—as the 120 mm cannon.

control. When my battalion entered Kuwait, we had three tank companies plus an infantry company, an engineer company, and a bunch of other attachments. This mixing of units is an army doctrine called "task organization." It allows ground forces to diversify so they can get things done quicker and more efficiently.

The Second Brigade of the Third Infantry Division was prestationed in Kuwait since September of 2002 for Operation Desert Spring. Now don't get confused; the name of this operation has changed a lot ever since the Gulf War ended in '91. But the idea was always the same: we kept a certain level of forces in Kuwait to deter Saddam Hussein from reinvading the country. The size of the force changed a lot, but when I was there, we had a brigade-size unit on the ground training for and anticipating going to war.[90]

M1 ABRAMS MAIN BATTLE TANK (MBT)

The M1 Abrams was named after the late General Creighton W. Abrams, former army chief of staff from 1972 to 1974 and commander of the Thirty-seventh Battalion. Abrams tanks provide the backbone for the armored regiments of the United States and its allied countries, notably Egypt, Saudi Arabia, and Kuwait.

Three versions of the Abrams tank are currently in service: the original M1 model, commissioned in the early 1980s; the M1A1, produced from 1985 through 1993; and the M1A2, which features upgrades from the M1A1, such as position navigation equipment and a digital data/radio interface unit that provides a common picture for tanks participating on a common battlefield.

Though originally fielded in 1980, the Abrams remained untested for ten years. In fact, during Iraq's invasion of Kuwait in 1990, many military experts became concerned that long months of continuous operation in desert terrain without proper maintenance would cripple the vehicles. Doubt existed over whether the

---

90. There are only ten active-duty divisions in the standing army, and each division has about 15,000 soldiers to it. A brigade, depending upon the number of attachments you carry with you, can number anywhere from 4,000 to 5,000.

tanks' complicated turret electronics could be counted on to survive the stressful conditions of combat. Also, due to the sheer size
and weight of each vehicle, Abrams tanks had to be deployed into
the Persian Gulf one at a time, using C-5 Galaxy airplanes, the
largest cargo aircraft in the U.S. Air Force. Despite these initial
concerns, the Abrams tanks soon proved themselves superior to
the wide array of Iraqi tanks they faced, mostly Soviet-made
T-72s and that vehicle's earlier models, the T-62 and T-54.

In the entire Gulf War, only eighteen Abrams tanks were removed from service due to battle damage. Of those eighteen, nine
were deemed repairable and returned to service. Not one Abrams
crewman was lost in battle.

We got our orders to invade Iraq on March 20. The first three days of
the strike were nonstop movement. We rolled out across the desert
bound for the city of Najaf. We had to get there as fast as we could; that
was the key strategy to the early stages of the war: take up battle positions fast and secure them. We didn't sleep for three days. The strike became an exercise in constant motion: move, move, move, refuel the
tanks, move again. By the end of that first three-day push, my ankles
swelled up so big that I couldn't get my boots off. I'd been standing up
the entire time in the commander's hatch, and it plays hell on your circulation.

We made no enemy contact on the march toward Najaf but one of
our sister battalions, the 1-64th Armored, radioed in on the twenty-
fourth that they had received fire. We figured we'd run into the same sort
of action so we braced ourselves for it, but it turned out we were clear.
We arrived at Najaf, and that turned out to be one of the most hectic
times in my life.

It was getting dark when we arrived. We'd been assigned to relieve Charlie Company 1-64 from their blocking position on the main roads at the
southern flank of the city. The plan was to stop any traffic exiting Najaf
so we could pass the First Brigade through our lines once they arrived.
We only had twenty minutes of light left, when one of my tanks got stuck

in the soft mud of a flood plain. The Euphrates River had receded; the tank had gone off-road and gotten mired in this clay. I had to leave a tank from my own platoon with the stuck tank to assist in extrication while I took over the blockade and set up my remaining tanks in the correct positions. It was difficult to do. The mud was making problems in other areas as well, so we had to set up our sectors of fire over very small patches of ground. Through all this, we had no idea what the enemy situation was. Intelligence reports were nonexistent.

To complicate matters further, I had a FIST [forward observer] team attached to me in a Bradley fighting vehicle. Their vehicle had broken down on the march up. I was waiting to hear back from the battalion XO [executive officer] to determine whether or not these guys would be brought up to the front; I was worried about where they were. Then one of my soldiers, First Sergeant Wilson, had *his* vehicle blow an engine so he was broken down somewhere behind me, too. Wilson's basically the right-hand man of our operation, the senior enlisted man, a pretty key guy in charge of logistical support. He controls the company combat trains, the medics, the mechanics; he's in charge of bringing in more ammunition and food when warranted. The Germans have a phrase for men of this stature in a company. They call the man Mother.

So darkness was falling. I was still struggling to jockey my tanks into blockade position. I had one stuck tank, a missing FIST team, Wilson maybe a kilometer or so behind me, best guess. I didn't know for sure because I couldn't get hold of him. I sent for another platoon to come forward and assist my blocking position, but that platoon had a tank get stuck in the mud, too. Right then, as if this situation couldn't possibly get any worse, we started to receive enemy fire.

First it was mortars but then it was rockets. Then small groups of insurgents started coming out of Najaf to pepper us with small arms fire. By that point, it was dark out. Our vehicles were blacked out, so the fire we received was highly inaccurate. Still, we were getting hit. We could hear shrapnel from the explosions bouncing off our vehicles. My first sergeant radioed in that he had mortars coming down close to his track. We identified the enemy mortar positions as originating from Najaf; they were firing Soviet-made 82 mm shells that carry a range of approximately 5,000 meters. The mortars were out of range for our tank weapons, so I called in a fire mission to a platoon of Task Force mortars organic to our battalion. The mortar platoon began to fire a mission on Najaf with four 120 mm mortars, maximum range 7,200 meters for each.

Now each brigade has an artillery battalion attached to it bearing 155 mm Howitzers, self-propelled guns with an average range of about 18 kilometers. We called them into action, and their fire missions were affective. We'd identified at least three enemy firing positions. Between the Howitzers and our mortars, we were able to destroy or suppress them all. We also engaged small groups of insurgents who came close enough to pepper us with AK-47 fire. This continued for the duration of the evening. I never got confirmed reports on dismounted enemy casualties, but I estimated that number to be somewhere less than ten. I think the insurgent activity was mostly of an exploratory nature, a bunch of men saying, "Hey, let's go see what's out there," then creeping out into the night to take some shots at us. Once they saw what was going on, it seems they crept back into Najaf.

A soldier sitting in an Abrams tank doesn't have a lot to fear from an AK-47, especially in the dark when fire accuracy drops to almost nothing. But if you're hanging around outside the hatch like the tank commander and the loader frequently do in order to see what's going on, you worry about catching a stray round. On rare occasions during my time in Iraq, I found the Iraqis had night-vision capability, and that's never a good thing. But my main concern was the enemy mortars. An 82 mm shell can do minimal damage to an Abrams, but the possibility of shrapnel hitting one of my soldiers concerned me greatly.

I'm sure my men would tell you that our first night in Najaf wasn't too exciting. I remember it because it was the first time I had to command my company under fire. I remember the chaos of the tanks getting stuck, and calling in fire missions to knock out enemy mortars. I remember the aggravation of wanting to have my first sergeant with me and the frustrating process of jockeying that FIST vehicle into location, which I eventually did once it entered radio range. We didn't take any casualties that night. The whole incident turned out to be more unsettling than dangerous. Our initial intelligence had said that Najaf was a friendly city where we'd encounter no resistance. Obviously, that hadn't been the case. Najaf turned out to be the first spot where we fell under enemy fire, and we hadn't been in the best position to receive it. It sure opened everybody's eyes. At daybreak, my company got new orders, "Pull up stakes and move north of Najaf, into the open desert." Meanwhile, part of the brigade stayed in our previous position to conduct operations in the city.

Life gets pretty cramped when you're rolling along, buttoned up inside a tank. As tank commander, I get the privilege of standing in the command hatch which, as I said, can go pretty rough on your ankles and legs if you do it too long. It'd be worse to ride inside, though. I'm six foot three and probably weighed about 245 or 250 at the time of the attack. My gunner was about the same size and sat right below me, cramped and contorted into his small seat. Gunners have the worst deal in the crew, as far as comfort goes. A gunner's whole view of the world is through a rifle scope that moves back and forth from three power magnification to ten. I guess I'd have to say the tank's driver scores the most comfortable position. His chair places him in a supine posture, so basically he just climbs into the tank, lies down, and goes to work.

Life inside a tank gets a little surreal. For instance, it's not as loud as you might think when you're inside, firing off the cannon. The tank's armor and the cannon's recoil mechanism deaden a lot of sound. Plus everyone on the team wears a special helmet with Bose speakers that cover your ears to minimize noise and enhance the volume of the radios and the intercom. You're very aware of the gun when it's firing, sure, but the noise won't rip your face off. That only happens when you're outside the tank.

I was mostly outside the tank whenever our cannon fired because I had to see where my company was maneuvering. Let me tell you: up close and in person? That gun is pretty loud. The shockwave is positively amazing. Your helmet's ear coverings still dampen a lot of the noise but the heat from the blast lashes back and hits you, rattling your bones. The inside of the command turret takes on the reek of cordite from the ordnance propellant; your clothes absorb it. Same thing when the machine guns fire. I love that smell. I'm used to it by now. That odor overpowers you and becomes part of your everyday life during the war.

The land north and west of Najaf was very barren. We reached our position and stayed out in the open desert for the next five days. Lucky us, we arrived just in time to get pounded by sandstorms.

You may have watched it on the news. The desert turned savage for two and a half days. Strong winds blew glowing, red-orange sand around at fantastic speeds. You couldn't see twenty feet in front of you. It was like being on the surface of Mars. The conditions were worse than anything I've seen before or since. The sandstorms struck maybe two days after we reached our mark. I remember glancing behind my tank one time in the middle of the day, broad daylight. I knew my Humvee was parked behind me, maybe twenty yards away, but I couldn't see a trace of it. The winds howled and blowing sand swallowed up everything.

We still had to conduct security zone exercises, regardless of the weather. Every night, I deployed our tanks and our scout platoon into a screen line ten kilometers long that strung out across the brigade front. This maneuver ensured there'd be no enemy infiltration into our ranks. We hunkered down as best we could, and rotated shifts. The tanks use thermal imaging systems and we all powered up our scanner sights to probe the desert to make sure no enemy was coming. I don't care what anyone tells you, though. With the sand blowing like that, you couldn't see a thing with the thermals. When we weren't doing maneuvers, we pulled our vehicles into what's called a desert box, a square formation with the armored vehicles forming the perimeter and the softer-skinned vehicles—your medics and your maintenance people—positioned in the middle.

This interval in the desert was sort of a tactical pause. We were waiting for the right conditions before continuing north. At the same time, we were waiting for our supply lines to catch up with us. We'd moved so hard and so fast those first few days that we'd outrun our refitting trucks. In fact, the only supplies we received were food and a little bit of water. No fuel, and fuel is essential for an Abrams tank whose 504-gallon-capacity disappears quickly when you're running the machine hard. At the rate we were moving, we required many refuelings per day. We had to consolidate supplies for two reasons. First, the operation being handled by Second Brigade in Najaf took priority. Second, the logistics vehicles were 5,000-gallon refueling tankers that pushed along miserably through soft sand. They kept getting stuck and we kept having to wait. It was a very difficult situation.

While the sandstorms raged, we stayed buttoned-up inside the tanks but I still had to get out and do things. I checked on my soldiers, walked from tank to tank, and attended meetings in the battalion TOC [tactical operations center; i.e., headquarters] from time to time to receive briefings and operations meetings. Thankfully, the temperature wasn't unbearable. It dropped into the 50s sometimes at night, very comfortable. When the sandstorms finally let up, we stayed in the desert two more days before orders came in and we moved on.

Our third mission assigned us to conduct a series of feints across the bridges of the Euphrates River. Different units were being tasked to run these missions at various times. We'd been assigned Objective Murray, to take the bridge near a town called Al Hindiyah, about ten kilometers west of Hillah where the old city of Babylon resides.

Up to that point in the war, Iraqi units seemed to have followed a procedure. Their units would shoot off artillery, then scramble to change positions. It wasn't the best strategy in the world since they never scrambled fast enough. Every time they fired their guns, they revealed their position to our air force, the marines, and the navy who'd launch aircraft and have a turkey shoot, destroying as many enemy units as they could find using MLRSs [multiple-launch rocket systems].

Eventually, the Iraqis decided to change tactics. They sat tight, hidden and silent, so we had no idea what the enemy picture was like in the region we were entering. For this reason, Operation Murray became as much about using our feint to draw Iraqi units out as much as it was about taking the bridge. My company would serve as the operation's exploitation force, meaning that we'd take the bridge, cross it, and seize a few highway intersections further east, closer to Hillah.

Our plan was simple. Our infantry attachment would storm the bridge while the tanks stood by, ready to cross. Meanwhile, a different company in our task force, Alpha Company, would spearhead an effort down a spur road leading west and conduct a blocking maneuver there. That way no one could surprise us while Murray was underway.

Well, my group didn't see a lot of action that day, but everyone else got their fair share. Alpha Company ran smack into a dismounted Iraqi infantry unit. Our own infantry company found out the hard way that the Murray bridge was being held by Baath Party loyalists; not an organized army unit but dangerous enough. Meanwhile, my company and I waited on a road. The division commander, a two-star general, showed up. We felt a little underutilized, but the division commander made it clear that the bridge in Operation Murray wasn't crucial, he didn't want to risk sending tanks into combat unless absolutely necessary. It wasn't, and the fighting on all fronts was quickly suppressed.

While we sat there waiting, though, someone started pelting us with small arms fire from a copse of woods nearby. It turns out that an Iraqi air defense company had assumed possession of a huge weapons cache stockpiled in the trees. I'm not sure if you've heard the stories about how Saddam Hussein turned the entire nation of Iraq into a giant stockpile of weapons, but it's all true. I'm not sure whether he'd planned this bizarre strategy or it was just poor organization. To give you an idea, one time our infantry company found an entire building stuffed with mortar tubes, which is surreal. Anyway, we engaged and killed a couple of these air defense soldiers, but most of them shed their uniforms and ran, disappearing into the woods and melting into the local population.

We entered the woods and found boxes upon boxes of uniforms, supplies, rifles, and ammunition, so many that it's hard to estimate the size of the cache. We started to destroy it, but it turned out to be so big that we actually had to call in our engineering company since they're better trained at handling demolitions. They had C-4[91] and were able to blow up the depot quite nicely.

Again, this wasn't a big fight for us, but it had the potential to be. More importantly, it gave us our first up-close look at this weird mixture of soldiers who'd formed the Iraqi resistance, a real hodge podge of military talent with regular army units supported by Baath Party loyalists and civilians. Over the course of my time in Iraq, I'd come to notice how some enemy units fought very well and some units didn't. The mixture of trained and untrained personnel in the Iraqi ranks always seemed a little unstable.

The best thing I saw stemming from these altercations was the maturing process taking place in my men. I began to notice how relaxed they were when receiving enemy fire, how seasoned their responses became. Their reports flowed more easily and efficiently, their tactics

---

91. A high-quality, high-velocity, military plastic explosive. C-4, like putty, can be kneaded and formed into almost any shape. The material possesses excellent mechanical and adhesive properties so that it can be stretched into long strands without breaking. It is especially popular for controlled explosives in that engineers can mold and shape an explosive charge to exact specifications.

became more and more professional. Najaf was the first time we came into enemy contact; Operation Murray was the first time we'd been given an operational objective. Even in that short scope of a few days, my men came a long way toward handling themselves like seasoned combat veterans. They were learning fast and that was good. As it turns out, we were going to see a lot more action before long.

We took seven prisoners after blowing the cache in the woods. My company had some zip strips, our word for those plastic flexi-cuffs the police use in riot or crowd situations. We'd search each prisoner and zip strip his wrists. At first, moving the prisoners presented a real challenge since our company trucks were positioned so far in the rear where they were safest from attack. We had to come up with an alternative method of transportation.

I give full credit to the Alpha Company commander for coming up with the brilliant idea of mounting prisoners on the front of a tank. We'd hoist him up onto the front plate and drive a bunch to the nearest prisoner collection point. From there they'd be moved back to the rear, separated, interrogated, and processed further back through various other installations until they reached the POW camps. The technique worked perfectly. We could put three men sitting Indian-style up on a tank's front slope like kids in car seats, utterly harmless to themselves or anyone else. Then we'd drive them slowly out to the prisoner collection point with another tank as escort. We never had any incidents.

After Operation Murray, we pulled out of Al Hindiyah and returned to a spot in the desert close to where we'd weathered the sandstorm. From there we were assigned orders once again.

Originally we were told to proceed east and avoid the Karbala Gap, a narrow piece of land between a lake and a river that offers direct passage to a bridge over the Euphrates. It turned out that the eastern road couldn't support much traffic, though. A battalion in front of us reported the route as impassable, so we had to change direction.

We were concerned about passing through the gap because it was a key piece of terrain which we'd been told the enemy would defend heavily. On a map, Karbala Gap seemed to present the perfect strategic position for the enemy to halt our offensive. Essentially, it's a bottleneck. On one side there were thousands of Iraqi irregulars in the city of Karbala. On the other were remnants of three of Saddam's best divisions—the Hammurabi, the Nebuchadnezzar, and the Medina.[92] In addition to all this, we'd heard there was an enemy artillery corps hiding nearby with their guns trained on the gap, waiting for us to pop out and provide them with a target-rich environment. The situation gave us pause. Everyone seemed to have a lot on their minds as we continued along our route of march.

All through the night the entire division moved along a narrow, one-lane road that snaked around Karbala toward the Euphrates. The logistics of passage became slow and crazy. Our battalion commander, Lieutenant Colonel DeCamp, had proceeded ahead of us by about three hours. From his forward position, he'd received a briefing from brigade on our next mission, to be staged the next day. Charlie Company was tasked to go over a bridge called Objective Peaches. So when we finally made it through the gap and came to the river after a long night's march, there was LTC DeCamp telling me I had twenty minutes to refuel my tanks and get ready to go. My company was assigned to pass through Peaches immediately and secure Highway 1, a thoroughfare heading west toward the Syrian border that intersected with Highway 8, which ran due south of Baghdad. Holding this position was a key to destroying the remaining garrisons of the Medina Division.[93] The Medina was rumored to have all their armored vehicles intact. Evidently, they were ready to defend Baghdad from a point southeast of the city.

We rolled forward, determined to seize our objective, destroy whatever vehicles we found, and eliminate any armed resistance we came into contact with. We moved across the Peaches bridge and headed for Objective Saints, which was the intersection of Highways 1 and 8.

I was shocked when the intersection of Highways 8 and 1 turned out to be exactly like the intersection of typical American superhighways. In other words, the roads this close to Baghdad were much more modern, much better maintained than any we'd seen before. We rolled closer to the intersection and suddenly found ourselves in contact with the enemy.

92. These three divisions are all Republican Guard units.
93. The Medina Division (Al Madina Al Munawara) was considered to be the crack unit of the Republican Guard.

They were Baathists for the most part, supported by three white Toyota pickup trucks situated off to the right side of the road. We took a lot of AK-47 and RPG fire going through the intersection. My third platoon, led by Lieutenant McKnight and Sergeant Marrero, started in on them.

Now here's where I just wasn't paying attention and something really ridiculous happened as a result. I was trying to coordinate the movements of third platoon while making sure the rest of my company could pass through the intersection. Sometimes you miss the obvious things when you're multitasking. My tank was proceeding down the road, there was an ammo truck parked to one side. Our turret was far over to one side and my loader wasn't paying attention—trust me when I say he had other things on his mind. I should have been watching him, too. We collided with the truck, which could have been really bad under the worst of circumstances.

The impact knocked off part of our bustle rack, the compartment located in the back of the turret where the tank crew packs its bags. Here we were in direct contact with the enemy and it turned into a comedy of errors with stuff falling off the back of the tank, guys in my crew going, "Hey, what's going on? My stuff!" and gunfire zipping all over the place while we were moving down on the road. Marrero and McKnight destroyed the trucks pretty easily, as it turns out. But again, my eyes were opened to how the little things can really screw up a good plan.

We made it through the intersection and got on Highway 1, which turned out to be a six-lane road. I left one platoon plus my executive officer behind to block the intersection and protect our rear flank from possible assault. I also left my medics, mechanics, and my first sergeant behind, basically all of my soft-skinned vehicles. Then I put my third platoon on one side of the highway, my first platoon on the other, and we rolled south side by side toward another key intersection objective we'd been asked to secure. This is where the worst fighting started to happen.

We started taking fire from insurgents in pickup trucks as we moved south on Highway 1. My executive officer, Lieutenant Dave Chen, and First Sergeant Wilson had the Second Platoon suppress the enemy using tank cannons and machine guns at about five hundred meters. They made short work of those guys in about five minutes, but I'm pretty sure all the gunfire alerted the enemy units we ran into next.

I suddenly saw big muzzle flashes up ahead. The flashes were pointed directly at us, which meant direct incoming fire. Then I got a report from Sergeant Lujan, my First Platoon sergeant saying he had visual contact with BMPs, specifically ten BMP IIs, which carry 30 mm chain gun cannons and antitank rockets.[94] The BMPs had set up a hasty defensive firing line a couple of kilometers ahead of us and dismounted their infantry. The Iraqi soldiers had already taken cover in the extensive irrigation canals running parallel to both sides of the highway carrying water from the Euphrates River to other locations. Along with all this, they also had a brace of three enemy MT-LBs.[95]

We rolled forward to meet them. The BMPs shot at us head on, and the Iraqi infantry pounded us with AK-47s and RPGs from the sides. I was in the middle of receiving my contact report when *Phsssseeeeeeeeewwww*, an RPG flew right over my head and hit the ground in front of my tank, exploding. I turned and looked back. Enemy troops were behind us now on an overpass we'd just passed under. They were raining fire on us from above. That's when, to use a technical term, all hell started to break loose.

Basically, the battle boiled down to a standoff between our nine tanks and the Iraqi's ten BMPs. The MT-LBs were only armed with machine guns, so they couldn't cause us any real damage. My platoon started identifying vehicles and using our main guns to engage them. BMPs have the capability to shoot missiles that can damage an M1 Abrams, but we got lucky that day; they only hit us with the 30 mm rounds, which didn't prove effective against our armor plating. We took only light damage. One of our gunners' primary sight was knocked out, and I had a tank commander take shrapnel in his eye. One of my soldiers, Specialist Martin, had a stray round pass through the vision block on his driver's

94. The BMP-II (Boyevaya Mashina Pyekhota) is a track-driven, fully amphibious fighting vehicle fielded in 1982 as an augmented version of the BMP I and proliferated in approximately twenty countries. A two-man gun turret mounts a 30-mm automatic with a long, thin barrel and double-baffle muzzle brake; this weapon is effective against aircraft and helicopters. An ATGM launcher can fire AT-4 Spigot or AT-5 Spandrel missiles. There are two roof hatches in the rear fighting compartment rather than four as in the case of the BMP-1. The BMP-2 accommodates seven passengers and three crewmen. Each side of the troop compartment has three firing ports with roof-mounted periscopes.
95. The MT-LB multipurpose armored vehicle is a lightly armored, amphibious, tracked vehicle equipped with a 7.62mm belt-fed machine gun. The MT-LB can carry ten troopers along with its two-man crew; handles snow and swamp operations with ease, thanks to the surety of its treads; and has a cargo capacity of up to 2.0 metric tons.

sight. It impacted a little high and missed his head by about five or six inches, scaring the shit out of him.

We focused on the BMPs and destroyed them all in about six to seven minutes. Then we worked on the MT-LBs and finished them off. After that our tanks engaged the infantrymen who were popping up from the canals by the sides of the road and shooting at us. It took about fifteen minutes to kill them all. If I were asked to give an unofficial count, I'd say they were a force of about forty-two men.

When it was all over, we found ourselves a little shocked by the encounter. It was our first armored vehicle–to–armored vehicle fight. I have to say the enemy fought well. Like I said, I'd begun to notice some trends in their behavior. Oddly enough, some of the smaller units fought especially well. I think that might have had something to do with the fact that the chain of command was so unstable from Saddam Hussein and his sons all the way down to the fighting units. The Iraqis didn't seem to know what was going on. As if to punctuate this, we routinely saw Iraqi uniforms cast off by the sides of the roads we traveled. Apparently they'd been left by soldiers who'd said to themselves, "I don't want to die for this cause when I have no idea what's going on."

In fact, I think there was a huge amount of disinformation, or lack of information, among these units. You know how you hear people arguing that we shouldn't have disbanded the Iraqi army? From what I saw, the army had already disbanded on its own. We never encountered Iraqi divisions or brigades, we only encountered remnants. The impression I got was that the army, as a whole, just gave up and melted away.

I know that an all-points bulletin was issued by the Hussein regime on April 1, which ordered all Medina Division units to return to Baghdad to assist in the city's defense. Our fight with the BMPs was on April 3, so maybe those units were moving up Highway 1 in response to the bulletin. I have a feeling it was just coincidence that we ran into each other. Highway 1's a major road. Those BMPs were probably just looking for the quickest way to get back to their garrison or defense positions. But they stood, they fought, and we defeated them.

At this point, I'd like to emphasize something. It's sort of an ongoing debate among soldiers who fight armored vehicles. Let me just say that our tanks were essential to the destruction of the BMPs. By that I mean, no other vehicle in our inventory could have won this engagement. I'm sure of it. This is very important to note since a lot of people in the army feel that the new Stryker vehicle is just as capable as the M1A1 tank. In my opinion, it is not.

After that fight, we consolidated and continued our march south. Eventually, we found the intersection we'd been searching for and sealed it off. With that done, no traffic could head north into Baghdad along Highway 1. Our mission was accomplished, but the next day we received new orders: Continue south along Highway 1 another forty kilometers and clear it of enemy presence.

A week before the war started, my company was issued five pairs of brand new M25 gyro-stabilized binoculars with magnification capability up to 14 power. These instruments were much better than others we'd used in the past. As we resumed our march southward, one of my loaders, Specialist Clement, was scanning the trees with a pair of these gyros when he thought he spied a gun barrel off in a grove of date palms. He immediately informed his platoon sergeant, who checked it out.

Clement was right. He'd caught sight of an enemy tank platoon, four T72s,[96] perfectly camouflaged in the trees. It turns out they were well-camouflaged but they weren't occupied, which is why we hadn't picked them up on our thermal scanners. These tanks hadn't been running—their engines were cold. We thought that maybe they'd been hidden in the grove to avoid being destroyed by our air force during a bomb strike. At any rate, we blew them up with our cannon.

The incident convinced us to be much more careful. We began to scrutinize every house we saw with great care, every tree, every potential point of concealment off either side of Highway 1. This really paid off. Wouldn't you know it? We started finding unoccupied Medina Division assets everywhere. Forty-nine BMP Is and IIs, forty-one enemy tanks, and I can't tell you how many caches of arms and supplies. The Iraqis

---

96. T-72s are Soviet-made tanks which first entered production in 1971 and were deployed within the former USSR and robustly exported in various models to non-Soviet Warsaw Pact countries, including Algeria, Yugoslavia, Croatia, Romania, Syria, the Ukraine, Armenia, Hungary, Iraq, Kazakhstan, and Uzbekistan. T-72s are designed for a crew of three, run on an 840 horsepower diesel engine, and can fire on the move at speeds up to 25 km/h. Its main weapon is a 125 mm cannon that like the M1A1 Abrams, fires a variety of rounds, though with maximum aimed range of 3,000 meters.

had squirreled stuff away all over the place. Like I said, the whole country was crawling with weapons.

The next two days turned out to be a turkey shoot for our 120s. We used the vehicles for target practice, and they all blew sky high; they'd been loaded with fuel and ammunition, readied for combat. There just weren't any Iraqis around to fight them. Looking back, I think I know why. During our trip south we'd seen fresh-dug trenches running along the side of Highway 1 which the Medina Division had filled with oil. My guess is they were anticipating the Coalition attack to roll straight up Highway 1 from Kuwait to the south. They'd planned to light the oil and cook us while we advanced. Unfortunately for them, we'd taken the Karbala Gap instead, and the Medina Division suddenly found itself with American armored troops rolling down from the north. They were cut off from Baghdad; they had nowhere to go. So they hid their gear and left.

Not every Iraqi abandoned their posts, though. On the Fourth of April, we came across a platoon of manned T72s hidden in another date palm grove about five hundred yards off the side of the road. They got off the first shot; they were aiming at my forward platoon and missed. By "missed" I mean to say that one round actually hit the platoon leader's tank, but it impacted just short of the tracks and caused no damage to speak of. We never gave them a chance to recover. My forward platoon perfectly executed what we call a contact drill. They turned their turrets at once and fired on the enemy tanks, destroying them all in about twenty seconds.

So we moved across the countryside from Iraqi garrison to garrison. In three more places we made contact with dismounted soldiers wearing green uniforms bearing AK-47s, recoilless rifles, and RPGs. They always fought in very small pockets, twos and threes for the most part. They always appeared to be completely cut off from any sort of help or information. They saw we were Americans and shot at us, but they weren't any real threat. I can't give you an accurate count of the soldiers we engaged since we were much more concerned with rolling fast, maintaining our pace, and covering all the places we'd been assigned to cover.

We went to five different garrisons, which is a lot. In three days, we put over 150 miles on each tank, quite a bit after all the driving we'd done already. At the end of our journey, we were really hurting. Tanks require an inordinate amount of maintenance. You have to keep them lubricated and you have to change off a lot of parts because sixty-eight tons of rolling, bouncing steel can wear out a vehicle's suspension system pretty fast. By the close of day on April 5, seven of my tanks were NMC [non-mission-capable]. Another company commander I talked to told me that ten of his tanks were down. We weren't getting any repair parts, either, thanks to the abominable failure of the logistical system I'm sure you've heard about.[97] Throughout the whole war, we never got a single repair part that our battalion didn't carry with us. In my opinion, this was a real failure of the American logistical system—a failure, by the way, which still exists.

At one point we found one of those huge ammunition supply points like the one you've been hearing about lately, ridiculous amounts of ammunition locked up behind high gates.[98] We couldn't stay and secure the site, though, we had orders to return to our original locations on Highway 1. We found out why soon enough. The entire 1-64th had already rolled down Highway 8 and into Baghdad International Airport to test the Iraqi defenses inside the city. This was the first "thunder run," an armored spearhead thrust into Baghdad. That was our new job.

That night, I received operations orders in the standard five-paragraph format. I met with my soldiers and briefed them out loud. Basically, we were ordered to take all our combat vehicles, the tanks and the Bradleys, and head into Baghdad. Everyone was quiet when I finished. Somber. No one was afraid, or at least they didn't show it. But there was cause to be. No one knew what Baghdad held in store for Coalition forces.

Part of our mood was shock. Before the war started, we'd never been

---

97. Consistent media coverage throughout 2004 brought home the point that American forces were universally suffering from a lack of timely supply shipments.

98. In late October 2004, Iraqi officials reported that thieves had looted some 377 tons of powerful explosives from a site left unguarded after the U.S. military invasion. Some of the explosives in question could be used to detonate a nuclear bomb, but the UN had allowed Iraq to keep them because they could also serve civilian and conventional military purposes. Following this revelation, which spurred some debate as the presidential election of 2004 drew near, a former UN weapons inspector informed the press that he had counted approximately one hundred additional unguarded weapons sites which may have been stripped of munitions eventually used against both U.S. soldiers and Iraqi civilians.

briefed we were going to take Baghdad; it simply wasn't part of the plan. From the beginning we'd been told, "Go up and destroy all the garrisons in the Medina Division. Secure the outside of the city. Wait for the light infantry to arrive." We were supposed to sit tight, wait for the 101st and the 82nd Airborne Division to clear out the city. When our orders changed so drastically, my buddy Phil Wolford, tank commander of Alpha Company, and I were just shocked. Mind you, we were pleased with the change of plans. But it still came as a surprise.

We didn't have a lot of time to dwell on what we'd gotten ourselves into; there were meetings to be held and plenty of preparations to see to before the attack got under way. The sixth of April became "Get Ready to Go into Baghdad" Day. My company faced tough odds with so many of our vehicles disabled and so few spare parts floating around. In the end, we resorted to cannibalizing the battalion S3's [battalion training officer's] tank for equipment to get our machines up to combat power.

While I'm on the subject of repairs, I can't speak highly enough about our mechanics. They're some of the toughest-working guys in the army. They bust their knuckles and work ridiculous hours to make sure my men ride out in suitable equipment, and let me tell you: it's appreciated. We had two guys: a BMT [battalion maintenance technician], Chief Warrant Officer Fil Vicente and one BMS [battalion maintenance specialist], Master Sergeant Mike Jones. They've each been mechanics for twenty years. Within a day, with almost nothing to work with, they got all of our tanks up and running.

We took everything flammable off the vehicles. We'd learned over the past several days that enemy RPGs could set them on fire. That meant removing our bags from the bustle racks and leaving them behind with our mechanics and tech personnel. For the strike, I let everyone in the company carry one personal bag small enough to fit inside the vehicle. For most guys, this boiled down to a shaving kit, a fresh T-shirt, and some extra socks. Aside from that, we carried water, ammunition, and medical supplies. That was it. We packed up the tanks with ammunition and topped them off with fuel. We kept busy, busy, busy and it was good, because being busy kept everyone's mind focused.

Here was the strategy to take Baghdad. 1-64 Armored would lead off and my battalion, 4-64, would follow them in accompanied by Alpha

Company Tank and Alpha Company Infantry. The infantry was necessary to secure things behind us once we'd penetrated the city. Once inside Baghdad, everyone had different mission objectives on the west side of the Tigris River, which formed our boundary with the Marines. We were all operating in or very close to the region we now call the Green Zone, near the Al-Rasheed Hotel, the Tomb of the Unknown Soldier, and Fourteenth of July Circle. In fact, one of my tank commanders compared our mission to storming the Iraqi equivalent of Washington, D.C., and seizing the National Mall, the Capitol, and the White House. Considering the similarity of targets, it was an apt comparison.

My company's particular objective was a road intersection and bridge that, once secured, would protect the brigade's entire southern flank and link the rest of our battalion. Strategically, it was a key point to winning the city. But I had to do this while short one tank platoon which task organization had loaned out to the infantry. I had some Bradleys with me to compensate.

We entered the city by marching up the wide stretch of Highway 8. The Iraqis had laid a minefield over it, but our engineers had worked hard the night before to clear it off. That was the first time I ever drove through a live minefield. A tank is vulnerable to mines. If they detonate against the tracks in just the right way, they'll render the vehicle immobile. And a mine exploding beneath a tank runs a chance of killing crewmen. We were concerned, but the engineers assured us it was safe to drive through. I found it especially interesting because that was the first time we'd seen the Iraqis use mines during the entire campaign.

Once we got past the minefield, the whole way up into Baghdad exploded into a fusillade of enemy fire. Rounds from recoilless rifles, AK-47s, and RPGs rained down on us from a hodgepodge of buildings on both sides of the road, apartment complexes, industrial buildings, factories, and an old military garrison where insurgents were hiding. Mostly everyone I saw engaging us was dressed in civilian clothes. There were a few uniformed soldiers, but not many.

I remember looking at the tanks in front of me and the Bradleys behind me. My team was shooting back at the Iraqis with everything we had, left and right. The fire got so heavy at some points that the tanks had all four weapons systems going at once. My loader was firing his 7.62, I was firing my .50 cal. My gunner switched back and forth between the coax and the main gun. It was intense. Through it all, our goal was to keep moving. 3-15 Infantry was behind us, protecting our lines of communication as we rolled into the city.

Once inside, the fire died down quite a bit. Before we got to our objective, we had another small engagement with about seven soldiers who jumped out of two cars but my second platoon was in the lead and destroyed them pretty quickly. We kept moving, got to Fourteenth of July Circle, and set up our holding maneuver. I left one platoon there to secure the circle and took my platoon up to the bridge to make sure there was no enemy presence on it.

No such luck. As we approached, we received all kinds of small arms fire from the bridge and the woods off to one side, down by the water. That attack lasted about ten minutes before we suppressed it. Then we basically set up a small ring, a company perimeter if you will, in order to defend the bridge. My tank faced directly toward the bridge; the other tanks had turned out and were staring down the intersections. We got organized just in time. Cars began to stream over the Fourteenth of July Bridge coming up from the Karada Peninsula.[99] They were mostly Chevy Caprices and Toyota pickup trucks loaded with men dressed in paramilitary uniforms hanging out the car doors, shooting machine guns, trying to ram their vehicles into us. We began to engage them with our machine guns and the 120s.

My biggest fear during this engagement was that the attacking vehicles were suicide cars loaded with explosives. If one of them got close enough to our tanks and detonated, we'd have hell to pay. Two of the vehicles we hit with our main guns exploded so violently that my suspicions were confirmed. Still, they kept coming. The bridge was a suspension type with a slight rise to it. You couldn't see the attackers until they'd crested the center and were coming right down on top of you. At least ten to twelve cars came at us in all.

One of my tanks was equipped with a mine plow in front. You drop

99. The Karada Peninsula in central Baghdad is a very busy district and the most prosperous zone in all of Baghdad City—perhaps in all of Iraq. It best exemplified the principles of economic reform taking place in the country and so became a target for suicide car bombers as in the March 17, 2004, bombing of the Mount Lebanon Hotel, which killed twenty-eight people and wounded forty. Experts speculate that the Mount Lebanon became a target because it was one of the small handful of new businesses that rushed to establish themselves after the Hussein regime fell. Under Saddam, maintaining a hotel business proved especially difficult because the Iraqi government insisted on owning hotels either wholly or in part.

the plow into soil and push it forward with the weight of the tank to clear
land mines. Staff Sergeant Smith had a brilliant idea. He dropped his
plow and began using it to shovel the cars we'd destroyed up onto the
bridge. Essentially, he used the wrecks to create a roadblock, which pre-
vented any more cars from driving at us. Another wave came and dis-
gorged infantry. We destroyed them pretty easily, though, and after that
the attacks stopped for a couple of hours.

It was midmorning on the seventh of April and there I was, standing
in the middle of fabled Baghdad as this eerie quiet descended over the
bridge after the battle. It seemed like we'd been at war for a very long
time, though it was only a few hard weeks. A weird feeling struck me, it's
difficult to describe. It was a good feeling because we had a saying in my
unit back then, "The road home leads through the city of Baghdad." But
it was also a bad feeling, bad because none of us knew what was going to
happen next.

The entire journey, we'd had an imbedded reporter with us, Jeff Mohan
from the *L.A. Times*. He climbed out the back of his truck and asked me
if he could call his editors back in California to tell them what was going
on. When he made that call, I felt this wild surge of hope. Maybe someone would radio back and tell us that was it, everything was finished.
"Thanks for the good job, everyone, war's over! Pack up and go home!"
But I knew that wasn't going to happen. We set up a secure perimeter in
the area. Later that day we had more contact with Iraqi infantry dismounts. It was all a little anticlimactic.

On the morning of the tenth, two Chevy Suburbans with TV sten-
ciled on their sides in big orange tape letters rolled up to my checkpoint.
Somehow, they'd come in from the west side of the city, a reporter from
Time magazine and a French reporter from *Le Monde*. They got out of
their vehicles and told me they'd snuck into Iraq by crossing the Jordanian border. They were trying to get to the Palestine Hotel, which lay
across the river. I thought the whole idea was insane, but I said okay and
let them through.

After that a reporter from Great Britain approached the bridge from
the opposite side of the Tigris wearing body armor and a helmet. We
struck up a conversation and I asked him what was going on across the
river, I wanted to use him as an intel source. He said that he hadn't seen

any insurgents that day or anybody with weapons at all, for that matter. He remarked that all of his shadows[100] had left, and that's when I got the sense that the Hussein regime was completely defunct. If reporters were running loose all over Baghdad, that was a real clue that things were going our way.

There were many more incidents with snipers and attack boats and so forth in the immediate days to follow. Basically, we stayed on in Baghdad until May and, no, we didn't see any sort of insurgency forming unless you count a few stray incidents with armed looters. Our duty basically became to stop looters, restore order, and make Baghdad a functioning city once again. We also stepped in to run a lot of gas stations because the lines were so long and so much illegal activity was going on within them. We stood guard over a lot of protective sights, too. The city back then was a different Baghdad than you see on the news today. There was still a Green Zone, but it wasn't as protected as it seems to be now. We patrolled the area and served as its administrators.

Later on, the First Armored Division arrived and we thought that would be our cue to go home. Command moved us to Fallujah instead, which had become a real hot spot for the insurgency. The rebels were definitely in full swing, though not nearly on the scale you're watching on the news right now.[101] But that's another story for another time, I guess.

100. People the Iraqi government had assigned to watch reporters.
101. In early November of 2004.

TO BE BOTH SOLDIER AND CHRISTIAN

✳

Captain Andrew J. DeKever

U.S. ARMY, 548TH CORPS SUPPORT BATTALION

Captain DeKever, age 31, is a career soldier with ten years of service including a year in Korea and a brief trip to Kosovo. The 548th is technically part of the Tenth Mountain Division but was attached to the 101st Airborne Division for Operation Iraqi Freedom.

Originally from Indiana, Captain DeKever graduated ROTC at the University of Notre Dame. He holds a master's degree in peace studies from Trinity University, Dublin. The army currently has him posted to West Point in the Department of Social Sciences, where he teaches international relations to cadets. He and his wife, Mary, live in upstate New York.

Very soon after we arrived in Kuwait—this was March of 2003—we were herded into a tent and given the procedures to follow in the event of a SCUD missile attack. It was all about following signals. There was an incoming missile siren, which sounded like the civil defense sirens you hear in the United States. When you heard this signal, you knew you had to put on all of your gear immediately, your gas mask and your chemical suit, which had a coat top and a trouser bottom. The older suits were charcoal lined, but the newer ones were made from thinner fabric and much more comfortable to wear. There were rubber boots that went on over your combat boots. Rubber gloves. On top of all this you'd wear your helmet, body armor, ammo pouches, and gear.

Anytime Iraq launched a SCUD anywhere in the theater, the entire Coalition force of 135,000 put their gear on no matter where the launch had come from. We were treating this very seriously.

We'd trained to put the chemical gear on during peacetime. Our instructors had impressed us with the fact that, in the event of an attack, you have fifteen seconds to stay alive. Nine seconds to put your mask over your face and clear it. Another six seconds to seal it. That was it, that was your window. If you missed that, you could be dead.

I'd always had a problem getting the mask on properly in peacetime training. The joke was that nobody would have a problem getting it on under an actual attack. After all, the choice was clear: get the mask on in time or get hit with all sorts of nasty stuff. Blister agents. Blood agents. Chemicals designed to cause problems with your breathing or kill you. In training we watched films of different laboratory animals being exposed to certain gases. Sure enough, they got fifteen seconds. After that, they were dead every time.

The first time I heard that siren, I put my mask on in record time.

Once you were into this get-up, you stayed in it until you heard the All Clear siren, which sounded sort of like a British police siren, an alternating tone.

My unit left Fort Drum in March, that's in upstate New York, just thirty miles from the Canadian border. Our bodies had acclimatized to cold, winter weather, but then we were suddenly flown into Kuwait where it's much, much hotter. The moment we arrived, they pulled us all into a tent so we could receive the missile attack procedures. The tent added to the heat.

ACCORDING TO THE ARMY STUDY GUIDE . . .

Name 3 types of NBC warnings.
  1. Verbal ("Gas! Gas! Gas!")
  2. Banging metal on metal
  3. Hand and arm signals

What forms do NBC contaminants come in?
  1. Solids
  2. Liquids
  3. Gases

> **What are three fundamentals of NBC defense?**
> 1. Avoid contamination
> 2. Protection
> 3. Decontamination
>
> **Your protective mask will not provide protection against what two type of gases?**
> Ammonia vapors or carbon monoxide.

When the first attack sirens sounded, I was amazed at the effort it suddenly took to put on all the heavy gear. Taking it off once the All Clear sounded was real exertion, too. I didn't know it at the time, but fatigue had already begun to take a toll on me. Then the sirens sounded again so on went the boots, the mask, the suit, everything. Then it was wait, wait, wait. Not much to do but sit there roasting and check on each other once in a while. Then the All Clear siren came so it was take it all off again. Attack siren: Put it on. All Clear: Take it off. And on and off and on and off. I lost track of how many times we did this during the first twenty-four hours in Kuwait. I know we did it four or five times during the first two hours alone and several times more after that. The attack sirens sounded in the middle of the night.

We hadn't gotten a chance to eat since landing and food would have been good right about then. You can drink from a canteen with your gas mask on and I made sure to drink a lot, but water isn't enough. Your body needs a lot of fuel under those circumstances. If you don't eat, you lose electrolytes and everything shuts down.

Eventually the fatigue sneak-attacked me. During one of the drills, I just lay down. I loosened my armor and took my helmet off. I'd overexerted myself. Slow, I thought. Just take everything slow. Settle down. Take it easy. Wait for the All Clear. I wanted to rip the mask off, but I knew what that could mean so I fought myself not to panic. I just lay there trying to shut my brain off.

This happened during drills. I don't want to think about what going through all that would be like under actual combat conditions. When I was stateside, I remember how I'd been so anxious to get into the war. I'd watched SCUD alerts on CNN just a few days before leaving for the theater and I thought, *How cool is that? I'm going to be experiencing one myself very soon.* I was an idiot. Later on I wrote in my journal, "Damn fool I am."

The first twenty-four hours were the worst. Put the suit on. Take the suit off. After that, the attack sirens came less and less frequently, tapering off to once every couple of days or so. Then, two or three weeks after we arrived they stopped altogether. Except for this one last time.

There was a huge explosion. The sirens didn't sound, but someone started yelling, "Gas! Gas! Gas!" and that was all it took; we scrambled for our masks and ran for the barracks. I looked to my left and saw this massive mushroom cloud rising hundreds of feet in the air less than a mile from our location. I held my breath for fear of inhaling chemicals. Part of me was in shock. I refused to believe that someone might actually be firing missiles at us. We did our drill and we waited.

Our battalion commander restored order shortly thereafter. He told us to take our masks off; no one had issued the order to don them. Word came around that the explosion hadn't come from a missile attack. We were occupying a former Iraqi airfield and there was a munitions depot outside the fence perimeter. Apparently someone had been trying to steal munitions and instead they'd sparked a detonation.

The regime fell on April 9, 2003. My unit went into Iraq on Easter Sunday, April 20. We were a supply outfit that participated in moving American military assets from Kuwait into Iraq. After that our objective would shift and we'd begin moving the assets to various locations around the country as needed. Some soldiers had already crossed the Kuwaiti border. We'd heard from them that the Iraqi people were warmly receptive to Americans. Well. I figured I'd wait until I saw it.

We entered the country and started driving north along the MSR [main supply route], the Iraqi equivalent of an American interstate highway. Our convoy consisted of hundreds of vehicles. We skirted the major cities, but every half an hour or so a small village would appear on the horizon—a dozen, maybe two dozen buildings. Here's where the drive became tense. Women, children, and men of military age would stand in the middle of the road to try and force us to stop. They wanted to sell us trinkets. They wanted to trade American dollars for money that had Saddam Hussein's face on it.

As an officer, I'd been assigned a driver. She was twenty years old, a specialist E-4[102] from my unit, and she'd never deployed before, so she didn't know the drill. She started to slow down when she saw the villagers in the road. But slowing down or stopping makes you a potential target for attack. My operations sergeant was sitting beside me, and he got on the radio to inform the rest of the convoy what we were experiencing. I yelled in my driver's ear, "Speed up! Don't slow down, they'll get out of the way." And they did. Every time we encountered Iraqi civilians, we'd speed up and they'd scatter just in time.

One of our vehicles broke down once, forcing us to stop the convoy. Now we had about twenty Humvees all in a line, just waiting to be shot at. I was in command so I immediately hustled my soldiers out of their vehicles and into security positions. The Iraqis immediately started walking toward our vehicles and I shooed them off: "Go! Go! Go!"

Part of me figured they were harmless but another part of me wasn't going to take a chance. What if one of them had a bomb strapped to them? There's no margin for error, we were always on our guard. We knew the Iraqi military and the Fedayeen[103] frequently intermixed with civilian populations. Even though the regime had technically fallen, insurgents have no qualms about killing ten of their own to kill one American. We've seen that a lot over this past year.[104]

---

102. Specialist E-4 (SPC) is one of the fourth-lowest enlisted ranks in the army, situated just above the rank of private first class and below the rank of sergeant. It is essentially the same rank as corporal, which is an NCO. Specialist E-4 rank is comparable to that of senior airman in the air force, Corporal in the marines, and petty officer third class in the navy.
103. Saddam Hussein's son, Uday, founded the paramilitary Fedayeen Saddam (translated as "Saddam's Men of Sacrifice") in 1995. The force, which numbered at times between 18,000 and 40,000 soldiers, was staffed with men from regions loyal to Saddam. In fact, the unit reported directly to the presidential palace rather than through the chain of command for the army of Iraq. Although the unit has often been referred to as an elite fighting force, experts maintain that their true value resided in the fierceness of their political loyalty. The unspoken rationale behind a loyalist autonomous army such as the Fedayeen was to quell potential domestic uprisings. As well, the Fedayeen frequently carried out the Iraqi police's dirty work. Though sometimes described as a collection of "bullies and country bumpkins," the Fedayeen were instrumental in maintaining Saddam Hussein's regime.
104. Meaning 2004, though it's also proven relevant in later times.

ACCORDING TO THE ARMY STUDY GUIDE . . .

What is meant by Biological Warfare?
The intentional use of germs or toxins to cause death and disease among personnel, animals, plants, or deteriorate material.

What are the best ways to protect against Biological Agents?
Immunization shots and personal hygiene

What is the current U.S. policy regarding the use of Biological Assets?
No Use

What are the four types of microorganisms found in Biological Agents?
1. Bacteria
2. Viruses
3. Fungi
4. Rickettsiae

Where would biological attacks prove most effective?
Against cities, animals, large troop concentrations, and vegetable crops.

The first thing that struck me about the Iraqi people was their poverty. They were living in these pathetic little huts made from dried mud, places that make low-income housing in the U.S. look like paradise. Sometimes Iraqi women would stand by the road as our convoy drove past. They'd motion with one hand as if they were waving to us but with the other they'd point to their mouths. They were begging for food.

People have to beg for food from an invading army? That told me a lot right away about how bad Saddam's regime was. Whatever money was in the country had gone toward the Iraqi military machine or for Saddam's personal use. None of it went to the people.

An officer and his or her driver tend to spend a lot of time together and develop a very close relationship. Early on, [my driver] told me frankly that she wasn't all for the war. She didn't understand the reasons we'd come to Iraq and what we were supposed to be doing there. Her opinion changed when we got further into Iraq and she saw firsthand the condition people were in.

This happened with a lot of soldiers I knew. They weren't quite sure what we were doing there until they saw the poverty and how glad the Iraqi people were to see us. Then it became less about a hunt for weapons of mass destruction and more about a humanitarian mission.

In the early days of the war, right after the regime fell, I didn't hear many soldiers talking about how proud they were that we were disarming Saddam Hussein of WMDs. Later on, though, I heard a lot of troops saying they were proud we were bringing aid to the people.

Once, we came across a bunch of Shiites on a religious pilgrimage to Karbala. Saddam had suppressed the Shiites for the past twenty years; no pilgrimages were allowed. But the moment his regime fell, the Shiites resurrected this age-old ritual. Pilgrims walked by the side of the road or drove by in trucks. You could always tell who they were because they carried bright green banners particular to their faith.

I found it very interesting that these people were suddenly practicing their religion again and were comfortable doing so in front of American troops. They seemed to understand that we didn't mind one bit. They didn't give us any problems and we didn't give them any in return. Eventually the MSR took us twenty miles north of Baghdad.

Later on in my mission, I took two flights across northern Iraq to Mosul, which is near the Turkish border. Man, you should see that country from the air. Mountains and river valleys, lush greenery with these majestic gold-topped mosques reflecting sunlight. It was just beautiful.

From up there, I could see some of Saddam's two hundred-plus palaces. They were scattered about the countryside. They had beautiful landscaping. Later on I got a chance to tour the palace in Mosul. It had an interior swimming pool and magnificent artwork in endless rooms. But I was struck by the extremes of what I'd seen. In a country roughly the size of California, one man had lived like a god while everyone else squatted in mud huts.

I'm a Catholic. I attended a Catholic university and I go to church every Sunday. I hold a master's in peace studies and I hate violence. I despise war. I don't kill ants and I don't swat mosquitoes. I'll never hunt, and I don't let my cat kill mice and birds. I hate the idea of life being taken. So do I have a problem reconciling all this with my military career? No problem whatsoever.

People in the military love peace more than anybody else. Think about it: when wars break out, soldiers have to fight them. We're the ones that suffer. But I'm a firm believer that a military, properly employed, can be one of the greatest promoters of peace in the world. There are people in this world who are willing to use violence in unlimited ways to advance their agenda. If we don't stop them, what happens? Six million Jews get killed—that's one-third of an entire population. Or maybe millions of innocent civilians get killed by their own government. Hussein did that during his reign of terror and it's unconscionable, an abomination of our species.

I'm sorry, you just can't allow people like that to function in this world, and the only way to counter them is to apply violence back at them in a limited fashion. I've heard people say, "Well, isn't that fighting fire with fire? Isn't that using psychology to rationalize making war to stop a war? What's the difference?" The difference is that America puts limits on what we do. We stop our action once evil has been defeated, and we'll pull out after providing support designed to give that region a chance to govern itself. Our ultimate objective isn't conquest. It's growth.

Look at the way we reconstructed Europe after World War II. Or how we liberated Kuwait in '91. Once Kuwait was liberated, we stopped our advance. In the current case of Iraq? Once the regime toppled, we immediately set about rebuilding the country's infrastructure. This, in my view, is the way a military should function.

Nobody likes war. But battles have to be fought sometimes in order to make the world a better place. It's perfectly logical. Places like Afghanistan and Iraq are more peaceful today than they were before U.S. intervention. The regimes of Saddam Hussein and the Taliban were brutal.

In the bigger picture, aren't these countries and their peoples better off because of the United States? The answer is yes. Absolutely. I defy you to tell me they aren't.

At the end of the day, it really depends on how you define peace, doesn't it? If you define peace as the mere absence of violence between two countries—some people call this "negative peace"—then perhaps you're happy with unrest so long as the people of one country aren't bombing and killing the people of another. I have a personal problem with that definition because it allows internal regimes such as those of Hitler, Milošević,[105] Saddam Hussein, and the Taliban to commit mass murder without anyone trying to stop them. In Bosnia and Kosovo, there were hundreds of thousands of people being killed in genocidal waves, but technically no war. Is that what you call a peace?

I think we need to look at peace in the positive sense and, specifically, we need to think of peace as justice. If you look at all these countries before and after the U.S. intervened and you examine how far these countries have come thanks to our presence, there's nothing to discuss.

You don't hear a lot about this perspective on the news, but that's the bottom-line truth of the situation. In fact, I wonder where the media puts their emphasis. My wife and I recently organized a support-the-troops rally at Syracuse University and I listened to this local TV news reporter interviewing an army captain and a marine lance corporal. The reporter was trying to lead the soldiers into saying things that would get them in trouble, pushing them to make comments on the Bush/Kerry election, which, at the time, was a week or so away. She didn't understand that we—as soldiers—can't talk about elections. We're in uniform, we're apolitical, and the truth is we'll work with whatever commander in chief is in office. The soldiers were being very blunt about this, but she kept pushing and pushing them.

Later on, I watched the broadcast she pieced together from the

---

105. Slobodan Milošević rose to power as president of Yugoslavia in 1987. He became head of the Yugoslav Communist Party and soon after the republics of Croatia and Slovenia declared themselves independent. The ensuing wars saw the Croats achieve victory over the Slovenians, though atrocities were alleged on both sides of the conflict. Additional tensions erupted when Bosnia-Herzegovina, a Muslim-majority province with significant Croat and Serb populations, declared secession in 1992 and the region was essentially carved into military fiefdoms, with Milošević having much of the blame for violence laid at his feet. Milošević was driven from power in October 2000 after another botched election fraud. By the time he left power, the entire region was in shambles.

footage. She made it sound like these two soldiers were trying to hide something by not answering her questions. It was ridiculous, a classic instance of something being taken out of context. But why? What agenda was she trying to promote? And who supports that agenda?

I want to emphasize that I was in Iraq during a certain early time frame. At that time the regime had just fallen. There was no insurgency. You could be 99 percent sure that the Iraqis you saw were harmless. Nowadays? That's totally different. Nowadays you never know. I meet a lot of soldiers coming back from Iraq now, and the consensus I get is that the Iraqi people are still extremely supportive of the American presence. The insurgency we're seeing is a very small percentage of the population and mostly comprised of Baathists who lost out when Saddam's regime collapsed. Plus you've got terrorists from outside Iraq who are now trickling into the country. But again, I emphasize: the Iraqi people are cooperating very much with U.S. efforts toward rebuilding the country.

They're also pointing out where insurgents are hiding. I know a marine that just got back from the theater a month ago. He tells a story about his time in Ramadi, one of the insurgency hotspots.[106] The marines stationed there set up a hotline for Iraqis to call if they wanted to provide information about insurgent activities. About half the phone calls the marines received on that hotline paid off and provided worthwhile intelligence which either stopped an ambush or brought in loose weapons. These are things you just don't hear about on the news. And this leads me to believe that there's a misperception being propagated by the media in our country, which tries to say that the Iraqi people are rising up against us, that they all want us gone. That's an absolute fallacy. The vast majority of Iraqis are glad we're there—they're very supportive. It's a slim minority that wants to kill us and the public needs to know this. This is not a wholesale uprising like I've seen portrayed on TV. If that was the case, you'd see far worse casualties than we've seen so far.

Let me use the example of Somalia on October 3 of 1993, the Black

---

106. Ramadi, known by other variants (Ramadiya, Ramadie, al-Ramadi, etc.) is a provincial capital, a town located about seventy miles west of Baghdad on the Euphrates River.

Hawk Down incident that was made into a movie. That was an example where thousands of people in Mogadishu rose up against an American military raid, and look at the casualties we suffered there. Of the 160 Americans trapped in Mogadishu, 18 were killed and 75 wounded. That's over 50 percent casualties. *That's* a popular uprising.

Contrast this to what's going on now in Iraq. Granted, the numbers are different but the ratio's about the same. We have somewhere close to 150,000 people in Iraq contending with a much greater population. But across the country we're only suffering a couple of casualties each day. So let's be clear: this is not a popular uprising. People in America need to understand that.

I'd really like to know what's going on in the corporate headquarters of CNN, NBC, and so forth because, when I watch the evening news, the things I hear reported don't correspond with the Iraq I saw when I was there or the Iraq I know from what people returning home tell me. Ask anybody who's come back recently if you don't believe me.

I fear that when history writes the story of Operation Iraqi Freedom, it'll dwell on is what the TV news showed each night. It'll totally forget how the Iraqi people are fighting for their freedom alongside America. This is a great moment in history! We need to prevail! This could be a great turning point in the world—an Arab country becoming a democracy. Imagine what that could mean.

The bottom line is that the mission in Iraq is a good thing. There's a lot of good things being accomplished. That's the story I want to hear told in the end.

Ed. Note: At the final editing of this story, Captain DeKever is now Major DeKever. He and his wife are expecting their firstborn, a son.

YOU'VE GOT TO TALK IT OUT

✳

Specialist Abbie Pickett
U.S. ARMY, 229TH COMBAT SUPPORT ENGINEERS

Hometown: Darlington, Wisconsin, a small farming community with a population of approximately 2,500. Abbie joined the Army National Guard during her junior year in high school; she was seventeen years old. She says she wanted to give something back to her country and to her community. The service seemed the best way to do that.

She wanted to be a medic but the army told her they had no slots available for that job. After completing her basic training, she was classified as a refueler and posted to the 229th. Abbie was twenty years old when, in February 2003, the 229th was called for active duty in Iraq. They were given less than 48 hours' notice.

Abbie, now age 23, remembers that time. She says she had conflicting thoughts about going to war. "I didn't think we had a solid platform [to be in Iraq]. I'd been reading a lot about the Vietnam War and drawing a lot of parallels. But I gave my word. I rolled the dice and they came up hot. Being in the military isn't about saying yes, I'll do that or no, that doesn't appeal to me. I was obligated to go, and there was no question in my mind but to fulfill my duty."

When we first arrived in Kuwait, there wasn't any mission for us and I had to take my watch off. That whole first week, I found myself obsessively checking the time. I'd look and it'd be ten ten in the morning. I'd wait for what seemed like an hour and check it again. Nope. It was only ten twenty. The days dragged on and we all started getting frustrated. It was a nerve-racking situation. We were in the middle of a war with nothing to do.

So my company planned to hop on board an engineering battalion headed to Tikrit. We sent an advance party first to see if there was enough work there to justify our going and they returned saying, "Oh yeah. There's work all right." We pushed forward in-country and got down to business.

For a long time we were assigned to stay on our own base and do general maintenance. We improved the runways, the roads, the buildings used to quarter troops, and the helo [helicopter] pads. None of these things were in fantastic condition when we found them so there was a lot to do, and I have to say morale improved a lot when we had jobs to keep us occupied.

Then we started getting assigned missions all over the country. Most of our orders kept us within the [Sunni] Triangle but at any given moment it might be "Go here! Go here! Go here!" Now we were building checkpoints on main Iraqi roads and setting up new bases. These were projects that expanded the Army's control of the country, and again we were very busy. My job was to drive a HEMTT [high-extended-mobility tactical truck; pronounced "Hemmet"] to support my unit. My truck could haul up to 2,300 gallons of diesel fuel.

For the most part, things went smoothly. I mean, compared to what a lot of soldiers have been through, I certainly can't complain about what happened to me, I'm back in one piece. But the incident that affected me most was the bombing incident that I talked about in the *New York Times*.[107] I want to talk about that here because I think it's important for people to know what happened and how long it can affect you. It's affecting me.

PTSD [post-tramatic stress disorder] is real. Right now, there's a lot of soldiers coming back from over there and they're having a hard time talking about what they experienced. Maybe it will help them to hear this.

It was in Baquba, at a base called Camp Warhorse. The camp's been renamed since I left, but even back then it had a reputation. We'd sent platoons down and every one of them came back saying how they'd spent time in bunkers getting shelled.

When my group got there, I admit, I was scared. But then your mind

---

107. "The Struggle to Gauge a War's Psychological Cost" by Benedict Carey, *The New York Times*, November 26, 2005.

takes over and starts to make everything routine. There was shelling all right but most of it was pretty distant. As crazy as this sounds, we all started joking about it pretty soon. In fact, we got a little pumped that we were finally able to yell, "Incoming!" and mean it. It was like, *Okay, check that off my list of things to do during the war.* Everything felt surreal, like being in a movie.

Usually the mortars fired in groups of three. When we heard one go off, we got used to looking at each other and asking, "Was that incoming? Outgoing?" A lot of times you couldn't tell if what you heard was them firing at us or us firing at them. If the explosions sounded like they were getting close, we'd head for the bunkers and wait it out. But then there was that night in October of 2003.

It was dark out, maybe seven or eight at night. I'd just had chow and was walking over to the Morale, Welfare, and Recreation [MWR] building. Picture a big building like an overgrown aluminum shed the size of a barn. Inside, soldiers were working out, watching TV, a few people were playing Ping Pong. It was the kind of setting where it's easy to forget you're in a war. Everybody's cutting loose and having a good time, dressed in workout clothes and army T-shirts. I took off my DCU [desert-camouflaged uniform] blouse and hung it on the back of a chair, said hello to some friends. Then I sat down and started tapping away on a public computer.

When the first shell came in, no one asked if it was incoming or outgoing. It was too close to joke about, it hit and hit hard. The blast shook everything, the building, our bodies, the furniture. I looked over at my buddies who'd been playing Ping-Pong, but they were already on the floor under the table. I remember seeing the look of terror on their faces and thinking, *This one's for real.* I dropped to the ground, too. I was like, *God help us.* Then came the terrible thought that it was only one shell. At least two more would follow. After that, things started to get a little blurry for me.

At some point, the lights went out and soldiers started hurrying past me toward the door. I grabbed for one of their uniforms because I was new to the base and not familiar with it. I yelled, "Take me to the bunker!" since I figured that's where everyone was going and I didn't want to get lost in the dark. There weren't any bunkers nearby, so everyone ran outside and got down on the ground by a bunch of HESCO barriers[108] planted maybe fifty feet away from the shed.

Mortars kept dropping and everything about the situation became surreal. Time started moving in slow motion. First we heard the shells drop in; they made a high-pitched squealing noise as they cut through the air. When they hit, the light from the explosion came first, then the concussion, so deep it shook the earth and blasted through our bodies. We were terrified.

Then a mortar fell right next to us, maybe thirty feet away, midway between the MWR shed and the HESCOs. We were definitely in the kill zone. By all accounts we should have been killed, but I guess the flak flew over our heads since we were flat on the ground. A female soldier lying very near to me started screaming. I remember there was a lot of smoke and a lot of dust. Fear and confusion. I couldn't get any fresh air. I was sure I was going to die.

The female soldier kept screaming and I realized I could make out her words. She said, "My bone's popping out," and started feeling her arm. She was hit, all right. The flak had torn her skin and she was bleeding, but it wasn't that bad. She had a small puncture wound in her arm caused by a small piece of flak. Her bone was intact as far as I could tell. I tried to reassure her. I told her she'd be all right. I said, "You're fine, look. There's no bone popping out of your arm." But she was hysterical. She kept on screaming.

I feel bad for saying this, but I had this crazy urge to punch her really hard and put her out of her misery. But then we heard shouts coming from inside the shed. "Medic! Medic!" I don't know why, but I got up and ran back toward the MWR. I went in alone.

Mortar shells were still falling but it suddenly didn't matter as much as helping whoever was left inside that shed. The lights were still off but I had a tiny, tactical blue light, which I pulled out and played around.

108. HESCO—Hercules Engineering Solutions Consortium, a company incorporated in Dubai whose principal activities include the supply of force protection and security systems for military, humanitarian, peacekeeping, and civilian operations. A HESCO barrier, or bastion (officially), is a collapsible, wire-mesh container lined with heavy-duty plastic. Using a front-end loader to fill the container with sand, dirt, or gravel creates a barrier to enemy fire that's nearly as good as concrete blocks. HESCO barriers come in a variety of sizes. Special "bunker kits" are also available.

Four bodies were lying on the floor: two Iraqi nationals, both male, and two American soldiers, a male and a female.

The American male had his hand over the female's neck. When he saw my light, he shouted, "She's hit! She's hit!" I moved in to help them but the whole situation was frustrating. It was pitch black inside the hut, and my light was so tiny. I could barely see what I was doing. I went to her and felt with my hands, checking her spine. I asked her to wiggle her extremities so we could figure out what was working and what wasn't. "Can you feel your toes?" I asked. "Can you feel your fingers? Move your hands, please. Can you move your hands?"

Then I felt blood on the ground, everywhere, pools of it. I yelled at the male soldier, "What's your assessment? Is this *her* blood?" I didn't know who the blood belonged to. He said, "I'm hit but I think she's worse." Which didn't answer my question. Whose blood was it? I was confused. All this while bombs kept exploding sporadically around us.

Looking back, the male soldier was definitely in shock. It was the way he kept repeating, "She's worse, take care of her!" I don't know how the two of them got wounded. It's possible some shrapnel flew in through the front door but I tend to think they were hit by pieces of the building, instead. When a bomb hits in or on or around a building, the building itself creates shrapnel. People inside get wounded because the ceiling collapses on them or a piece of wall explodes in their face.

Really, it's irrelevant, though. This much was certain: we had three soldiers wounded at least, probably more, with no medics on hand, no kits, nothing. At this point, another soldier entered the hut. He started looking after the female soldier so I turned my attention to the guy who'd had his hand on her neck. Turns out he'd been wrong. His wounds were much worse than hers.

One look at his lower arm under the blue light and I knew he'd hit a vein. Blood was spurting out of him with each heartbeat, like something you see in a horror movie. I lunged for the chair where I'd hung my DCU blouse and grabbed it, shoved it onto his arm, and applied pressure to stop the bleeding. Then I tried to get him to raise his arm over his head. I wanted to get the wound over his heart, and that's when I saw how bad the damage was. The inside of his arm was shredded, too. He'd hit the artery that runs through there and blood was spraying all over the place. I wound the shirt into a tourniquet.

At some point shortly thereafter, people started pouring in through the door. Somebody had a medical bag and we started getting the wounded outside. We loaded the male and the female American soldiers into a Humvee, plus the two Iraqis who'd also been hit, plus the woman from the HESCO. We needed to get everyone to the hospital ASAP but we couldn't turn our lights on and risk giving away our position. The hospital wasn't far, maybe three-quarters of a mile, but in the dark with all the excitement and panic and people bleeding all over the place, let's just say it wasn't a pleasant trip.

I worked with the soldier with the bad arm along the way. It dawned on me at some point that I didn't recognize him, we'd never met on base. I remember saying, "You're gonna be okay, you're gonna be fine," and I started asking him questions. I remember everything he told me. His name was Sergeant Hill and he was thirty-two years old. He was married and had O positive blood. It's funny the things that stick in your mind in a situation like that.

When we got to the hospital, a nurse approached the Humvee. She asked what was wrong and what popped out of my mouth was, "This is Sergeant Hill. He's thirty-two years old, he's married, and he has O positive blood." Which must be the weirdest way to introduce somebody but that's what I could manage at the time. Then I told the nurse, "He needs blood right away," and she snapped at me. "What makes you so sure?" She was looking at all the blood on me and I said, "No, no. None of this is mine. It's all his." This seemed to make sense to her.

My group wasn't the only one who got pounded that night. Wounded started pouring through the hospital doors. Pretty soon it became apparent that this tiny field hospital wasn't equipped to handle that kind of influx. Then things got a whole lot worse. The enemy shelled the hospital.

From a tactical standpoint it seems pretty clear they waited for us to move our wounded so they could identify the hospital and recalibrate their aim. A shell dropped in and someone yelled, "Cover your patients!" so that's what we did. We laid ourselves over the wounded and used our own bodies to shield them from whatever might come next.

Again, we were close. The hospital had a tiny psychiatric ward, not an inpatient facility or anything like that, more of a combat stress area where soldiers could sit and unwind after trauma. We found out later that a mortar actually hit the ward but didn't detonate. That would've been close. That would've been much too close.

When the shelling stopped all attention turned back to the wounded. Turned out Sergeant Hill was the worst injury of the night. They didn't have blood on the base to treat him, so they loaded him onto a medevac and off he went.

The next day, I was out working at a project site when an enlisted man, a specialist, I forget his name, came around and introduced himself. He said he was a counselor, a mental health specialist. He wanted to know if anyone who'd been under fire wanted to talk about what happened and, specifically, he wanted to talk to me. He said, "I understand you saw a lot of stuff last night." And I said, "Yeah, I guess we did."

He said, "Well, if you want to talk about it, I'm here." But I didn't want to. I didn't feel ready to say anything to anybody, especially not a complete stranger, not just then.

Later on I talked to one of my NCOs, Sergeant Chad Freymiller. He was my superior in the chain of command, the soldier I turned to for practically everything. We'd become friends during my time in Iraq, and I feel like I owe him a lot because he was always a very generous listener. Whether he knows it or not, he really pulled me through some rough times.

Sergeant Freymiller came around one night later on and said, "Listen, I have something to tell you." He made sure I was sitting down. He said, "I don't want you to hear this from anyone else. But I heard Sergeant Hill lost his arm from the wounds he received."

That was the straw. I lost it. I broke down. All I remember after that is Sergeant Freymiller saying, "It's all right. I know. It's gonna be okay." But I said, "No, it's *not* gonna be okay. He's thirty-two years old and he doesn't have an arm and it's all my fault." I really thought it was.

See, you run through every possible scenario in your head, everything you could have done better or faster. I shouldn't have listened when Sergeant Hill said he was okay. I should have wrapped his arm sooner and elevated it higher. I could have run faster, I could have been smarter. I could have done more. Anything. Just *more*. You run through every possible scenario in your head, and in every one you come up short.

I started having difficulty sleeping. I got moody. The base doctor prescribed me sleeping pills and Prozac. I kept going out on missions.

I think it's a major misconception that you have to be under fire or see wounded to get stressed out. One time we had a guy whose vehicle hit an IED. It was enough to put the whole unit on edge, it didn't matter if it was you. It could have been. It might be still.

I'm back in school now with a double major in political science and psychology. I'm not really sure what I'm going to do after college, but I'm leaning toward helping veterans in some capacity. To this day, any loud sound I hear makes my hair stand on end.

There have been other effects, too. Now that I'm home, I've done some work with groups like Afghanistan and Iraq Veterans of America [AIVA] and another one called Vets for Vets. These are fine organizations committed to making sure soldiers' voices are heard. I had a chance to meet other vets, and it was always a powerful experience. With these men and women, I finally felt like I belonged to a group that understood me, and whom I understood.

I really clicked with a veteran named Robert Acosta, a specialist my own age who'd been stationed at Baghdad International Airport in July of 2003. Meeting Rob made a major impact on my life. When Rob was in Iraq, he and a buddy drove off base one day in a Humvee to get a few cans of soda from a street peddler. Someone threw a hand grenade in through the window. It bounced onto the floor and Rob was reaching for it to throw it back out; he got it six inches off the floor before it exploded. The blast took off his right arm and shattered his left ankle and foot.

I mention this because the moment Rob and I met, we instantly became friends. Something fit, something about what I'd been through and what happened to him. We spent some time together in Washington, D.C., at an AIVA event, and a very strange thing started happening to me. It's difficult to describe, but I suddenly began to see people with missing right arms. I'm not sure if you'd call this a hallucination or a vision or what. It only lasted a few days. But, you know, that's crazy.

Later on, I visited another friend in New York City. I stayed at her apartment and we were there, talking. In the middle of saying something, I glanced over at her. She was missing her right arm. The panic came back. I had to slow myself down and force myself to look again. I told myself, *See? Everything's okay. She's got both her arms and everything's fine.* I never mentioned the incident to my friend, but I was certainly freaked out.

When you're coming home, everyone talks about the things they're going to start doing again, things you can only do in the States. They caution you, "Don't expect any parades or anything like that. You don't want to get your hopes too high." That was fine by me. When people asked me, "What's the number one thing you're looking forward to when you get home?" I always answered, "Indoor plumbing." I think my expectations were pretty realistic.

But I thought I'd come back and be the same type of person, the same type of woman, the same type of student I was before. No. Not hardly. When I first got back, I didn't realize how screwed up I was. On any given day, I'd feel jumpy. I'd have panic attacks in the grocery store. Some days, the symptoms were mild. On other days, they were completely incapacitating.

I lived with friends when I first got back. They never told me this at the time, but a few months ago, two full years after I'd returned from overseas, one of them confided in me. "You know," she said. "You were a real zombie when you got back." I said, "I was?" "Yes. And we all made a secret pact. We promised that we'd stick by you and see you through no matter what. But honestly we didn't know what to do for you."

That figures. I went from being an honors student carrying eighteen credits to a near dropout carrying four. Whereas I used to be a goal-oriented person, I don't do that much anymore. I still set my eyes on a few things, but I'm much more conscious that you can never really know what each day will bring. It's best not to hold on too tight.

I get scared on the days where I feel really good because I know that a day will follow where I bottom out. I go into that frame of mind where essentially I'm on autopilot. For a few days or weeks, maybe even a whole semester at a time I'm just doing the work, putting in the hours and getting by. Nothing affects me; I'm in the zone. My grandmother passed away, and a kid I used to baby-sit for was diagnosed with cancer. I didn't feel anything at all.

But then, suddenly, the low time comes. The feelings rush back in like a dam's broken open inside me. It's such an overwhelming experience that sometimes I'm not sure if I can take it. I've felt that I don't want to live anymore, and that's a horrible thing to say. It's selfish and awful and you'd never want to put your family and your friends through it. But I can't pretend it's not the truth. Over many days and nights, I wished I'd died in the mortar attack.

Talking to other veterans is the only thing that's helped me get through the bad times. I think it's the most important thing a soldier can do: Find other soldiers who've been through similar experiences. Sit down with them. Share. I know it's hard on our families, but they just don't understand. Guys and gals come home from a war. Families see their moms or dads, husbands, wives, or brothers and sisters struggling, but they don't know how to help them. And soldiers don't want to talk. What is there to talk about? You want to shield your loved ones from all the crap you experienced over there, you don't want to drag them down in it.

It's hard to let somebody go. I know the temptation. You want to help them heal. You want to hear their story. But it has to be done in the proper time.

Ed. Note: Specialist Pickett wished to thank two organizations who have helped connect her to other veterans: Afghanistan and Iraq Veterans of America, and Vets for Vets. Also, a special thanks to Paul Rieckhoff of AIVA, "for helping me find an outlet where my voice could be heard. Thank you."

STORMING BAGHDAD

✷

Staff Sergeant John Murray
101ST AIRBORNE DIVISION (ON LOAN TO DELTA COMPANY,
THIRD BATTALION, 187[109])

John joined the army as a career choice in April '96. Now age 27, he has two sons, Michael, six, and Gunner, two. They live in Kentucky.

John's unit was activated and shipped to the Middle East in November 2001. The following March, Delta Company pulled duty in Afghanistan to replace a Marine Corps unit. They stayed in Afghanistan until August 2002, first in Kandahar, then in Baghram, and finally in Kabul, where Delta Company assisted members of the Special Forces as they trained the Afghan National Army. Delta Company primarily ran routine security patrols and secured the American embassy against possible attack. They were sent home for a spell before receiving orders to mobilize to Iraq.

"We'd only been back stateside a little bit before we had to head down to Louisiana for supplementary training," John says. "Which meant that something was going to happen. Sure enough, when we finished training, they gave us some leave and after that it was time to go." He laughs. "Man, did that suck."

John's voice is full of warmth as he recounts his story. He tends to laugh a lot, bringing a natural sense of humor to bear on circumstances that might otherwise prove overwhelming. He gives the impression of a man who's very comfortable with himself.

Listen, if it's all the same to you? Make sure you get this story down right. My unit had a problem with *Soldier of Fortune* magazine. They did a piece about our firefighting in Baghdad and, man, when we read it? We all started laughing. They made it sound like we were fixing bay-

---

109. Also known as the Rakkasans, a Japanese word for "falling-down umbrellas."

onets on our rifles, charging the enemy, screaming at the tops of our lungs. We all sat there scratching our heads going, "I don't remember it being like that. That sounds more like World War I." I guess it sold a lot of magazines, though.

I'm glad to have a chance to talk to somebody. I tell you, it means a lot to have someone wonder what went on over there.

We deployed to Kuwait and weren't there very long before they told us, "You're going in." We continued to train every day, nonstop. By that point we were veterans of Afghanistan, so we sort of understood the situation. But honestly? Things were very different. It's like I told my wife. I said, "Baby, Afghanistan was the playoffs. Iraq is the Super Bowl, and all the big stars are playing."

My unit pushed in behind Third ID [Infantry Division] and then the sandstorm hit. Let me tell you, that sucked. The Iraqis would hit some of our Patriot missile sites with their attack vehicles and we'd start to chase after them, but by the time we got out there, they'd disappeared into the desert. It was frustrating.

Then we got word that the next day we'd take Saddam International Airport and, man, that got us excited. Our attitude was, "Holy shit, you've got to be kidding, right?!" They weren't.

The attack scenario changed a couple of times. First we planned on doing an air assault, but that got nixed because the Iraqis had so much antiaircraft capability. Our air force had knocked out a lot of their guns, and frankly, the Iraqis weren't great shots to begin with. But we'd already run a few advance patrols around the airport and ascertained that they had enough antiaircraft capability to take out a few of us at least if we went in by helicopter. We figured better safe than sorry.

Again, we pushed in behind Third ID. We had Bradleys and tanks supporting our front. My unit was an antiarmor detail equipped with .50 cals, 119s, and TOW missiles mounted on our Humvees. Our job was to provide security for what we call the line dogs—infantry soldiers walking the ground in long columns beside the vehicles. We were going in with a whole battalion. That's at least seven hundred soldiers, a lot of people to protect. But there was nothing going on. We marched right on in and it was like we were on parade or something, nobody put up a fight. Nobody was *around*. It was like we'd already won.

Then right before dusk I remember we were moving down the highway. Ahead of us, we could see a vehicle burning in the middle of the road. It wasn't an uncommon sight, so we didn't think much of it; we kept driving forward. I remember there was an old man standing on the side of the road, waving at us as we passed by. The land all around us looked like potato fields and it stretched away in all directions, empty, just mile after mile of rolling land dotted with the occasional mud hut typical of the Iraqi style. Then, all of a sudden, *bam! bam! boom!* From out of nowhere, they started shooting at us.

It started out with a barrage of RPGs aimed at our LMTV [light medium tactical vehicle]. There had to be at least fifteen shooters because rounds started kicking off like crazy all at once. Total mayhem. The Iraqis must have used that burning vehicle on the road as their targeting point because that's where they directed their line of fire.

I got lucky. My own vehicle had passed that area and left it about a quarter mile behind but the rest of the unit got stuck. For some reason the vehicle carrying our soldiers stopped, not a good thing to do, it should have kept on going. But since they didn't, the Iraqis pinned them down with AK-47 fire.

Now I'm not sure what was going through the Iraqis' minds. Maybe they thought they were attacking an easy target, like a supply convoy. Instead, they'd attacked an infantry battalion, which meant that they'd blundered into a situation where fifteen guys or however many they had were squared off against a couple hundred heavily armed Americans who were on their toes and ready for a fight. That's a pretty big "oops." We fought that battle and killed them all.

Interestingly, none of our guys got hit. And they should've. I mean, we'd been ambushed, after all. Logically speaking, we had to expect to lose somebody. Our attackers had hidden themselves really well in the uneven ground and farmhouses maybe a hundred and fifty yards off the road. They should have had us dead to rights. Some of our trucks got hit with RPG fire, but none of the rockets exploded. Just lucky, I guess.

We pushed on after that battle and stopped at one of Saddam's palaces to prepare for the night. It was a really nice place on the southern end of the airport complex. Way up ahead of us, we could hear arms fire rattling away as the darkness came on. Once we'd oriented ourselves, we pushed in a bit further and took a southern part of the airport, encountering no resistance.

We figured we'd hit a good place to settle down for the night, so we pulled all our vehicles into some empty hangers where the airport mechanics must've performed maintenance on the planes. The planes were all gone; don't know what happened to them. We could still hear the arms fire blasting away ahead of us, much closer now that we were actually in the airport complex, but we didn't think much of it. We made ourselves as comfortable as we could and slept on our trucks.

It's funny. You learn to follow certain habits in a combat situation. As it turns out, you don't actually *think* too much about anything, you just *do*. Finding cover, for instance, becomes a default instinct. Keeping your rifle clean becomes second nature, like breathing or keeping your eyes peeled. You give yourself over to some very strange attitudes under combat conditions, attitudes like, "If tonight's my time to die, so be it. For now, though, I'm gonna get behind this wall and grab a little sleep." In retrospect, sure, it's a little fatalistic. Almost surreal. But that kind of thinking makes about as much sense as anything when you're over there. You learn to roll with it almost to the point where you forget there was any other way of being.

Another strange thing: you never really sleep when you're in a combat zone. You shut your eyes and drift off, but it's more like you enter this weird kind of daze. When we holed up in those airplane hangers, I remember squinting down at my boots, which I'd just taken off and left on the ground beside me. I remember thinking, *Damn. What do I do first if we get hit? Put my boots on or my helmet? Boots or helmet? Helmet or boots?* It was such a big question, you know? I couldn't think straight. *Boots? Or helmet?* Hell, I was barely awake let alone functioning at full mental capacity.

All night, our tanks were still pushing through the zone, shooting off rounds, moving eastward, trying to clear through the airport and head into downtown Baghdad. They encountered resistance. The Iraqis might have been lax letting us proceed up to that point, but they sure as hell weren't going to let Baghdad slip through their fingers without a fight.

In the middle of the night a stray Iraqi round hit the ground really close to us. We were so damn tired that nobody cared much, but one guy jumped up to his feet and started screaming, "Oh my god, they're coming in! Get up! Everybody! Get up!" Someone else yelled out, "Lay down and go to sleep. Jesus. Don't worry about it." So the guy did. He lay back down, but I doubt he got any more sleep that night. He was wound up too tight for that.

The next morning, our commanders said, "First platoon and Fifth. You've got your orders. Go in and clear the rest of the airport." I was part of First platoon. I was going into a battle zone.

Now during the break my unit had between our assignment in Afghanistan and shipping out to Iraq, we went to Louisiana and trained in a fictitious village called Shugart-Gordon. It was a pretty good urban combat scenario named after two of the American Delta Force snipers who lost their lives in Somalia.[110] At Shugart-Gordon, we learned to clear rooms and clear them well, but I tell you: My whole time in the army, nothing really prepared me for the taking of Baghdad Airport. That was my first firefight and I'll never forget it as long as I live.

Baghdad International had three terminals. Third ID had already cleared one up ahead of us, but apparently they'd been more focused on pushing through to secure the airport's outer perimeter. They hadn't stopped to do an extensive search, leaving large portions of the inner perimeter unsecured. Recon duty fell to us and recon duty can be pretty dangerous. I don't mind saying I was pretty scared. The terminal buildings were all modern glass structures, like a lot of airport buildings you'd see here in the States. You could tell that the facility hadn't been used in quite a while, so we didn't expect to encounter unfriendlies. But glass walls were the last things I wanted to see from a safety perspective. Glass

110. Sgt. First Class Randy Shugart and Master Sergeant Gary Gordon, two Delta Force snipers who were inserted via helicopter by their own request to rescue a wounded Black Hawk pilot, Mike Durant, from approaching Somalis on October 3–4, 1993, in what later became known as the Black Hawk Down incident. Both soldiers were later killed by a mob of Somali militiamen who swarmed the site. Both soldiers posthumously received the Medal of Honor.

walls mean shrapnel and shrapnel can kill. I was on edge, I can tell you that.

All for nothing, though, as it turns out. We reconned around the buildings and didn't see anything, so we went back and reported All Clear. After that, we came up with a plan of attack and moved in to take over the buildings.

For this phase of the assault my unit provided cover and security for the line dogs, same as usual. We pointed our guns toward the windows of a building to cover soldiers while they made their formations and burst in through the front doors. For the most part, that meant we sat around waiting to receive sniper fire. As it turns out, we weren't disappointed.

Some Psy Ops guys pulled up in a Humvee equipped with projection loudspeakers. This was standard procedure. Psy Ops traveled around with a bunch of guys who spoke Arabic, nationals who wore patches on their sleeves that said FIF, which I believe stood for Free Iraqi Forces. A lot of these guys were Iraqis who'd immigrated to the States and returned to their native country to act as translators during the war. They'd climb onto the loudspeakers at appropriate moments and say things in Arabic like, "Stop! The Americans mean you no harm! Throw down your weapons!" That kind of thing.

One of my buddies went over to talk to the Psy Ops guy and the next thing I knew he comes back with this huge grin on his face. I asked him what was up but he didn't say anything. Not yet. I remember leaning against my truck, trying to relax, waiting to see what would happen next when all of a sudden I started hearing American heavy metal. *Really* loud. I thought I was imagining it, at first. Then I was like, "What the hell, does one of my guys have a CD player?" No, it was coming from the speakers on the Psy Ops Humvee, this death metal bass beat pounding out loud enough to make the air shimmer. Took a second for me to recognize the band: this group called Drowning Pool doing a song called "Bodies":

Let the bodies hit the floor . . .

Everybody went nuts. Guys started to cheer. I thought the whole thing was kind of cool, but my CO got pretty mad. He stormed up to the Hummer and told them to turn it off, turn it off now, turn it off immediately, which the Psy Ops guys did. After that everything was quiet for a few minutes. Then the line dogs went in and started to clear the building.

While they were in there, I turned on a shortwave radio I kept with me at all times. We didn't know a damn thing about what was going on in the outside world apart from what little we heard from Command and I always sort of thought they weren't telling us the whole story. So I had this little radio with me I could use to tune in and listen to the news if I caught a good signal. The only one I ever got came from the BBC, but it was something.

I was sitting in my truck watching our infantrymen kick in the doors of a terminal building and stream inside when the voice of a BBC commentator broke over the radio and started saying, "Coalition forces are, at this very moment, taking Saddam International Airport." I thought, *Holy shit! That's pretty up-to-the-minute commentary!* The commentator went on to say that the Coalition had not yet taken any casualties, which was true as far as I knew, and that a certain Iraqi general was broadcasting announcements that the army of Iraq had, in fact, retaken the airport, killing a bunch of American forces in the process. According to this Iraqi general, the Coalition had been beaten badly in the fight for the airport and were now in the process of surrendering. I thought it was some of the funniest shit I'd ever heard.

I called up my platoon sergeant on the truck radio and said, "Hey, man. You been listening to the radio?" He said, "No, what's up?" "Apparently the Iraqis are kicking our asses right now. Hear them tell it, they just took over the airport."

My sarge was like, "Shit. Don't that beat all? Guess we just underestimated them, that's all." I'm watching a squad of our guys come out of the airport terminal lighting cigarettes and clapping each other on the back. They looked like they were on their way to a barbeque, not back from an urban assault. "I guess we'll never learn," I said. "Those Iraqis are tough as nails."

That night we got to relax a bit. Our mission priority shifted toward providing inner perimeter security for our attack forces that were ahead of us on the front lines, pushing into Baghdad.

Later on we got word that we'd been selected to refit[111] the Third ID Cav, a front line unit. The push into downtown Baghdad was already underway with the front line ahead of us, we could tell from the constant racket of gunfire. We knew we were close but we never knew just *how* goddamn close we were until we started moving into position. Turns out the front line lay just a few landing strips away from the terminal, on the eastern side of the airport, near the road that takes you from Saddam Hussein International into the guts of Baghdad, a highway called Ambush Alley.

We went in and refitted Third ID Cav, which turned out to be a little hairy since they were in Bradley fighting vehicles and we were in plain, unarmored Humvees. The lack of armor hadn't really mattered to us before, since our whole mentality up to that point had been geared toward standoffs. We knew, for instance, that Soviet tanks could only fire their ordnance effectively from ranges that paled in comparison to our own. So we'd considered ourselves relatively safe from heavy incoming barrages. A lack of armor was never an issue for the work we'd been tasked to do.

But this place was a totally different story. We were smack dab in the middle of the hottest zone in the war. Iraqi forces weren't just aware of us, they were *aiming* at us. And they weren't way off in the distance, either, this was practically hand-to-hand combat. There was another palace up in that area, plus the Secretariat,[112] a walled complex with trees everywhere and buildings and wide open fields, a crazy situation from an attack-defense standpoint. If I thought I was nervous before, my nuts were up around my throat now, you know?

I had four gun trucks in my platoon with alternating weapon types. The first truck had a .50 cal machine gun, the second truck had a Mark 19 automatic grenade launcher. The third and fourth trucks had a .50

111. *Refitting* is a military term used to describe when one unit spells, or relieves, another: the unit being refitted gets a chance to stand down from the rigors of their post, relax, resupply themselves on ammunition, and perform whatever maintenance is necessary for their vehicles to continue in optimum performance.
112. The Iraqi equivalent of the Pentagon.

cal and a Mark 19, respectively. Every truck was equipped with a TOW system and a SAW gun, too. There was also a cargo truck, our fifth vehicle, which served as the platoon sergeant's command post. The cargo truck carried ammo, food, water, gasoline, and so forth. My platoon's supplies also supported Alpha Company, a company of line dogs whom we protected.

The whole battalion dug in, making a big half-moon configuration from wall to wall between two complexes on either side of the road, everyone facing toward downtown Baghdad. The arms fire from up ahead began to accelerate, if anything, which didn't do much to ease our nerves. In the formation, my truck ended up facing down an asphalt road with a big open field sprawling off to the left and a grove of trees lining each side of the road. I remember thinking, *Man, this sucks.* Because I felt like we were wide out in the open, sitting ducks for any idiot who wanted to use us as target practice.

To make matters worse, there was no soft ground to dig in and make fortifications. See, every time we stopped the column, we'd dig indirect pits by the sides of the road for us to scramble into in the event of incoming artillery or mortar fire. Totally impossible in this region. The ground on either side of the asphalt was too tough. Farther out, the root systems of the trees from the groves made the turf impenetrable. So we had nowhere to hide in case shells started dropping in. None of us were happy campers.

As it turns out, I took my machete and went off to one side of the road, started cutting down trees which we used to camouflage the trucks. Word of advice: machetes are not the proper tool for cutting down trees. Use an ax. Use a chainsaw. Use explosives. Use anything, just don't use a machete; it's an exercise in futility. We did it that way since we didn't have any other means, but it wasn't easy.

Up until that point, I thought it was ridiculous that we were out in the desert fighting in trucks that still had woodland camouflage. But it all worked to our advantage on that road in Baghdad. The woodland camouflage worked perfectly for trucks covered with trees.

The soldiers we replaced were relieved to see us; they'd been out on the front for a long time and badly needed a break. We talked with them a bit while preparing our position, and they gave us a situation report on the activity they'd seen in the area. I couldn't help noticing a blown-up tank right behind our location, so I asked about it, I said, "Jesus, what's been hitting you guys?" Anything powerful enough to take out a tank was something I wanted to know about far in advance of hunkering into a position and staying there for any length of time.

The guys from the Third ID Cav just shook their heads. They all had this weird punch-drunk quality to their movements and expressions, the kind of behavior you see in people who haven't slept in a very long time. Their eyes were dreamy and distant, like sleepwalkers. "Nah," one of them said. "Don't worry about it. It's nothing. Every once in a while a guy'll pop up from over there someplace." He waved his hand in the general direction ahead of us like he was pointing out features on a golf course. "They'll shoot off an RPG or try to plug you with small arms fire. Ain't nothing. They're lousy shots."

I was like, Okay. Yeah. Sure. They were so relaxed about everything, I just didn't understand it. Now I understand it's all a question of perspective. Iraq was my first experience taking fire; I'd never seen combat in Afghanistan. Oh we did a lot of patrolling, but my unit never got the chance to really get it on with the Taliban. Actually, I take that back. *Some* of the guys in my unit saw action, they were the veterans of Operation Anaconda.[113] But not me. Uh uh. No firefights.

So I'm standing around feeling really naked, like I said—out in the open, no cover, no pits, no idea what's going to happen next. Night was falling and my gunner put on his night-vision goggles. Words got passed down the line to the effect of, "Anybody you see out there is the enemy. There are no, repeat: no! friendly personnel in this zone." Which in a way was pretty cool; I could take some comfort in that because at least I wouldn't have to stop and think, *Should I fire or should I not?* if I spotted anyone moving toward us.

I was actually discussing this very same situation with my platoon sergeant when my gunner started yelling, "Hey! Hey, Sergeant Murray! Hey, I see somebody out there!" I said, "Talk to me. What've you got?"

And he said, "I see . . . I see . . . I see, I don't know . . . five guys? Maybe seven! They're running around out there and it looks like— Jesus, it looks like they're using flashlights to get around!" I was like,

---

113. Operation Anaconda is the code name for the U.S. invasion of Afghanistan in March 2002. Coalition forces made a massive push against about five hundred to one thousand al Qaeda and Taliban forces in the Shahi-Kot Valley and Arma Mountains southeast of Zormat.

"Flashlights? What the hell are you talking about?" So I put on my night-vision and looked out to where he was pointing.

Yup. There they were. A group of guys way down the road running around trying to act real stealthy, sneaking around in the dark so they could pull a recon on us. They had flashlights, all right; Iraqis weren't equipped with night-vision goggles. Bad for them but good for us. Our goggles made the darkness bright as day.

The guy next to me was the SAW gunner and he said, "Open up on 'em!" but I wanted to follow procedure. So I picked up the handset and called it in on the radio: "Hey, we've got five to seven guys running around through here—" but that was it, that was all I had a chance to say. The SAW gunner opened up and the shooting started. At first I was screaming, "No, no, no!" but then I just sort of went with it. There wasn't much left to be done by that point. I told my gunner to lay in with the .50 cal to lend support and he did.

Part of my job is to command and control a fight when it happens. With everybody already blasting away, I figured the best way to command and control was to get involved. Plus, I have to confess. I saw this as my chance to really do something. Hell, we had the advantage, right? So I got out of my truck and opened up with my own weapon, an M-4[114] rifle with a laser light scope.

Getting into a shooting match is scary. Obviously, you don't want to get hit, you don't want to die. When it happens, it happens so fast that you just leap into attack mode. You kind of get into that space of "Fuck you, Asshole!" and after that, it's not hard to start shooting. Suddenly the night turned into a whole lot of smoke and noise.

I want to say that the distance between us and our targets was three hundred yards, give or take. With all that land between us, you have to rely almost entirely on the four fundamentals of shooting. There's Breathing, control your breathing when you fire a weapon. There's Proper Position, meaning situate yourself in a good firing stance before you begin. Sight Picture, which means that you keep aiming at the same spot every time you fire. And Trigger Action: Squeeze the trigger, don't pull. If you integrate these four parts correctly, it's pretty much a no-brainer; you're

114. The shortened variant of the M-16A2 rifle.

going to hit your target. If you end up missing, it's because something's deficient in one of those four fundamental areas. Find out what it is, correct it, and keep shooting.

I was standing right beside my truck, opening up with my weapon, when it occurred to me I was wide open in the middle of the road, no cover. Totally stupid move. I didn't take a knee or anything, I was standing right out there in the middle of the friggin' road, doing everything I'd been trained *not* to do. The thought hit me like a brick between the eyes: *What the hell am I doing, for God's sake?* I covered my gunners during their reload interval. When they picked up firing, I corrected my position and got behind my truck to reload my own weapon.

I heard the radio chattering away, so I called in. Everybody up and down the line wanted to know what was happening, what we were seeing. I gave a quick report, five to seven guys probing us from up ahead, targets engaged. What I didn't know at the time was that another of our platoons had just then begun engaging another cluster of enemy soldiers nearby, on a different side of the wall. Somebody else down the line was on the phone, too, calling this action in.

Well. Evidently the other guy on the phone called in an artillery strike because, the next thing I knew, there was this huge explosion. You know all that crap you see in the movies, where you hear the whistle of the incoming shells right before they impact? It's bullshit. Honestly. I didn't hear shit. That damn artillery dropped so close to us, it blew up maybe a hundred feet away. There was a bright spark of white phosphorous[115]—that stuff is hot enough to set anything it touches on fire. Right after that, everything went white.

---

115. On Tuesday, November 15, 2005, the BBC reported the Pentagon's confirmation that the U.S. had used white phosphorous (WP) weaponry during the 2004 Coalition offensive to occupy the city of Fallujah. Pentagon spokesman Lt. Col. Barry Venable said, "Yes, [WP] was used as an incendiary weapon against enemy combatants. When you have enemy forces that are in covered positions that your high explosive artillery rounds are not having an impact on and you wish to get them out of those positions, one technique is to fire a white phosphorus round into the position because the combined effects of the fire and smoke—and in some case the terror brought about by the explosion on the ground—will drive them out of the holes so that you can kill them with high explosives (i.e., 'shake and bake')." Venable went on to note that phosphorous was used as an incendiary weapon against enemy combatants only—not against civilians. This statement, however, contradicted the U.S.'s earlier denial that WP weapons were used in Fallujah at all. Venable further stated that white phosphorous rounds were "conventional munitions" rather than chemical weapons, and therefore the rounds were neither "outlawed or illegal." The Pentagon's official standpoint, reiterated on November 30 by General Peter Pace, was that the use of WP rounds is not prohibited, and that any previous denial of use was based on "poor information." Article 2, Protocol III of the 1980 UN Convention on Certain Weapons bans the use of white phosphorous rounds against civilians.

I remember dropping my radio handset and jumping to the ground with another soldier next to me. Everyone's screaming, "Add! Add!" which signals to the artillery guys that a shell's landing too close: add distance. More rounds came in. After that, it was total destruction.

I tell you all this because this was the best part of the war for me, and before you go making any assumptions about what I might be talking about, let me explain. It was the best part of the war because, at that point, we were given everything we needed to win. We had airplanes, we had artillery, we had ammo. We were psyched about our tools and psyched about our training. We were willing to do whatever needed to be done. I tell you, and I know I've said this already. It was like going to the Super Bowl.

The fighting started at seven o'clock. I remember that because I'd happened to look at my watch just before the shooting started. When a lull came on and we all started to relax, I thought that maybe an hour had passed. But I checked my watch again and I couldn't believe it. It was eleven o'clock in the evening. I thought, *Holy shit!* You know? I couldn't understand how all that time had passed so quickly. Suddenly all the adrenaline drained right out of me and I was so, so tired. That's another thing you learn very quickly: combat is exhausting.

Throughout the night, we saw something burning on the road a few hundred meters down from our position, right where the phosphorous had hit. We didn't know what it was until daylight came up again and we were able to get a better look. Turns out it was a dead guy. Turns out one of the Iraqis got a chunk of that white phosphorous caught in him and it just kept burning. The guy's body had been on fire for a couple of hours. Crazy. The next day, Third Infantry pushed into downtown Baghdad.

There was another palace directly down the road from where we were facing. Saddam had so many palaces over there, it was completely ridiculous. Our airplanes had already dropped some JDAMs onto the buildings of this particular complex, and apparently there'd been some construction going on there before the invasion started because there were cranes all over the place. We were about to find out the hard way that the Iraqis had put people up in those cranes to spot us as we approached. From that altitude, they could track us pretty easily.

THE USE OF WHITE PHOSPHOROUS ROUNDS IN MODERN WARFARE

Sometimes known as Willy Pete or WP in military lingo, white phosphorous is a common allotrope of the chemical element phosphorous that has found extensive military application as a chemical found in tracer rounds, smokescreen agents, and antipersonnel incendiaries capable of causing serious burns.

During the second major Coalition assault on the Iraqi city of Fallujah (Operation Phantom Fury, November 2004), *Washington Post* reporters embedded with Task Force 2-2, Regimental Combat Team 7, wrote: "Some artillery guns fired white phosphorous rounds that create a screen of fire that cannot be extinguished with water." This tactic, at first blush, would appear to be an acceptable use of WP as outlined in the 1980 UN Convention banning certain weapons.

However, controversy was fueled by an article appearing in the U.S. Army's *Field Artillery Magazine* in the spring of '05. In this article, a captain, a first lieutenant, and a sergeant reviewed battle tactics they had practiced in Fallujah, writing: "WP proved to be an effective and versatile munition. We used it for screening missions at two breeches and, later in the fight, as a potent psychological weapon against the insurgents in trench lines and spider holes where we could not get effects on them with HE [high explosives]. We fired 'shake and bake' missions at the insurgents, using WP to flush them out and HE to take them out." In another passage the authors noted that they could have used other smoke munitions and "saved our WP for lethal missions."

The term "shake and bake" refers to a seasoning made by Kraft that is put into a plastic bag with chicken and shaken before baking. Its use as field artillery jargon seems to imply that U.S. soldiers purposefully used WP in the Battle of Fallujah to entrap enemy soldiers before destroying them with HE. Is this, then, a noncombative use of WP?

The military tactic of forcing opponents out of cover is hardly a new one. Indeed, WP weapons were used extensively during the Vietnam War to force North Vietnamese troops to leave their positions. But, as postulated by Paul Reynolds, world affairs correspondent for the BBC, "One wonders of course if, in Falluja [*sic*], WP was used more directly to kill insurgents and not just to flush them out. In battle, soldiers take short cuts and this seems an obvious one."

As of November 30, 2005, Pentagon officials have denied any civilian casualties related to WP strikes during the Battle of Fallujah. These reports, however, have been contradicted by the *Guardian* newspaper of London, Italian documentary filmmaker Sigfrido Rannuci (*Fallujah: The Hidden Massacre*), and several independent journalists. Ranucci in particular claims that U.S. forces killed civilians in Fallujah, using a combination of WP armament and air-dropped MK-77 bombs. MK-77 is essentially a modernized form of napalm.

As we approached the palace, I could see the complex had security turrets on some of the walls. Apparently someone in one of those towers shot an RPG at one of our gun trucks as we moved in. I say "apparently," because I sure as hell didn't hear it. Again with this not hearing the artillery. Like I said, combat's nothing like the movies. All I heard was a bunch of guys suddenly yelling for fire command and there I was thinking, *What the hell's going on now?*

Then I heard the *pa-pow*! of a missile launching and all of a sudden one of the security towers burst into flames. Somebody from our group must've launched a TOW at it. I jumped on the phone and started requesting information, I desperately wanted to know what was going on. "What the fuck's happening? We got a whole bunch of guys out there or what? What's the damn story here?"

The soldier on the other end of the line said, "They're shooting at us, Sarge! We fired back!" I said, "That's bullshit," but this guy says, "No, honest! They just launched an RPG at us!"

I hurried over to this soldier's position. Sure enough, there was an

RPG round sticking in the ground a few meters short of the gun truck that had fired the TOW. The RPG hadn't exploded. It was just sitting there in the ground. I thought, *Damn. That's pretty wild. Well. All right.* I didn't know what else to say to my guys. That round could've killed them if it exploded. So I said, "Good job. Keep up the good work."

Looking back, maybe I remember the war in Iraq more from funny experiences like that. Like the day our battalion commander, battalion sergeant major, first sergeant, and company commander all paid us an unexpected visit. We'd gotten into some pretty heavy fighting the day before, so being a little tired and having a different attitude about life in general, I woke up that morning and said, "Fuck it. Today, I'm not gonna shave." That's against regulations, we're supposed to shave every day no matter how dirty or tired or shell shocked we are. Suddenly I saw all four of the Big Guys coming my way and, man, did I ever get cold feet. All of a sudden not shaving didn't seem like the hottest idea in the world, know what I mean?

One of them walked right up to me and looked me square in the eye. I saluted and he returned it. Then he says to me, "Heard you guys did some shooting last night." I heard myself say, "Oh, Roger that. Yes, sir. Yeah, you know. We were . . . we were doin' some shooting." But in my head all I'm thinking is, *Please don't say anything about my beard! Please don't even look at my chin, oh pleasepleaseplease.*

I know he noticed it. He didn't say a word. The way the Big Guys talked to us, the way they looked us over, it was obvious they thought we were exhausted. We were. Adrenaline was keeping us going once things got kicking. Once that adrenaline dropped, we were sapped. Done.

I shaved the moment they left.

Now it was our turn to go on the attack. We had a simple plan: One company would go in first and clear out the Secretariat, a barracks, and a training grounds for Iraqi soldiers. Another company would storm what we called the Spiral Hill, a high rise of ground which the Iraqi artillery were using to call down mortar fire on us. Meanwhile my group would take out an underground complex that led toward the airport and palace.

We had just under one hundred men in Delta Company plus some

Bradleys to lend support. An A-10[116] led the strike by flying in and dropping bombs. They let loose with a whole lot of firepower, but I'll say one thing for the Iraqis, they make some pretty strong walls. We hit those damn things with missiles, and the A-10s pounded them with their Gattling guns. Nothing. No way. Those walls refused to crumble. We punched a few holes in them, but that was it.

We checked our satellite imagery and found a possible alternative. If we used explosives to blow through two walls, our infantry guys could swarm in right behind us. We could clear out two buildings in the complex, make sure they were empty of enemy personnel, and continue forward into the large field that lay just beyond. From there, it was a straight shot up to the palace which had this huge lake next to it with a bunch of mini-palaces dotting the shoreline. Evidently, this was a popular area for the Baath Party.

I was in the lead truck and I always hated being on point. For good reason, too. I completely bypassed the spot we were supposed to enter, a gate between two buildings. It really wasn't my fault, looking back. The area looked so big on the satellite shot but in actuality it was much, much smaller. I shot right past it and kept following the road as it ran along the wall for the complex. When I finally realized my mistake, I told my driver, "All right, holy shit, I made a mistake, back up, back up, back up."

We backtracked to the original position and realized, okay, the gate wasn't as big as we'd thought. Not a problem when you're equipped with a bunch of explosives. We backed the truck up and tried blowing through the walls with our missiles, but it was such a confined area that our missiles couldn't cover the distance required for their warheads to activate. No matter how we positioned ourselves, we were barely going to meet that criterion. Even if we did, we had the back blast to consider, and the added detriment of the percussion an explosion would cause in such a tight spot. Missiles weren't the answer.

As it turned out, our Bradleys solved the problem with their 25 mm

116. The A-10 is one of the first aircraft specially designed to lend close air support to ground troops. These are simple, hearty, and effective twin-engine planes which can be used against all ground targets—infantry, tanks, and other armored vehicles. The A-10 was primarily designed for day and night close air combat support for friendly combat forces in low- and high-risk situations, while acting as forward air controller to coordinate friendly-fire targeting. The A-10's secondary mission is to support search and rescue operations for the Special Forces. Its specs list it as possessing limited capabilities for interdiction.

machine guns. The 25s brought the wall down quick and we moved through, but again we were stopped. The spot of ground between the first and second walls was pure marsh, not good for equipment, not good for foot soldiers. Man, it was all so frustrating, the best-laid plans of mice and men. But we'd come that far, you know? We'd pushed the vehicles over the first hump. At that point, it seemed ridiculous to turn back. So the Bradleys moved in and started shooting again. The line dogs took positions along the second wall, ready to move in the moment a gap opened up. Then I got a call from one of the Bradley commanders saying, "Hold up! Change of plans, change of plans! Move everyone out again."

He said he had an idea, which was this: "What we're gonna do, we're gonna go back down the road we were on first." Meaning the road I'd shot down after I first missed the gate. The Bradley commander said, "We'll keep going down that road because there's another gate down there, a back gate. We should secure that first, anyway, because, if anybody flees out that gate, we'll catch 'em right there." Apparently the back gate was pretty evident on another satellite shot I hadn't seen. Those satellite images can be pulled off any computer in the headquarters unit, printed out, copied, and forwarded up to the line so the front guys see what they're doing. It's a totally awesome capability.

So we went around back. We drove down the road and, as we went, we noticed a hole in the wall, looked like a missile had blown right through it. A point of interest but only for a moment. We were driving along, being careful, watching out for booby traps, which the Iraqis are justifiably famous for leaving all over the place. At about the same moment we noticed the hole in the wall, we also caught sight of this wire strung across the road. I say "we noticed" it, but actually, my driver didn't see the wire at all. He kept moving forward and a few of us finally got it through our heads that he was oblivious. We started calling out, "Stop!! Hey! Stop!"

Humvees are loud machines. The driver didn't hear us right away. But we kept screaming, "Stop! Dammit! Stop!" and finally he hit the brakes. The truck ground to a halt but not until the barrel of our machine gun came within two feet of this copper wire, much too close for comfort. Shit, we *really* didn't want to hit that wire, see? If that'd been a booby trap, some kind of trip wire for a grenade or an IED . . . ? Shit, they'd be picking pieces of us off the ground for weeks. We'd heard of cases where the Iraqis pulled tricks just like the VC did in Nam. String piano wire up at head height and wait for a convoy to drive through with men standing up in the backs of the vehicle. If the trucks are going fast enough? Instant decapitation. This wire was strung up just high enough to take the head off of my gunner who was standing upright in the back of the Hummer.

So there we were, stopped there, staring at the wire. Everyone gets out and scurries to pull security detail until we can figure out what the fuck's going on. The driver gets out, too, so he can assist in making the hasty perimeter. He pulls the emergency brake, which is standard procedure, we always pull the emergency brake so the truck won't roll. But as he gets out of the truck, the lanyard on the grip of his holstered 9 mm pistol gets caught on the emergency brake lever. The lanyard pulls, the emergency brake drops out of gear. Now the truck starts rolling forward again, straight toward the wire. Everybody's shouting, "No, no, no! Holy shit!"

We grab the truck anywhere we can and start pulling hard. Not enough. The damn thing keeps rolling and everybody's screaming, "The brake! Hit the goddamn brake!" The driver jumps back in and stopped the vehicle, just in time. After that there was a long, deathly silence which breaks wide open when everybody lands on the driver like flies on shit. I am the biggest fly. We're yelling, "What the fuck were you thinking? Jesus!" and this poor guy's screaming back, "Sorry, sir! Oh God, sir, I'm sorry!" It was fucking crazy.

Turns out the wire was one of ours. Remember the day before? We'd shot TOW missiles at the defense towers. One of them must have passed on through and blown a hole in the wall that we'd seen. Now, TOW missiles are what we call command-guided ordnance. They're a little more primitive than the Javelins, which are fire-and-forget.[117] When you fire a TOW, the warhead goes out and unspools a line of copper wiring behind itself. The wire's connected to the firing system, which is in your hands and enables you to guide the missile toward a target via a computer console that displays imagery via target-acquisitioning lasers inside the warhead. We're talking about a very sophisticated piece

117. A military term for a type of missile that does not require further guidance after launch.

of equipment here. Hell, we've got missiles capable of flying over a target and dropping smaller warheads right down on top of it, where reactive armor plating is usually a lot more vulnerable, like in the case of tanks, for instance. Like I said, we were playing in the damn Super Bowl of ordnance.

Anyway, with TOW missiles we're talking about a lot of wire. A TOW's got a maximum effective range of something like 3,750 meters, but that's the maximum *effective* range. Maximum *range* is a whole lot further. That wire will unspool itself until . . . well, until forever. Even though it was our weapon, I'm glad we saw it. Copper wire is sharp as shit. That would have done serious damage to my gunner. Might've even killed him.

Let me say this, while we're on the subject of sophisticated weaponry: high-tech weapons are all fine and good when you're fighting against an army. Truthfully? With all the tricks we had up our sleeves, there's no way *any* army could beat us. Mind you, none of those fancy toys help you one bit when you're fighting insurgents. Let me give you an example.

When I served in Afghanistan, you knew which people were Taliban members. You could just tell. They might not be wearing the traditional tribal dress the Taliban favored but that didn't matter. When they gave you that look? That's all you needed to know who you were dealing with. That look that said, "You piece of American puke, I want to step on you like a bug." It was good to see that look on people's faces. As a soldier, it let me know right away where the battle lines were. Catching a look like that made you think, *Okay, I see where you're coming from. So do something wrong, please. Do something wrong right now, that way I can kill you before you try to kill me.* That's the problem with the war in Iraq right now; the war began after we *won* the war. These insurgents blend seamlessly into civilian populations. They can ambush you from any vantage point and melt away like ghosts. They'll plant a dozen IEDs before having breakfast and wait all day for them to go off. Fighting an army is easy. Fighting terrorists is not.

Storming Baghdad was easy, but Baghdad was just the beginning. Once the Super Bowl ended, we came up against situations that were much more complicated. For instance, we'd receive intelligence that one man was a terrorist. We'd go in and question him using a show of force. Now maybe the reports we got were true, maybe he was linked to a few bad guys. But just as likely, maybe he wasn't. In the end, it's really tough to tell over there.

Let's suppose that he isn't. Let's suppose that he's actually on the side of the Coalition. Now he's really pissed off and all of *his* people are pissed off because we just busted in this guy's front door and made a big stink. This problem happened to us a lot in Baghdad after the fighting was supposedly over and we started focusing on peace keeping ops. By that point, we were patrolling the city from small outposts set up within the inner-city districts. People would drive right up to our positions and say in broken English, "Oh! I know where Baath Party member is!" To which we'd say, "Okay. Cool. Show us where he's at."

We'd follow these citizens out to a house. They'd point out someone leaving and say, "This man! This man is Baath Party!" We'd move in, form a perimeter, bust down the door, the shouting, the screaming, the whole show. It was a bust, of course. That guy in the house wasn't a Baath Party member, the informant just didn't like him because of, hell, because of any number of ethnic issues. Maybe the guy in the house was Syrian, Egyptian, Shiite, or Sunni. There were so many cultural clashes going on over there, and we didn't know a damn thing about any of it. We were just trying to do our jobs, working off whatever information came our way. In one situation, the guy in the house wasn't a Baath Party member, but we later learned that everyone else on that block was. The people who'd pointed out the other guy were. Now didn't we feel stupid?

Another complication: not all Baath Party members were terrorists. Some of them were ordinary people who'd joined the Baathists in order to survive the political climate of Iraq. For instance, let's say you were an Iraqi citizen who worked a shit job at the local gas station. Your life was pretty bad as it was. Why complicate matters by resisting the Baath Party who might torture you if you didn't join them, or kill a member of your family, your wife, or maybe your child? It's not worth the risk. So you say, "Okay, fine, I'll join the club, call me a Baath Party member, just leave my family alone." And just like that, they let you go on your merry way.

I remember one guy we talked to who was a veteran of the Iraqi

Army, retired. He was very up front with us. He said, "I fought against Americans in the first Gulf War. We don't want any problems here. There's no bad guys, just people trying to make a living. People trying to survive, just like you." Like a lot of Iraqis, this guy was a legitimate citizen just trying to make a life for himself and his family. I can sure as hell understand that.

But let's turn it around. Because I have to say: I can also understand why people would join the terrorists without much provocation. Let's face it, if you live in a country where the government's trying to come along and there's no system in place that will attend to the needs of your family, what else are you going to do? You have to do something. Why not go with the strongest game in town? Wouldn't you side with them if you thought they offered the safest road to a better life for your family?

Sure, there's a bunch of hard-core people who thrive on conflict and want to turn the whole conflict into some sort of religious epiphany. And some of those people are more fanatical than others; you get that in any population. But you've got to separate the fanatics out from the ordinary guy who's got no electricity in his house while his wife's pregnant. He's lost his job because of the war, he's got to put food on the table, and he'll do it any way he can. Put yourself in that guy's shoes. Go on, I'm serious. What would you do if you were that guy? Someone contacts you and says, "We'll give you food if you drive this ammunition truck to the location marked on this map." Doesn't sound too bad, right? So you say okay, just to put food on the table, just this one time.

But then they tell you, "Take a rifle with you for protection, because if the Americans spot you, they'll shoot." Well, that's not so good, but you still have to feed your family. So you take the rifle and you hop in the truck and you hope that nothing happens. This is how it starts with a lot of Iraqis over there. It starts from desperation. It starts from commitment to children and family.

What would you do if conditions here in America were like that? Wouldn't you hop in the truck, too? Just to put food on the table. Just that one time.

It's so damned complicated. Because, no matter how much I sympathize for the guy in the truck trying to feed his family, if he decides to point that weapon at me, I'll shoot him. I want to go home and put food on *my* family's table. The way I see it, the bottom line is this: it's him or me. In that equation, it doesn't take a lot of brain power to figure out which one it's going to be.

Some of my soldiers would tell me, "Sergeant Murray, you can be a real asshole sometimes." A lot of soldiers who didn't work with me would say, "Sergeant Murray, you're so cool! But we're confused. The guys who work with you tell us you can be a real asshole. What gives?"

They're both right. It's like I told my guys all the time, "The way I look at it, we can be cool, cool, cool. But when it comes down to doing our jobs? If I tell you to do something, you do it. I'm telling you because I've got a damn good reason, and I'm sure as hell not going to have some incompetent kid get my ass killed because he did something dumb, all right? I'm going be a hard-ass because when that airplane touches down on American soil, I'm not getting carried off in a body bag, I'm *walking* off, and I want you there doing the same."

Yeah, I feel bad sometimes when I go into asshole mode with my soldiers. I can really put it on them when I do. But you know what? It's for everyone's benefit. Having served in Afghanistan, I knew the dangers. I was always nervous about land mines, for instance. Over there, they had mines all over the damn place. When you drove down a road, you had to *stay* on that road. You had to assume that everything else, the land all around you, was rigged somehow to explode. If you got ambushed in Afghanistan? That's it. You're dead. There's nothing out there, nowhere to hide, it's dead terrain. Standard procedure for an ambush says, get off the road, find some cover, and fight. But anybody staging an ambush would more than likely do it in a spot where getting off the road meant stepping on a land mine. So you're damned if you do and damned if you don't.

That's why in Iraq I told my guys, "Be careful here. Don't take street corners too tight when you're driving." Hell, I was the guy riding in the passenger seat, you know? You take a corner too sharp and your wheels go off the road into the shoulder even just a little bit, it's *ka-boom!* Goodbye. My guys would do it anyway, you know? A civilian habit. And I'd get pissed, I'd smoke 'em, yell at 'em, make em do push-ups. Twenty-five push-ups the first time, fifty the next. If they were stupid enough to let it happen again, it'd be fifty good ones dressed in full body armor and pack. That shit'll smoke the hell out of you.

Or maybe I'd make them stand guard with all their gear on in that godawful desert heat. The punishment didn't matter. I was trying to get them to understand that they needed to stop being a dumb-ass, wake up, and think of everybody else in the unit. I told them, "Listen, asshole. You drive off this road and get my legs blown off, I will shoot you myself, do you hear me?" They shouldn't take it personally. That's just how you are when you're a noncommissioned officer in the United States Army. Your job is to train your soldiers. It's an area where a lot of sergeants mess up, by the way. They try to be friends with their soldiers, and yes, you need to be friends, that's part of the game. But you can't let friendship override the fact that, when you tell them something, they have to listen to you. That's the way of the beast.

After all the combat we saw in Baghdad, the Eighty-second Airborne came in and replaced us. We moved north to Talifar, west of Mosul, and got a new job taking care of the Syrian-Turkish border. It was May and command kept telling us, "Relax, boys! We'll all be home by the Fourth of July!" You should have heard us cheer. We thought it would be a six-month rotation. By this point, we were having very few problems, a couple of attacks here and there, but our attitude was like, "Oh, some Baath Party dudes are still pissed off. No big deal." But when July came, they told us, "Sorry, July isn't going to happen, we'd be going home in September." When September came, we heard, "Home by Halloween." After that it was, "Don't even talk about redeployment. We're gonna be here for a while, end of story." When they finally got around to breaking it to us we'd be there a year, the shock was over.

What really sucked was I'd made staff sergeant in Afghanistan, so I needed to go to noncommissioned officer's school back in the States. I'd actually been scheduled to go just before deploying to Iraq. The deployment bumped me. Command took me aside while I was in Baghdad and said, "You're going to BNOC [Basic Noncommissioned Officer's School] in October." At the time, October had seemed so far away. I got to leave Iraq in late September to go back to school. The rest of my boys stayed until January 2003. They'd been gone since early February of 2002. Yeah, I felt bad because I got out early. Those were my boys. But at the same time, coming home—you're just glad to be back, no questions asked.

My wife was pregnant with my youngest son when I was in

Afghanistan. Communications over there sucked. You got ten minutes per call, and you had to use a military operator to call a stateside operator who connected you to the place you wanted. The effort to connect took most of your minutes. By the time I got to hear my wife's voice, my call was down to practically nothing.

At one point, I asked her, "Look, what're we gonna name our son?" She said, "I don't know." We started picking names real fast since we didn't have a lot of time. Nothing worked and I got frustrated. I said, "What about Gunner Harding Murray?"

She said, "Yeah, yeah. That's good!"

"Okay. Gotta go. Love you."

"I love you, too."

It wasn't until I started walking back to my guys that I thought, *Oh, hang on here a second, wait a minute.* When I finally told my guys what I'd named the kid, they razzed me but good. Know what, though? That name fits that kid. He's crazy as hell, that one, just like his old man.

WE WERE GOING HOME . . .

✹

Second Class Petty Officer Christopher L. Siddall ("Doc")
COMBAT MEDIC, U.S. NAVY RESERVE, ATTACHED TO CHARLIE COMPANY, FIRST LIGHT ARMORED RECONNAISSANCE DIVISION, USMC

"Doc" Siddall was born on-base at Camp Lejeune, North Carolina. His father was a marine who'd served two tours in Vietnam. Ever since he could remember, Christopher felt the corps running through his blood. He grew up in southeastern Pennsylvania, close to Philadelphia, and joined the full-time U.S. Navy in 1994. In the navy, he underwent the arduous training to become a corpsman, or medic. After that, destiny reclaimed him. While most navy medics are placed on duty assignments aboard ship or at base hospitals, Siddall was loaned out to the U.S. Marine Corps.

The Marine Corps falls under the Department of the Navy. However, the corps has no medical personnel among its MOS [military occupational specialties]. For this reason, whenever marine ground troops deploy for battle, U.S. Navy medics accompany them.

Siddall, now age 35, has served in the naval reserve since leaving the full-time navy in 1999. He volunteered for duty in Iraq, where he served for six months.

Charlie Company was light-armored reconnaissance, meaning we'd deploy ahead of the main attack force. They weren't my usual unit. For years, I'd worked with an air defense platoon. Problem was, Iraq didn't have much use for that kind of unit. So Command broke my unit apart and shipped us out in pieces. The guys in Charlie Company were complete strangers to me. I had to start from scratch getting to know all ninety-six of them. That's a lot to handle when you've been working with a unit for years, twice as hard when it's all brand new, ten times harder when you're on a battlefield getting shot at. I was the only medic in that group. I felt like I had my work cut out for me.

Our group consisted of eighteen light-armored vehicles, which I'm sure you've seen on television. They look like small tanks that have eight black tires instead of treads. There are several different versions of these things.[118] The guns on them are deadly. My LAV had a modified, six-barrel Gattling gun that fired 25 mm rounds at enormous volumes. It was great for taking out missiles, UAVs [unmanned aerial vehicles], helicopters, anything that flew. When you loaded that thing up with depleted uranium rounds? Man, it could tear through anything. It even mowed down armored units.

If the guns didn't work, you had another option: infantry squads could disembark from the vehicles and patrol on foot alongside. Mind you, we weren't trying to engage the enemy. We were actually trying to ferret out their locations, estimate troop strengths, and survey the topography. Check out what kind of equipment they had and report everything back to base. The idea was to *probe* the enemy. If anything, we wanted to avoid combat. That was our plan, at any rate. The Iraqis had different ideas.

We breached the border under cover of night the evening of March 18. We went in down by Basra in southeastern Iraq. None of us had ever been to combat before. Everybody was tense. I was the oldest guy in the group and the only thing I knew about fighting came from the stories my father told me about his two tours in Vietnam. My grandfather'd served in the Second World War II; he was a medic, too. So I grew up hearing all this stuff about combat but it didn't measure up to what I was feeling.

I don't know how to describe the mental state. Thoughts come spinning at you one hundred miles an hour. First I tried to anticipate anything and everything that could happen, which of course is completely impossible, but I tried to do it anyway. I found myself making mental checklists for every wound I'd ever studied. First I'll do this. Then I'll do this. Third step is this. Sanitize, bandage, evac. Job is done. My head was abuzz with all this mental traffic. Organizing. Prioritizing. Preparing. Bracing. Then nothing happened. No shots fired, no rockets launched, no shouts, nothing. And this went on, this period of intense anticipation, intense fear, apprehension, waiting, for three or four days.

118. Siddall explains: "Most LAVs carry 25 mm guns, three operators—a driver, a gunner, and a loader, plus a small squad of deployable infantry. Some LAVs carry mortars and antitank measures—I believe those have a five-soldier crew—plus their squad. And some LAVs carry supplies—these have a crew of six soldiers."

That's what combat is really like. It's not about the moment they start shooting at you. That's actually sort of a release. It's more about the waiting. The anticipation. Waiting, waiting, waiting. We hit Basra and nothing happened. Kept moving north, toward Naziriyah.

Now the real danger sets in. Again, it's not from combat. All this time you've been waiting and waiting causes thinking and thinking is a trap. Your head attempts to justify the silence. *Well,* you think. *This isn't so bad. Obviously, the Iraqis understand how outgunned they are. Their situation is hopeless. Maybe they'll lay down their weapons and we can get this over with real quick. Go back home, see the kids, take a hot shower. Man, I'd really love a hot shower right about now. . . .*

That's when the first ambush hits.

It snaps you awake, I tell you. First comes the weird thought of, *Wow, they're really shooting at us.* Then you watch your own hands pull your weapon up in slow-motion and mount it against your shoulder, like you're watching this on a film. You feel your finger click the safety off, site a target, and start squeezing off shots. Now comes another weird thought: *I'm shooting bullets at live human beings.*

Yes, corpsmen engage in combat. I carried an M-16 and a 9 mm M-9 pistol. According to the Geneva Conference, medics are designated noncombatants, but we're allowed to fire our weapons in defense of ourselves or our patients. Good luck interpreting that one. I've already tried. For instance, is it defending yourself if someone else is already firing at you? Or do you have to wait for one of your men to get hit? What about an ambush? Doesn't the very fact that you've been sneak-attacked put you immediately in a defensive posture? I found myself wishing someone had given me a bit more guidance on the subtleties involved with Geneva.

My grandfather told me that medics wore white armbands with red crosses back in the day. Grandpop called the insignias "targets," said he always took his off during combat. Lo and behold, he saved a few lives and got to come home alive. And did you know that a reason modern medics are issued rifles is because of Vietnam? In Vietnam, medics were only given pistols. It wasn't a great move. The Vietcong figured out pretty fast that the only people carrying pistols were officers, com-guys, and medics. Read: highly desirable targets. The whole designation of medics as noncombatants is ridiculous. If you're in a war zone, trust me, you're a combatant. They shot at me, so I shot back. End of story.

The ambushes would spring up out of nowhere. All hell would break loose for a while as we fought them off as best we could. Then the enemy would, for no reason at all, cease fire as quickly as they'd begun and melt away into nowhere, like ghosts.

Unless we got pinned down by heavy fire, we stayed constantly on the move, especially during those first few weeks. In fact, we kept up such a brisk pace that our drivers weren't getting adequate rest. Then we had supply problems. We outran our lines once we left Hilla. This was right about the time the whole Jessica Lynch incident happened, by the way; we heard about it over the radio and our vehicle commander gave us the details. Private Lynch was part of a supply convoy that had fallen under attack. That whole incident seemed completely indicative of our current problem. The push to strike at Iraq so hard and fast had stretched our supply routes until they snapped under the tension. The enemy saw the opening and took it.

Up until that point, we'd engaged in sporadic contact and gotten some close shaves. The Lynch thing made us take things more seriously. That hit my unit like a wake-up call. That's when we figured this shit was serious.

Nasiriyah, Diwaniyah, Hilla, and Tikrit. Our intelligence always seemed pretty unintelligent. Not that reports were ever completely divorced from reality. But when they indicated we'd find hordes of Iraqi troops, we found a few guardsmen taking a piss in the desert. When they said we'd find the next outpost "lightly fortified," we'd stumble onto a massive fortress brimming with mortars, rockets, artillery, and infantry. After a while, we stopped paying attention to intelligence.

The ambushes kept coming stronger now, heavy fire from AK-47s, RPGs, and mortars. The mortar fire in particular got pretty good at zeroing in on us, which made us nervous. LAVs are called light-skinned vehicles because they aren't armored to the same degree as, say, an M1 Abrams. I don't know the armor plating's technical specifications, but they're practically impenetrable to rifle fire. Not RPGs and mortars, though, that can damage them. At one point, one of our vehicles got whacked with a 20 mm canon round. It damaged the vehicle but didn't penetrate the armor. As far as I know, none of our LAVs experienced an armor breach, but that was cold comfort. You never wanted to push that envelope too far.

I remember the first wound I had to treat. We were caught in an ambush and I was in the process of returning fire when I heard the call. "Corpsman! I'm hit!" Then it's you thinking, *Oh, shit. Here we go.*

THE TRUTH (?) BEHIND JESSICA LYNCH

On March 23, 2003, Iraqi soldiers ambushed the army 507th Maintenance Company in the city of Nasiriyah. Jessica Lynch, a twenty-year-old female private from West Virginia, was abducted during the raid. The *Washington Post* reported that Lynch "sustained multiple gunshot wounds," and was stabbed as she "fought fiercely and shot several enemy soldiers . . . firing her weapon until she ran out of ammunition." According to a U.S. military official cited anonymously in the article, Private Lynch was seen "fighting to the death." Naturally, within days, this story buzzed across headlines around the world.

Army Rangers and navy SEALS were mobilized for a rescue raid on the Nasiriyah hospital where Lynch was being held. The mission proved successful and Private Lynch was liberated. But even as the raid was being hailed as a testament to American bravery, discrepancies began to appear within the accounts of Lynch's capture and liberation.

First of all, Lynch did not appear to be as damaged as some reports had indicated. Intense pressure was levied against the *Washington Post* to confirm its reporting but the paper's ombudsman, Michael Getler, eventually concluded that, despite the *Post*'s gripping account of Lynch's heroics, "what really happened is still not clear."

As more and more disturbing evidence accumulated, the entire incident, including the Ranger/SEAL raid, began to look more and more like the product of U.S. military propaganda. Lynch herself did little to clarify matters. Her handlers begged off from answering specific questions, stating that Lynch had "amnesia," had been "raped," "tortured," and worse. But no hard evidence surfaced to substantiate any of these claims. If anything, contradictory stories ruled the day.

Lynch later received a million-dollar book deal for *I Am a Soldier, Too* (Knopf, 2003). The author, Rick Bragg, is a former *New York Times* reporter and Pulitzer Prize–winner who quit his paper after admitting that freelancers did much of his reporting for him. Critics lambasted Bragg's writing in *I Am a Soldier, Too*, noting that he'd tossed aside fact-based journalism in favor of cinematic storytelling. For instance, Bragg wrote: "Everyone knew what Saddam's soldiers did to women captives . . . In [Lynch's] worst nightmares, she stood alone in that desert as the trucks of her own army pulled away." The intimation of rape is clear. The evidence, if any exists to corroborate the crime, is not.

An Iraqi lawyer, Mohammed al-Rehaief, later claimed that he helped Lynch during her imprisonment. Lynch, in turn, contradicted nearly all of al-Rehaief's contentions and furthermore stated she'd never met him. Nevertheless, NBC Studios coproduced a made-for-TV movie, *Saving Jessica Lynch*, based on al-Rehaief's account. Lynch refused to cooperate with the making of the film.

In the end, the Jessica Lynch incident may best be remembered as an early barometer for American public sentiment toward the war in Iraq. To citizens who wholeheartedly supported "Shock and Awe," Jessica Lynch became a polarizing symbol of patriotism and human rights. But for those still wondering why weapons of mass destruction were never found in Iraq—and what link, if any, Iraq had to the terrorist attacks of 9/11—the story of Jessica Lynch became another disturbing example of government propaganda's inciting Americans to war.

Ten years of military training led up to that moment. I grabbed my bag and moved. It's not a cliché. Your training really does take over. Once I shrugged off the shock of things blowing up all around me, the chatter-box of incoming and outgoing fire, shell fragments and debris ricochet-ing off steel, rock and sand, the sight of real blood, believe it or not, it's really not all that different from doing exercises on the training ground.

The marine who'd called me had a shrapnel wound. An RPG blew up next to him and sent hot metal into the meat of his shoulder and leg. Relatively minor, the shoulder was worse than the leg. Neither injury was immediately life-threatening so long as we got him on the next chopper out. I set about prepping him for that. While I was bandaging him, I told the guy, "You're lucky," which became a sort of catchphrase for me when dealing with the wounded. The way I saw it, anybody alive enough to hear me while I patched them up *was* lucky.

Treating that first wound was a turning point for me. It made me re-alize that yeah, I could do this. But the best part about treating that first soldier was when I'd finished bandaging him. The medevac chopper was coming in, he looked at me and said, "Thanks, Doc." Made my day? That came close to making my whole life.

See, every corpsman who goes out into the field relinquishes a tiny piece of himself. It's the only way we can function. Your rank, for instance, doesn't matter anymore. Rank's not important to a guy who's bleeding, so you leave it behind. Where you come from, where you're going, that doesn't matter, either. Nobody cares if you're a smart aleck, an asshole, or Mother Teresa. They care about your technique, that's it. How good are you at your job? When the shells start dropping and the guns begin to chatter and everything's smoke and dust and fire, a medic even leaves his name behind. Every corpsman in the history of the armed forces goes by the same title. Everyone calls us "Doc."

It's such a simple word, like "Mom" or "Bro" or "Dad." Corpsmen cherish it. Were we trying to pass ourselves off as physicians, hell no. Medics know that our job isn't to heal wounds, it's to stabilize them. We never overstep our link in the chain of aid. We prep wounded soldiers so we can pass them on to the doctors who heal them, that's it. We love the name "Doc" for other reasons. Because when someone calls out for "Doc," an instinct kicks in. I don't know what to call it. Your job? Your essence? Your training? It's something vital to who you are, that's all I know.

"Doc" is like a synonym for "Help me." It could be a cry of pain that means, "I'm hit!" or maybe it's a confession: "Heal me, please, I want to live." When someone calls you "Doc," you realize why you've devoted your life to your job, why you worked your skills for years on end. It was all so that, one day, you could stand the ground that runs between a man's life and his death, and maybe make a difference. You might be the one person who decides whether a fellow soldier, your brother, goes home with a scar and a scary story to tell his family, or in a body bag. On the battlefield, there's so much destruction. To be the guy who embodies, I don't know, life? Another day, a return trip home? Hope? That's an awesome thing, and that's what a medic in combat becomes.

There's no such thing as a standardized load for a combat medic's pack. I stocked my bag with whatever I thought my guys would need in the field: Lots of IVs, morphine, and sedatives, lots and lots of bandages, plus a general assortment of what I call the comfort medications, stuff to treat headaches, minor aches and pains, fever sweats, upset stomachs. I carried antidotes for nerve and chemical agents, I had epinephrine and atropine and this one antinerve agent, I don't remember the name, which came in a purple auto-injector. You'd break the seal on the device, pop it out, and slap it against your thigh or buttocks. The spring-loader would inject a needle into your muscle and deliver the right amount of medication. Simple. Each marine carried his own supply of this medicine. If we got hit by bio-chem agents, everyone was expected to self-treat before being overcome by the toxin.

This was a good procedure. Imagine how busy a medic would be if someone shouted, "Nerve gas!" and all of a sudden the entire platoon started swarming over me to grab an antidote injector. I kept antidote reserves in case I had to treat someone who'd been incapacitated, but we never needed them. Iraq had no chemical weapons.

In our travels, we ended up with six wounded and one KIA [killed in action]. The fatality didn't come from combat, we had a vehicle accident. Since we were in the reconnaissance business, we conducted most of our movement at night. Darkness allowed us to keep a low profile. Iraq is basically a third-world country, so the roads we were typically moving along were dirt roads. A lot of times we found ourselves traveling parallel to the banks of the Tigris River, which had steep and sudden declines in elevation. One night we were driving near the banks, when the road gave out from under a 25 mm turret vehicle. The LAV rolled off the bank, down the slope, flipping over two or three times, and wound up perched on its side. The crew's loader was stationed in the back of the vehicle. When the vehicle rolled, all the equipment packed within started flying around inside it, ammunition, machine parts, you name it. The loader was injured in the crash.

He didn't die right away. We pulled him from the vehicle comatose. He never regained consciousness. He had a lot of intercranial swelling, so the cause of death was listed as head trauma. Something must have clipped him on pretty good. There was nothing we could do.

The irony of it. Such a stupid way to go. I felt horrible. Here I was, a medic in a combat zone. People were shooting guns and rockets at us day in and day out like someone had painted targets on our backs and, in the middle of all that, something stupid happens and claims the life of a good man. Believe it or not, vehicle accidents and other stupid things have been responsible for more injuries and death than enemy fire in Iraq.

One of our guys turned out to be extremely lucky. We got hit with an ambush when his LAV wasn't buttoned down.[119] He was sitting up front and an enemy soldier shot him with an AK-47 through the window.

Charlie Company'd been issued flak jackets without the armored SAPI plates which slide into the pouches. The AK round went through the front of his supposedly bullet-proof vest. Clean entry and clean exit, a flesh wound right through the soft tissue of his flank. Very, very lucky. AK-47s use 7.62 mm rounds that tumble through the air a certain distance after discharge. All that tumbling turns the bullet into a jagged shard of metal that'll tear an awfully big wound in human flesh. We're talking about rounds that are markedly larger than the 5.56 mm round used in the standard U.S. issue M-16. AK rounds hit with a tremendous impact and incredible terminal force, creating a very large shockwave.

AK-47 rounds cause what we call large cavitation wounds. You know how you drop a pebble in a pool of standing water and a ring spreads out? That's a shockwave. In ballistics-speak: cavitation. Bullets do the

119. The armored hatches on the vehicle weren't closed.

same thing when they hit soft tissue and AK-47 rounds are so large, move so fast that they cause cavitation waves which can displace organs and cause incredible internal damage. You have to keep this in mind when you're tending your wounded. Thank God no one in my platoon was struck directly in the torso or head. Medic friends from other units told me awful stories. One guy had a soldier get shot in the head by an AK-47. The round tore the back of his skull off.

Another Charlie Company soldier got shot in the arm. He'd been standing up in the back of the vehicle when he got ambushed. While I was bandaging him, he told me he hadn't even realized he'd been wounded at first. He thought that hot brass had ejected from the gun of the soldier standing next to him and maybe slid under his sleeve. That turned out not to be the case. The fighting was over by the time he'd figured out what had really happened. By that point, he'd had a chance to calm himself down so I didn't treat him in a heat-of-the-battle *Saving Private Ryan* type of moment. It was more of an "Okay, show's over, enemy's dead," and "Geez, will you look at what the hell happened to me?" kind of thing.

I told him he was lucky, too, and I meant it. A few inches to one side or the other and the flesh wound he was griping about could have disemboweled him. Also, this guy got off without any broken bones, which are very common when someone takes an AK round in a limb. This gentleman got hit in his forearm, the round passed right between the radius and ulna bones. Unbelievably lucky.

We had a couple more soldiers suffer fragmentation wounds from RPGs that exploded in close proximity. But all in all, aside from the one KIA, we were incredibly lucky soldiers.

The lack of personal armor pissed us off, sure. Our flak jackets were like vests, heavy pieces of equipment like the lead blankets a doctor or a dentist drapes over your body when you have an X-ray taken. They're designed to stop shrapnel from grenades, artillery, and mortar explosions. Supposedly, they'll stop any round moving at pistol velocity but I wouldn't want to test that. They specifically do *not* stop rifle rounds, so the army came up with the SAPI plates, which could be added to a vest's front and back. The plates slide into prestitched pouches and do a pretty good job of protecting the vital organs of the torso, the heart, lungs, the majority of the spinal column, and so forth.

Obviously, the lack of body armor's been a big point of contention. My unit, for instance, was told we'd receive the insert plates prior to crossing into Iraq. We got barely enough to armor our drivers; the rest of the unit had to go without. It pissed us off a little, but morale was pretty high overall. Most civilians don't understand this but anyone who's been in the military for a while accepts getting the short end of the stick. The lack of delivery on SAPI plates didn't strike us as any great surprise. None of us really counted on them. When they didn't come, we shrugged and were like, "What are you gonna do? You still have to fight the war, right?"

Some funny stories? Sure, I've got a few. One time we were pulling patrol a lot up near Tikrit. By this point, the president had declared an end to major combat operations, which actually didn't achieve much. From where we stood, we were still getting shot at just as frequently. We'd stopped moving around so much and set up checkpoints so that every day we were searching civilians for weapons. We were living in concentration and, as normally happens in that situation, someone caught a bug and, man, did he pass it around. Call it a natural consequence of being in a foreign country where sanitation standards and hygiene practices are, for lack of a better word, backward. Or call it viral gastroenteritis. Whatever it was, it ripped through our platoon, vomiting, diarrhea, the shakes. It was awful and it hit everyone. As corpsman, I wasn't immune.

One night we were out on patrol and I had a bad case of diarrhea. You know that old saying, "When you gotta go, you gotta go"? I assure you, no truer words were ever spoken. I signaled the patrol leader who called a halt to the column. Everyone dropped down, took a knee, and started scanning the darkness, searching. I didn't worry about modesty, I scuttled off the road like a crab, dropped trow, and went to work. I was right in the middle of my procedure when I turned my head left and noticed a tunnel.

We called them spider holes. Iraqi insurgents had dug them all over the country, they were deadly little places. Men could stuff inside, packed to the gills, waiting for the right opportunity to burst forth and start shooting like madmen. Spider holes meant ambush, and here I was, literally with my pants down, squatting a few feet away from one. The first thought that went through my head was, *Oh shit.* Fittingly enough.

I groped for my weapon and tried to bring it around at the same time I heaved myself to my feet, bare-assed, staggering, flailing my arms so I didn't step in my own mess. I was torn between screaming for help and trying not to make a sound. I didn't know what was down that hole and I sure didn't want to find out while my shorts were around my ankles. So I started shuffle-stepping toward the road, that step you do when your pants have roped your ankles together. I was so damn scared I thought my heart was going to burst out my rib cage. When I got to what I thought was a safe distance I started hollering like hell.

We investigated the spider hole. It was abandoned—a stockpile of RPG rounds inside, nothing else. Then the jokes started: "Hey! Hear what happened to Doc? He got the shit scared out of him." "Naw, he was just outta ammo, had to use whatever he could." "Doc, is that really a spider hole? I mean shit, Doc. *Shit!* Is that really a spider hole?"

I think I would have preferred the ambush.

Combat marines joke about everything. It keeps them sane. My guys laughed about their gunshot wounds. The soldier who was sitting in the LAV, for instance. He got hit in the flank and kept howling how he deserved the Purple Heart. "I'm gonna get my Purple Heart! Hyeeeah! Purple Heart, baby! Bring it! Now!"

I told him to shut up, for the love of God. I had a simple rule when dealing with combat wounds: no morphine meant no Purple Heart. This guy didn't need morphine, he needed a cold beer and a hot shower. "Don't even ask," I told him. "Don't even ask." "Aw, come on, Doc. Pleeeease?"

I love the marines. They're like a different breed of animal altogether. I'd never go into combat with anybody else. To say that Marines are gung ho[120] is an understatement. They're *very* intense soldiers. They operate from a singular mind-set: get the job done, period. Make no mis-

---

120. *Gung ho* is a military expression first introduced by Lieutenant Colonel Evans F. Carlson and adopted by the U.S. Marine Corps Second Raider Battalion in 1942. Apparently, the word derives from the Mandarin Chinese abbreviation for the Chinese Industrial Cooperative Society, a Communist organization that Carlson admired greatly. Literally, the words *kung* and *ho* mean "work" and "peace/harmony," respectively. Evidently, Carlson introduced the phrase to his men as an imperative for them to work together. Amusingly enough, this interpretation has nothing to do with the actual Chinese etymology. Also amusing is the fact that a phrase with such a strong background in communism became the unofficial mantra of the U.S. Marine Corps as far back as the early '40s. The phrase *gung ho* has since expanded in meaning to indicate incredible spirit, zealousness, courage, or loyalty. The phrase has also been used disparagingly to indicate an unthinking excess of these qualities.

take, though, these men are not robots. They're the most highly trained, incredibly disciplined fighting force on the planet. They fear God, they love their country and their brother soldiers. They fight to win and accept nothing less.

You know what else? To a man, marines possess a sense of honor which I've never seen matched in any other branch of the U.S. armed services, including the navy. When you're in combat with a marine, you never doubt that somebody's got your back. You can count on those men to give everything they have to any situation, any situation at all. I'm humbled to have stood beside them in service to our country. They never said it in words because marines don't say things like this. But it was clear that they accepted me as one of their own. Who needs a medal or a commendation after that? The respect of a marine is the highest military honor any soldier can hope to receive.

Another time in Tikrit we stopped an old Toyota truck because it had blue license plates. In Iraq, blue plates indicated that the driver was Baath Party. There were three guys in the truck. One of them had papers which he kept thrusting at us over and over. We couldn't tell what the documents said since they were written in Arabic. Even though they looked official, we decided to detain these gentlemen. We'd take them down to Intel where they had translators, let Intel figure the whole thing out, interrogate them or do whatever it was they did; it wasn't our problem. We had the Iraqis get out of the Toyota.

We bound their wrists with flexi-cuffs and put them in the LAV for transport. But no one knew what to do with their truck. We couldn't just leave it there for someone to come and steal so we decided to impound it, drive it back to the base and hand it over along with the Iraqis. Me and a couple guys climbed into the truck, cranked the motor and followed the LAVs home.

Well, have you ever taken a cab in Tijuana, Mexico? Vehicles in Iraq were like that: not in the best of repair. We were driving along behind the transports and we'd worked up a pretty good head of speed when we discovered the truck didn't have any brakes. The driver started stomping the pedal, but his boot just crushed the damn thing down against the firewall. He started screaming, "Okay! No brakes! No brakes!" This was not a good situation. Of course, by this point, we'd reached the base gates and the LAVs had stopped ahead of us. We were practically on top of them and gaining real fast.

The driver said, "Shit!" and we all went *Whooooooaaaa!* He twisted the wheel and swerved us out of the way just in time to avoid collision with the LAVs. But the swerve steered us right in line with the base's front gate. We were barreling toward it like a missile. You could see the faces of the soldiers standing guard, the way their eyes widened when they saw this Iraqi wreck coming in, jumping the curb at high speed. With all the dust and confusion, they had no idea American soldiers were inside. The guards swung their automatic weapon around, took a bead, and were about to open fire when we crashed into the concrete median. We hit it head on and broke the truck's axle among other things. The crash was horrendous. We were tossed around like rag dolls in the truck's interior. Some guys ended up hanging out the windows with their weapons dangling. All in all, the crash was pretty fortunate. If we hadn't stopped the truck, that gun would have opened up on us and torn the Toyota to tissue paper.

Nobody was hurt, it was just another close call. Again the jokes started coming in. Everyone called us Delta Force.[121] Apparently, with all of us hanging out the windows like that, we looked like a Delta mission trying to crash the gates, disembark, and attack. Man, they just wouldn't let that quit for a long, long while: "Ooh, look! It's Delta Force! The *elite* have arrived! My, my! How disciplined you guys are! We hear you're the best. Not just the best, they're the best of the best!"

(Sigh.)

What's the saddest thing I saw happen over there? Unfortunately, two incidents come to mind. One of them showed me how war affected the Iraqis, the other showed me how the war had affected us.

In the early days of April we were holding down a section southwest of Baghdad called Sadr City. The fighting there was intense; we experienced heavy incoming fire on a routine basis. One day, an Iraqi man came running up to us holding a child, a baby boy who couldn't have

---

121. The army's First Special Forces Operational Detachment—Delta (First SFOD-D) is perhaps the premiere counterterrorism unit in the United States military. The Pentagon keeps a tight lid on what is known publicly about this unit, but it's clear that Delta Force soldiers are mainly recruited from the Green Berets and Rangers. Delta Force's main function is hostage rescue.

been more than a year old. The baby'd been shot. A bullet had entered his torso under the right arm and exited out the other side. The child was dead, but the Iraqi man didn't understand that. Or maybe it's more accurate to say he hadn't accepted it yet. He'd brought the child to us and he was screaming in Arabic. We couldn't understand a word of what he was saying. It was obvious he was pleading with us to do something—we didn't need an interpreter to figure that out—but the child was dead, there was nothing we could do. We tried explaining that to this man right there in the middle of the gunfire, the explosions, the shouting, the smoke. The baby was gone but he wouldn't believe it. He had this crazy hope in his eyes that went beyond all reason.

Seeing an innocent child meet an end like that was difficult, I have two kids of my own. But to see that man—maybe he was the boy's father, I don't know. To see that man trying to will that baby back to life with every fiber of his being . . . It broke my heart.

Then something else happened, much later. It's been almost two years since this occurred and I still don't know what to make of it. It wakes me up in the middle of the night.

My platoon finished its tour and crossed the border back into the safety of Kuwait. The plane was coming for us. We had less than thirty-six hours left in the Middle East. Do you get what I'm saying here? In less than thirty-six hours, we'd board a plane and fly back to the States. We were going home.

Me and a bunch of maybe twenty guys were playing football in the field outside our barracks tent. We heard a gunshot. Everyone froze. We thought it was a round exploding in one of the amnesty pits.[122] It wasn't. A moment later, this guy comes tearing out of a tent. He's got an M-16 in his hands and he sees us, he freezes. Everybody's like a statue, we're all looking at each other, no one knows what to do. Then the marine pointed his weapon at us.

122. Siddall explains: "Before you ship home, soldiers go through stages of preparation. You're not allowed to bring any weapons or ammunition back to the States so you turn all that in. But if, for example, you forget to turn something in—which happens a lot over there—a few pits have been dug around base—we call them amnesty pits. And before anyone finds out you're holding a piece of contraband, you can toss it in the amnesty pits and that's it—you're off the hook, no questions asked. Those pits fill up with everything you can imagine. Lots of ammunition. It's not unusual for someone to find a stray round in their packs, for instance—so they throw it in the pit and that's what we thought had happened: somehow a bullet had fired itself off. Evidently not, though."

He didn't have a magazine in the rifle; you learn to notice things like this when you've been in combat. The only danger he could've posed came from the one round he might have kept in the chamber, the one round he'd apparently fired already. The next thing I knew, someone started screaming for a medic from inside the tent. Nobody said a word. In an instant, everyone dropped the football game and ran down the marine with the rifle, beat the crap out of him. I ran inside the tent to see what had happened.

I burst in. The first thing I saw was a bunch of marines standing around, shocked, and another soldier, one of our own, lying on the floor. There was blood everywhere. My first impression was that he'd taken one in the head and was dead as a doornail. But then he started moving. His eyes blinked open and he said, very clearly, "I've been shot," which snapped me into another mode altogether. I moved in to do my job.

The first thing to do was find the entry wound. It took me a few seconds, but there it was, slightly left-of-center on the neck, left of the trachea, beneath the jaw. I couldn't figure out how he'd gotten hit so high up, but then I was looking for the second thing, the exit wound. I couldn't find that, either, at first. With a neck wound, I didn't want to move the marine around too much; that could lead to spinal compromise which might paralyze him if he wasn't there already. All the same, I had to control the bleeding. We had to find where that round went out, if indeed it exited at all.

Then, all of a sudden, there it was. The shot had traveled down at a severe angle and blasted out the soldier's back, through his left shoulder blade. He must have been sitting on the floor or something when somebody, the marine with the M-16, came up practically right on top of him, pointed the rifle barrel down at his neck, and pulled the trigger, point-blank range, blowing him away. I thought this kid was going to die right there and then. By all rights, he should have been dead already. There aren't many places in the neck you can take a bullet without receiving a fatal wound. The way blood was spurting, I figured the shot had hit the jugular and that was that. Anytime the carotid or jugular is compromised you've got about thirty seconds before the victim bleeds out and dies.

Remember I said the soldier who'd been hit in the flank was *one* of the luckiest guys I've ever seen? This neck wound kid had him beat. By far, this kid was *the* luckiest man in the world. Thirty seconds had already expired and there he was, still talking and moving. I started to think, Maybe he's got a chance after all. Amazingly, he never lost consciousness the whole time I was with him. I kept monitoring his pulse, it was strong and steady. He was talking and moving and saying all the usual shit somebody says when they get hit, "My God, my God. Help me, please, don't let me die."

Eventually we pieced together what had happened. Jesus Christ, it was so stupid.

The marine who got shot was a vehicle commander. The gentleman who shot him was a member of his own crew. Apparently, the crewman wanted to get something from their vehicle, but it had already been sealed for the voyage home. That's standard procedure. After final inspection, vehicles are locked. From that point on, no one but the vehicle's commander has access to them. This is done to prevent theft and smuggling. The two men had some sort of verbal exchange, which escalated into physical confrontation, a lot of pushing and shoving. After that, the crewmember left, and everyone thought that was the end of it. Apparently not. He came back three hours later. The vehicle commander was sitting on the floor of the barracks tent, playing cards with a few other guys. The crewmember walked right up and shot him with his M-16, point-blank range.

Like I said, we were less than thirty-six hours from going home. Now the one kid, the shooter, he's going to spend the rest of his life in Leavenworth.[123] And the other? The kid who got shot? It's unbelievable that kid lived. Trust me: unbelievable. The point-blank shot turned out to be fortunate, as was the fact that the bullet was one of our own 5.56 rounds. At such close range, the bullet didn't have a chance to start spinning and tumbling. It was a smaller round, and it didn't do a whole lot of damage before it tore out a chunk of his shoulder and exited his body. Plus, when the shooter pressed the muzzle of the gun against his comman-

---

123. Leavenworth Federal Penitentiary, located 15 miles northwest of Kansas City, Kansas, began incarcerating inmates from the nearby army disciplinary barracks in 1903. Today, Leavenworth is the largest maximum security prison and houses some two thousand inmates—many of them U.S. soldiers who have committed serious crimes.

der's neck, he missed the vital blood vessels. Call that a one-in-a-million chance. The shot nicked the carotid and that was serious—that was what caused the spurting blood. The carotid's like a high-pressure hose; one tiny point of compromise and it'll tear itself open within seconds. You bleed out. Even a nick in the carotid can kill you. I tell you, God must have been watching over this kid.

Another fortunate circumstance: the incident occurred on base. We had a dozen corpsmen plus a physician in the tent within five minutes. I held the wound closed and applied pressure to stop the bleeding until they arrived. When the doctor came in and squatted down, he took a good look at the kid and determined he was having trouble breathing. The force of the shot had blown the victim's trachea over to one side. We performed an emergency tracheotomy,[124] which had to be done without anesthesia due to the nature of the injury. The surgeon had a hard time performing the procedure because the trachea had shifted so much with the force of the shot. I know for a fact that it caused a lot of pain for the kid. There was nothing to be done, though. That procedure, however painful, saved the kid's life.

He was stabilized and flown by medevac to a hospital in Kuwait. From there, I hear he went to Frankfurt, Germany, where the U.S. military has a big hospital. I also heard that he started hemorrhaging again on the way over. They had to perform another emergency surgery on the plane.

A little epilogue. Later on, stateside, I was on base when I ran into that kid. He had a lot of bandages around his neck and he wasn't out of the woods just yet, but he was healing. He was walking and talking and living. That's the happy ending.

Don't ask me what causes an incident like that. Don't ask me what was going through the shooter's mind to take out one of his own buddies—over what? Over nothing. Call it psychotic behavior. Call it an incident of post-traumatic stress. Go ahead and call it anything you want. It doesn't matter. It happened, that's all that's important. I don't think we'll ever know what caused it, not really. I didn't know either one of the

124. A tracheotomy is a surgical procedure that creates a temporary opening in the trachea to facilitate breathing when the windpipe is otherwise blocked. The hole itself is called a tracheotomy. The tube which is placed through this hole in order to conduct the passage of air is called a tracheotomy tube.

men involved, they were from a different unit. But I tell you, I had a lot of nightmares after that wherein I tried to figure out what went wrong. I still have nightmares.

I mean, after all we'd been through. We were going home. You understand that, right? We were going home.

Ed. Note: "Doc" Siddall currently lives in Southern California, just north of the 29 Palms marine base. He is divorced and working to raise his two sons—ages thirteen and eight—while completing his degree in criminal justice.

THE MATURITY COMBAT
TEACHES

✴

Sergeant Jason Adamiec
UNITED STATES MARINES, GOLF COMPANY, 2ND BATTALION,
2ND MARINES

Sergeant Adamiec, age 24, hails from a military family in Lombard, Illinois, a suburb of Chicago. He joined the U.S. Marines in 1999 and served on active duty for almost five years. Currently he is enrolled as a full-time student at Eastern Illinois University. His military status is listed as Inactive Reserve, but he plans to reenlist in the Active Reserve as soon as possible.

Eastern Illinois is a medium-sized university that boasts approximately ten thousand matriculating full-time students. In this busy environment, surrounded by younger incoming students who haven't had the experience of fighting a war in a foreign country, Sergeant Adamiec treasures the discipline taught to him by the United States Marine Corps.

I had a very big mouth and I ran it off to a lot of people my freshman and sophomore years in high school. I got into lots of fights with teachers because I had a great big problem with authority. My GPA [grade point average] was horrible. Picture me back then: I was wearing shorts that came down to my ankles and a Mr. T starter kit—three fat gold chains around my neck. I thought I was a Little Bad Ass.

Then I started dating this girl my junior year. I became friends with her older brother and things started to change. This guy was on the other side of the spectrum. He gave me the third degree for a long time because he wanted to know what kind of guy was dating his sister. I didn't get angry at him, I sort of respected that. I understood he was just looking out for his little sister. And the more I respected this guy, the more I started to change my ways. At the time, I was very concerned about the status of my social life; this guy showed me you can do good in school and have a social life, too. We became best friends and I worked my butt off junior and senior years trying to make up for the damage I'd already done.

I ended up graduating in the top half of my class. Not a fantastic showing but that's okay. Enlisting in the marines was the best move I ever made.

I've had some experiences that set me apart from the average college freshman. The other students I know repeat the media's point of view on the war. A few agree that the U.S. should be in Iraq, but most are extreme liberals who don't see any sense in what we're doing there.

I remember when the Abu Ghraib[125] scandal hit. The story seemed like no big deal at first. Then the pictures began to surface on the news, and details began to circulate. After that, the American public wanted answers and students on my campus saw it as another reason to pull out of Iraq. I was mad as hell about it, same as everyone else. I was mad for a different reason, though. To me, Abu Ghraib was a scandal because it gave the totally wrong representation of the majority of American forces functioning abroad.

The whole thing was an embarrassment to me. I remember watching one interview with a soldier, I believe he was an army staff sergeant. He said he'd received no formal training in the handling of prisoners of war, as if this was his justification for stripping prisoners naked, handcuffing them, and beating them. I don't know how they do things in the army, but in the United States Marine Corps everybody from a buck private on up is given very specific orders to follow the Geneva Conventions. We're told to regard prisoners as people. We also, by the way, have something called common sense.

We took prisoners when I was in Iraq. In Kut Al Hai in April 2003, one of our platoons captured seven prisoners from a building they'd raided. But everything was done by the book. No mistreatment. No un-

---

125. The Abu Ghraib story was exposed to the media on January 13, 2005, when Joseph Darby, a young military policeman assigned to the Abu Ghraib prisoner facility, reported repeated and bizarre cruelties to prisoners held there to army's Criminal Investigation Division. As well as outraging the American public, the incident allegedly involved depicted key members of the presidential cabinet—notably Secretary of Defense Donald Rumsfeld and National Security Advisor Condoleezza Rice. For a thorough article detailing the far-reaching ramifications of the Abu Ghraib scandal, see: "Anals of National Security: The Gray Zone" by Seymour M. Hersh, writing for *The New Yorker* magazine, May 24, 2005.

necessary hitting. These men were not mistreated in any way, they were no longer considered combatants. As such, they were to be treated as human beings and taken to the holding area where Intel would debrief them humanely. We'd been given specific instructions on how not to overstep the boundaries of the Geneva Conventions. In fact, we'd even been given little plastic laminated cards that had the Geneva Convention codes typed out.

The other side of the card had the CFLCC[126] Rules for Engagement. It spelled out procedures such as No Warning Shots, the rationale behind that being that gunfire tends to escalate a situation rather than defuse it, especially in a war zone. If you saw a situation happening and you felt the urge to fire your weapon and assert your authority—no. There's another rule for engagement called the Escalation of Force rule. Meaning: Always apply the lowest measure of force to a situation in order to get the job done. If the opposition chooses to escalate force, that's their decision. We don't operate that way, we try to calm the situation down until we have no other option but to kill every enemy in sight.

CFLCC ROE CARD

On order, enemy military and paramilitary forces are declared hostile and may be attacked subject to the following instructions:

a) Positive identification (PID) is required prior to engagement. PID is a reasonable certainty that the proposed target is a legitimate military target. If no PID, contact your next higher commander for decision.

b) Do not engage anyone who has surrendered or is out of battle due to sickness or wounds.

c) Do not target or strike any of the following except in self-defense to protect yourself, your unit, friendly forces, and designated persons or property under your control: Civilians,

---

126. Coalition Forces Land Component Command—these laminated cards were distributed to all U.S. Army and Marine personnel in Iraq.

Hospitals, mosques, national monuments, and any other historical and cultural sites.

d) Do not fire into civilian populated areas or buildings unless the enemy is using them for military purposes or if necessary for your self-defense. Minimize collateral damage.

e) Do not target enemy infrastructure (public works, commercial communication facilities, dams), Lines of Communication (roads, highways, tunnels, bridges, railways) and Economic Objects (commercial storage facilities, pipelines) unless necessary for self-defense or if ordered by your commander. If you must fire on these objects to engage a hostile force, disable and disrupt but avoid destruction of these objects, if possible.

The use of force, including deadly force, is authorized to protect the following: Yourself, your unit, and friendly forces.

Enemy Prisoners of War

1. Civilians from crimes that are likely to cause death or serious bodily harm, such as murder or rape.

2. Designated civilians and/or property, such as personnel of the Red Cross/Crescent, UN, and US/UN supported organizations.

3. Treat all civilians and their property with respect and dignity. Do not seize civilian property, including vehicles, unless you have the permission of a company level commander and you give a receipt to the property's owner.

Detain civilians if they interfere with mission accomplishment or if required for self-defense. CENTCOM General Order No. 1A remains in effect. Looting and the taking of war trophies are prohibited.

REMEMBER
Attack enemy forces and military targets.
Spare civilians and civilian property, if possible.

Conduct yourself with dignity and honor.
Comply with the Law of War. If you see a violation, report it.
These ROE will remain in effect until your commander orders
you to transition to post-hostilities ROE.

Every marine had to have this card on him at all time. When in doubt, you checked the card or asked a superior for clarification. I don't think you can get a procedure much simpler than that, so to me what happened in Abu Ghraib was an isolated incident of poor discipline and poor leadership. Unfortunately it gave a black eye to the entire United States military.

When my group first entered Iraq, our protocol for engagement was this: if you see someone with an AK-47, shoot them. After the initial invasion, that protocol changed. AK-47s were floating around all over Iraq and a large percentage of the population carried them for personal protection. So the rule became more or less like this: if you see someone with an AK-47, that's permissible. If they raise the rifle in a gesture of attack? Then you could shoot them.

We did a lot of vehicle check points and performed some raids. In a town called Al kel Zakar we worked side by side with the Iraqi police, going door to door to inspect houses. Unfortunately, the Iraqi police were extremely corrupt. They were basically under Baath Party control, so they'd take every opportunity to steer us in the wrong direction when we'd go out on patrol. They never led us to the houses of Baath Party members, they showed us the homes of regular families. The deception started to become pretty obvious, though. The Iraqi police would take our lieutenant aside and say, "Yes, yes. This is a Baath Party house, right over there." Our whole unit would get pumped up because this was potentially dangerous work. It didn't matter if we were going into the most innocent-looking place you could imagine, we never cleared a building half-assed. You always had to consider that maybe you were walking into a house full of well-armed Baathists. So we'd get pumped up and enter the house. What would we find? Six little kids and two old ladies sitting around on the floor, staring at us. These people weren't Baath-related at all, they were harmless. They also had no idea what we were doing there. After doing that a couple times, we caught on pretty quick. The police weren't helping, so we changed our procedure. We kept uniformed Iraqi policemen with us but we started approaching whatever houses we felt posed a threat.

It was stressful work, we were constantly on our toes. Adding to the pressure was the fact that Iraqi children would come out into the streets in packs and follow our patrols. Adults never did that, they seemed to understand we were only there to do our job, and they certainly seemed to understand the repercussion of approaching our troops without reason or warning. But children are innocent. They're curious. Hundreds of cheering, welcoming kids came out with us on every patrol. So now, instead of just watching your own back and the backs of your buddies, we also had to mind what the kids were doing because no one wanted them to get hurt.

We used a rotation schedule that kept one platoon on patrol, one on perimeter security, and one getting rest. Each platoon consisted of thirty to thirty-five soldiers, and we used every last man to search a single house. Why so many? We weren't taking any chances. We always took Intel guys along and some translators, too. Depending on the size of the building, sometimes one squad would stay outside and set up a defensive perimeter so we couldn't be attacked while checking the place. The rest of us would go inside.

We'd take up ready positions while our lieutenants, the interpreters, and the Iraqi police approached the door. The lieutenant would knock. Someone from inside would answer and the lieutenant would use the interpreters to say, "We have reason to suspect you are hiding weapons here. May we search the house?" If the person said yes, we entered and maintained our readiness as if active combatants were waiting on the other side of the door. If they said no, we went in anyway, but much more tactically and aggressively. Very few people said no.

We went into buildings of all different sizes. Iraqi architecture is very different from Western-style buildings, so it was difficult to figure the layout. For instance, you could never tell how many rooms a place might have. In America you sort of expect every building to have a main entrance in the front plus maybe a back door. Not in Iraq. Every single building we entered was completely different. Sometimes a door would open into an alley and sometimes it would open into a large garden courtyard in the middle of the house that you couldn't see from the outside. The structural irregularities gave us another reason to keep on our toes.

Most of the buildings were made from dilapidated mud bricks. We found some places that had been bombed or shot through by tanks, probably from the first wave of American military that swept through the area.

Inside the houses, the walls were almost always bare. It was common to see ornate rugs on the floors. Most of the houses we saw had couches like American homes, but the furniture was much more eccentric in color and style. I saw some very old-model televisions, like 1980 Zeniths, stuff that went that far back. Didn't notice many other electric appliances and absolutely no microwave ovens. Convenience items were pretty much nonexistent, including toilets, sewage, and plumbing works. The houses in Kel Zakar at least had electric lights. And you could tell these were religious people since each house would have a small prayer room with a shrine in it.

We followed explicit orders to respect the Iraqis' property. Yes, we were there to search for weapons but under no circumstances would we violate the peoples' confidence in us. Part of our job in those raids was to win their perception of the American soldier. Hearts and minds. We didn't rip things up and throw them on the ground, we were gentle. Our procedure was calm and smooth.

We checked cabinets, closets, rooms, under beds and furniture. It was a relatively preliminary search procedure, especially if it appeared we'd entered the house of an innocent family. We didn't check under the floors or look for hidden compartments in the walls or ceilings, for instance. Frankly, we didn't have time for that. There were suspicious buildings all over the city, and we had to move fast in order to search them all. Our patrols lasted four hours on about average, though it was really up to our lieutenant's discretion. Within that time we generally covered six or seven buildings scattered several miles about the city. That's a pretty heavy load when you're clearing rooms using urban warfare–style tactics.

Every time we disturbed a family, our translators did a good job making sure that everyone understood what was going on. By and large, the people seemed comfortable with what we were doing. A couple of them even asked to have their pictures taken with us. Overall, I got an impression that we were very welcome indeed. We allowed each house to keep one AK-47 along with two magazines of ammunition for personal protection. Anything more than that was confiscated.

As a general rule, Iraqi adults never came to our compound in broad daylight. They were too scared for their lives, fearful of reprisals from Baath Party members. Instead, they'd run to us under cover of night and deliver information on where the Baathists were. They'd point out which streets and houses we should focus our attention on. Some of them told us how they'd been tortured under Saddam. I remember one Iraqi man in his thirties or forties who was very happy to see us. He took off his shirt and showed us the scars from whip marks covering his back. He kept asking us, "Is Saddam dead? Is Saddam dead?" over and over and over again. We also saw a little girl who'd been maimed. I'm not sure if her nose had been burned off or cut off, but she'd been disfigured by Saddam's men, probably in reprisal for something her parents had done. Ruthless behavior. Suffice it say these Iraqis were, in the majority where we were, the downtrodden. They were thrilled that we'd arrived, that we were disarming the Baathists who'd served as Saddam's right arm and carried out his campaign of fear.

From what I saw, the Baath Party in Iraq was like a ruling class. They had all the power and all the money. You could tell who they were from their personal appearance alone; Baath Party members were clean kept and dressed in good-quality clothes while the rest of the Iraqis ran around in rags they couldn't afford to keep clean. Baathists lived comfortable lives of wealth and privilege, while the rest of their countrymen were starving. For this reason, we eventually started targeting the more lavish buildings for searches. If a place had high walls and iron fences, we could assume that the people inside carried influence, and influence meant the Baath Party.

I recall how, on one patrol, we walked past a particularly extravagant house. As we moved past, seven or eight men came outside to watch us. They definitely did not look happy we were there. We were surrounded by a bunch of smiling, happy Iraqi children but these men weren't smiling at all. One of them broke from the rest and started following my platoon. I saw him grab one of the children trailing us and hold the child close while he walked along counting the number of troops in our patrol.

I notified my squad leader who had our staff sergeant halt the platoon. Then my squad leader and I held a quick conference with my lieutenant and staff sergeant. I told them what was going on, that the house we'd just passed had to be a Baathist house. We glanced backward and, sure enough, more men were massing at the corner of the building now, watching us. My lieutenant looked at the man holding the child and asked to speak with him. The man came over and the platoon closed ranks around him in a circle.

My lieutenant asked, "Are you Baath Party?" The man said, "Yes." So the lieutenant said, "We're going to search your house. You have one hour to turn in your weapons."

The man just looked at him and replied, "How long are you going to be here?" He spoke very good English. It was obvious he understood everything we were saying, but for the rest of the conversation, he kept repeating the same question, "How long are you going to be here? How long are you going to be here?" Finally my lieutenant answered, "Until our job is done."

It was pretty clear to me what the guy wanted. He couldn't wait to see us leave the city. He felt like he was losing his grip over the populace. If we left, he and his buddies could pick up where they'd left off and start punishing the people who'd embraced our forces. The terror would start all over again.

We entered this extravagant house and confiscated some AK-47s and ammunition. We also confiscated an antiaircraft gun so old I don't even know if it would have worked. It was too heavy to drag back to headquarters, so I dismantled the barrel and threw it over a nearby bridge. It was a temporary measure that hopefully would throw a monkey wrench in the works of the city's crooked, oppressive leaders. We knew that American Civil Development forces were coming up behind us and they could ensure that men like the ones in that house would cause no more harm. The Civil Development plan would rebuild the Iraqi police force using volunteers; we heard this was already being done from convoys that rolled through our area. We hoped that the plan would create an environment where the Iraqi people could see they had options. There'd be a ruling democratic force in place to protect them so they'd no longer be forced to succumb to Baath Party tyranny.

See, that's what I feel America's role is in Iraq. You know how everyone says that President Bush was wrong because there were no weapons of mass destruction in Iraq? I personally feel that Saddam Hussein *was* a weapon of mass destruction. He murdered thousands of his own people and imprisoned many more for no justifiable reason whatsoever. Other people say we went in for oil, to which I say, Why not? Why shouldn't we get something out of this deal? That's just business, right? What did my unit help to do in Iraq? We showed an enslaved people that they can be free from tyranny. We showed them what freedom is. We're helping them build it. I think that's a noble duty. It's a duty I believe in.

I've got a lot more discipline because of my time in the marines. I look around my campus now and I see a lot of freshmen who are eighteen years old, normal age for freshmen. It's their first time away from home, they're partying like mad, and they tend to forget what they came here to do, which is learn. Don't get me wrong. Everybody parties. It's a question of moderation, that's all. You have to balance everything against your schoolwork, which is your primary objective. I notice a lot of freshmen don't come back after their first semester at college. They just can't handle the experience. They screwed up their GPAs early on and, after that, they just give up rather than fall further behind.

I have two classes a day Monday through Friday. As soon as I get back to my place, I sit down and make note cards for myself on the material we learned. I study. I eat lunch, go to another class, repeat the note card procedure, and then I get to relax a bit. Then it's back to studying again. I definitely wasn't a 4.0 student before I went into the military. Now I'm pulling around a 3.8. I don't feel like the people I'm going to school with understand or appreciate the military. To me it's always been a different culture, maybe even one I prefer. There's so many things that I get from the military that I don't get from the civilian world. You'll never make friends like the ones you make in the service. The bond you form is tight. American society is so divided into cliques. You have your hip-hop guys, your country boys, your preppy people. But in the military, when everyone's wearing camo BDUs [battle dress uniforms], you're all the same. Sometimes you're working under terrible conditions in adverse weather, staying up for endless hours pulling guard duty in a fighting hole. It's not glamorous. But that only serves to bring people together.

You learn to take care of the guy sitting next to you. In a foxhole, everyone's the same. But if you all go out to let loose on the town, you see something really extraordinary. When soldiers wear civilian clothes, you've got a preppy standing next to a guy with a cowboy hat and boots standing next to a dude with gold chains around his neck. It's a crazy assortment from all walks of life, and you're all the best of friends. That's amazing to me. I overhear some of the younger students saying things like, "Oh my god, look what that guy's wearing! I could never be friends with him or her!" They entertain discriminations. It's ridiculous but I also find some humor in it. I know these people don't have any experiences to draw from that would teach them any differently.

I'm majoring in speech pathology, minoring in psychology. Eventually, I want to work with early intervention autistic children or clients with traumatic brain injuries. I think I chose my major because it allows me to help people. Maybe that's the reason I miss the military, too. I helped a lot of people in Iraq and that's a really good feeling.

Can I say one more thing? I voted for George Bush [in 2004] because I think he's a strong wartime leader, and we need a strong leader to get the job done in Iraq. I think he's the man for the job. It appears that the nation agreed with me. For all those people who think we're not doing anything good in Iraq, let me tell you. When you look at a kid who's never seen the inside of an elementary school being afforded that opportunity because we were there, because we removed a madman from power? Well, that can't be a bad thing.

ROADSIDE BOMBS, JORDANIAN WHISKEY, AND SERIOUS QUESTIONS FOR PRESIDENT BUSH

✴

Sergeant Chad Vance
ARMY NATIONAL GUARD, 1245TH TRANSPORTATION COMPANY
OUT OF ARDMORE, OKLAHOMA

Sergeant Vance, age 31, comes from a small town in north-central Oklahoma. His father worked oil fields and his mother held a job in a convenience store. "Actually," says Chad, "She got a better job later on in the billing department of a hospital. Can you make a note of that? I don't want her to feel shortchanged when she reads this. After serving in the war, I've come to realize how important family is. Over in Iraq, we had a few days where things got quiet and we forgot to worry. Families never take a day off from worrying when their loved ones are overseas. Especially Moms."

Chad joined the National Guard during his junior year of high school and found himself working alongside a diverse population. The 1245th was comprised of approximately 130 soldiers. Some were college students and some were journeymen machine shop workers. Some were farmers, retail store workers, and truck drivers. Most soldiers of the 1245th were in their early twenties but some were much older. Some had served in Vietnam, the Gulf War, or both.

The sudden mobilization of a National Guard unit can create a great deal of tension within the unit's members. Too, the guard's unique position as a part-time fighting force doesn't always integrate well with the culture of a full-time standing army. As Chad tells it:

We got activated on February 10, 2003. It was especially difficult for my unit because we were given only two days' notice to report for duty. The call came in on a Monday afternoon, telling us to report to Oklahoma City on Wednesday.

When a Guardsman receives orders to mobilize, it essentially means he's now a full-time professional soldier employed by the United States government. This is a very large adjustment to make. For some people it meant squaring away an apartment lease and putting everything they owned in storage. For everyone it meant leaving a family and a personal life and most of your identity behind. Then there's the money to consider. Going on active-duty salary turned out to be a big pay cut from the money a lot of guys were making at their civilian jobs, so there's additional stress in that now they had to support their families on reduced incomes. To top it all off, there's the talk you have with your employer that goes something like this: "Well, I'm going overseas for a while. Can't really say when I'll be back. Hope you can get along without me, and I hope I'll have a job when I return." Believe me. That's a lot of stuff to deal with in two days' time.

Our orders stated we would serve one year in the theater with a possible yearlong extension. Nobody believed we'd be gone that long. We were all using Desert Storm as a basis for comparison. The Guard and Reserve troops in Desert Storm didn't stay longer than six months in the theater, by and large, so we assumed we'd get the same deal. Well, I guess you know what happens when you assume something.

Actually, I was lucky. I was single and living with my grandparents when our deployment orders came in. Full-time active service in Iraq meant I'd pull in about $30,000 a year, more money than I was making at home. And as far as upheaval went, I basically had to make sure my bills and credit cards would get paid on time. No big deal.

What was the general sentiment in my unit over our deployment? It depended on who you talked to. The younger folks were nervous about going to Iraq, but they were nervous in an eager, ready-to-go kind of way. The older guys weren't excited at all. In fact, they seemed pretty resigned. They just told a lot of old war stories. I think they were trying to get the younger troops in the right frame of mind for what we might face in Iraq. Those of us who hadn't been to war before were all ears. It was reassuring to us that we'd be going into combat with guys who'd been there before.

In the end, the stories didn't make a whole lot of difference. There's only so much someone can say to prepare you.

We spent about six weeks at Fort Sill in Lawton, Oklahoma, for deployment training. Everyone had to qualify with our weapons. For most people, that meant the M-16 but we also had gunners who qualified on the SAWs and the .50 cals. We did first-aid training and learned how to don the new chemical masks and suits, what they called the JSLISTs, although I don't know what that stands for.[127] Before that, we'd trained using the older, heavier suits, so this was all new.

From early on at Fort Sill, a lot of guys tried hooking up with the females in our unit. About 90 percent of my unit was male, so the competition level for female attention ran pretty high. Some guys made it pretty obvious they were trying to find a partner for the deployment. On the whole, there was a lot of sex going on in my unit. Unfortunately, it wasn't something I participated in.

In fact, while we were in Iraq one of our female soldiers eventually discovered she was pregnant, which is a huge military no-no. That's court martial material. The females were given pregnancy tests while we were still at Fort Sill so, given the timing of everything, she must have conceived right before we left for Iraq or immediately after we landed. That soldier was sent back to Fort Sill and served the remainder of her duty at home.

Actually, by the time we came home, my unit of 130 was down to 110. We didn't suffer any combat casualties per se, but lots of folks were sent home for medical reasons. One guy had a bad back. The girl who got pregnant left. One of our older guys, a Vietnam vet, got sent home with a heart problem. Stuff like this became sort of routine.

We were sent to Kuwait with the 345th Support Battalion, our home battalion in Ardmore. We knew those guys pretty well since we'd all drilled together in the same building. But in Kuwait it became clear that my company would proceed immediately into Iraq once our vehicles ar-

---

127. Joint service lightweight integrated suit technology—when combined with a chemical protective mask, the JSLISTs provide protection against chemical and biological agents, radioactive fallout particles, and battlefield contaminants. JSLISTs entered service in 1997 and replaced the older, heavier battle dress overgarment (BDO).

rived by boat. The 345th would stay behind. We ended up getting attached to another group, the 485th Combat Support Battalion, an active-duty unit out of Germany.

We had to wait ten days for our trucks to arrive. Then it took us a few more days to put ring mounts on some of them to accommodate the .50 cal machine guns; we handled this work ourselves. As a general rule, transportation companies provide security for themselves. So these gun trucks were very important; they'd form the core defense mechanism for our shipping convoys.

The 345th never made it to Iraq. We found out in October that they'd be home by Thanksgiving; their deployment orders came in and, just like that, they were out of there. This was the same day my unit found out that we wouldn't be home by Christmas despite the fact that we'd been told we'd "definitely be out of the theater of operations" in early December. When I heard that our deal had fallen through, I knew it meant we'd have another three to four months in Iraq, at least. Hearing that news, I laid back in my cot because it felt like someone was sitting on my chest. It was definitely not a good day. Not knowing when you'd get to go home was definitely one of the worst parts of the war for me.

We set up our base camp at a place called Camp Dogwood, about thirty miles south of Baghdad. The location of that camp was one of the first things that amazed me about Iraq. The Tigris-Euphrates river valley was lush and green. There were farms and groves and the countryside was beautiful, just beautiful. Everything outside the valley was barren wasteland. Camp Dogwood was set up in a really unfortunate spot. Just across the road to the east, we could see the lush green river valley, but out where we were there was nothing but sand and desert. To the west, the wastelands stretched as far away as the eye could see.

It didn't take us long to figure out the way things ran over there. Our job was pretty simple. Basically, U.S. forces had set up a handful of large, logistical bases that stockpiled food, water, ammunition, and repair parts. You've probably heard of some of these bases. One of them was out at Baghdad International Airport, BIAP for short. Another was Camp Anaconda, which is in the news a lot these days; it's located about fifty miles north of Baghdad, near Balad. These bases became the supply source for dozens of smaller, more remote camps scattered across the countryside. Essentially, transport companies were responsible for picking up supplies from a logistical base and hauling them out to the smaller camps as needed.

The system worked liked this: the small camps requisitioned supplies and a battalion was chosen for the delivery mission. The selected battalion then handed the order to a company in its command. They chose the company by comparing the load being requisitioned and each company's specific capabilities. The orders to a company would come in the form of basic instructions, like "Five systems[128] will pick up x amount of MREs at Camp Anaconda and deliver them to MEK." MEK was a camp posted about seven miles from Fallujah. Our company commander would read over the orders he'd received from the battalion and select a platoon for the mission. Our company was divided into three platoons, each staffed with about thirty soldiers. If your platoon got selected, you usually found out a day before the mission at our nightly platoon meeting. The next morning, the convoy commander would hold a briefing to go over the mission. Then it was time to start rolling.

A typical mission went like this: we'd start out early in the morning from Camp Dogwood and cross the Euphrates River, driving north through the city of Baghdad. We'd arrive at Camp Anaconda by midmorning. Then it was time to load the trucks.

The systems we drove were called PLSs [palleted load systems], equipped with huge hydraulically-powered hooks. A flat rack would be positioned on the ground and loaded with goods, usually via forklift. Then the PLS driver backed his truck up close to the rack and employed the hook, which extended out behind the truck, picked up the rack, and deposited it on the load bed.

A lot of times, if we were hauling MREs, we'd have to secure the pallets of boxes to the flat rack using tie-down ratchet straps. In the heat and blowing sand of the summer, this was not a lot of fun. But sometimes we'd haul Connexes [huge metal shipping boxes], which were usually filled with bottled water. They had these massive lifting vehicles called wretches that picked up the loaded Connex boxes and placed them on the load bed. We preferred dealing with Connexes since it

---

128. A system is composed of a truck and trailer.

meant less work for us. You'd pull up to a loading area and the machine would slap the Connexes on your truck back. Simple. Once you locked them down, you were good to go.

The loads varied according to each mission. The goods we hauled came in different forms. We hauled a lot of bottled water bought from local vendors, which had Arabic writing on the labels. We hauled U.S.-issue MREs that came in boxes of twelve. Other times, we hauled repair parts and ammunition. Once, I hauled a huge crate of plastic explosives and assorted ammunition; that mission couldn't have ended soon enough for me. One RPG or AK-47 burst and my ass would be all done.

We'd head out to our delivery point which might have been Baghdad Airport, for instance. We'd get there, unload, and usually stay the night, sleeping on the big flat roofs of the truck cabs in the open air. Sleeping bags weren't necessary usually, especially during the summer when it got so hot. The next morning we'd wake up and head back to Camp Dogwood.

Everyone was fairly nervous when we first got to Iraq. We didn't know what to expect. The war had been going on for about two weeks by the time we entered the country. Everything was chaotic. At that point, everyone was still anticipating chemical attacks so we took our gas masks and suits with us everywhere we went. We had MP escorts our first few trips out, plus our gun trucks with the mounted .50 cal machine guns for protection. After a while, though, it became obvious that the threats we'd feared weren't going to materialize. We began to leave our chemical equipment behind; for my unit, it became a matter of personal preference. If you wanted to take your chemical gear along, fine. If you didn't, no one was going to say anything. The MP units were in high demand and stretched pretty thin, so we began to see less and less of them. Soon enough we were providing our own security. All in all, we found our own groove and things started to go a lot easier.

When we weren't working, we did anything we could to keep our minds busy. We played cards a lot; Spades and Hearts were the rage for a while. Then somebody brought in a set of dominoes and we got hooked on that. We finally got a PX at Camp Dogwood in August or September, and a few guys bought a TV and an Xbox. That was the end of the card games. Guys suddenly started staying up all night playing video games.

A lot of us would read to pass the time. We played a lot of sports, too. Volleyball and horseshoes made perfect sense since our base was basically located in a giant sand pit. Soccer games followed and then flag football. We organized intramural teams and played in a battalion league.

I kept a journal while I was in Iraq—that was another way of keeping busy when times were slow. I'd never kept a journal before, but the idea came to me at Fort Sill. I'd add something to my diary once or twice a week, and it turned out to be pretty helpful. I could write down whatever was on my mind and vent it that way. I also played my banjo a lot; I usually took it with me on missions. Sometimes one of the other guys in the unit, Sergeant Schoonover, a guitar picker, would sit in and we'd play together.

We also did a lot of drinking since alcohol's pretty easy to come by when you're in a transportation unit. We were on the road 90 percent of the time, and the road was where you could buy all sorts of black market goods. Iraqis would hang out on street corners or any place where you had to slow your vehicles down. If you were on a rural road, for instance, and the road took a sudden dip, the whole convoy would gear down in order to negotiate the terrain. The moment we slowed to a certain speed? Boom! The Iraqis seized the moment and ran up to our trucks, hawking whatever goods they had and trying to exchange dinars for dollars. Considering that dinars were practically worthless at that point, they were pretty zealous in this endeavor. They got a lot of takers, though, since we all wanted dinars to take home as souvenirs. The Iraqis were very pleased to trade a 250 dinar note for a dollar. As a rule, five bucks American could buy you almost anything they had to sell. Five bucks was a good unit to use since we never had time to stop and haggle. Slowing down was dangerous enough when you rode a convoy.

Right. Alcohol. We bought that on the road, too. Mostly we picked up this shit-tasting Jordanian whiskey, really harsh stuff. You were never really sure if drinking it was going to kill you or not so we had this ritual where we'd pour a little whiskey into the bottle cap and light it to make sure the flame burned blue. Rumor had it that blue-flame whiskey was safe to drink, red-flame meant the whiskey was bad. I'm not sure of the validity of that. Occasionally the market price for whiskey would spike and you'd end up paying ten or fifteen bucks a bottle, which, considering the quality, was outrageous.

Sometimes we found beer was available and we'd pay anything for it, twenty to thirty bucks a case. Beer was a lot harder to come by, though. If we found it at all, it was usually at Baghdad International Airport. The locals there peddled light, canned lagers, foreign labels, mostly Petra and Atlas, stuff that makes Bud Light taste like high-quality brew. We could buy block ice from the Iraqis outside of Anaconda, too. Beer and ice meant instant party.

Technically, drinking was illegal. But most of the people we knew were doing it, both in the Guard and the regular army. I think our commanders just looked the other way, that's all. They seemed to understand that we were under a lot of pressure, so they never made an issue out of it unless somebody got really out of hand and did something stupid.

Like this one time, my buddy John got really hammered. John was a wild man, and on this particular occasion he dressed up in jeans and knee-high cowboy boots and was walking around the base drunker than shit. On this particular occasion, he was feeling absolutely no pain so he paid a visit to the battalion commander's quarters, kicked on the guy's door, and broke in a window with his fist. Then he passed out spread eagle on the grass. When they found him, he was dead to the world and sure enough, we had a contraband inspection after that. Everybody's locker got searched. John got in a little trouble, but they didn't crack down on him too hard. They needed every person they had over there. You had to do something really creatively stupid in Iraq if you wanted to get arrested by the MPs. You basically had to pose a threat either to yourself or your fellow soldiers, but I never saw anything get out of hand like that. I just saw a lot of people blowing off steam. A couple of guys smoked hash, too.

When we weren't working, our days were basically ours to do with as we pleased unless we needed to perform maintenance on the trucks or you pulled a detail. Details were regular chores that needed to be done around camp, like taking out the trash and burning it, burning our shit from the latrines, kitchen police duty, that kind of thing. We had nightly platoon meetings and a company meeting once a week or so, they held those to disseminate information. Most of the time our superiors would herd us all together and squelch rumors that we were going home.

Nope, they'd say. Not true. You're still screwed. Make the best of it. And we'd be like, "Well, thanks for sharing." Then it was right back to the grind, waiting for missions to come down and figuring out ways to kill time.

During the whole year we drove through Iraq, we never came in contact with the Iraqi military; they'd all been defeated or dissolved by the time we were in full swing. During one mission early on, one of our convoys wandered into the wrong area. They got lost trying to find Camp Anaconda and drove through a manned Iraqi checkpoint. But no shots were fired. We never fell under small arms fire from insurgents or RPG ambushes. No, my unit was really lucky. Mostly, we just had to contend with the roadside bomb attacks.

There were unsecured stockpiles of arms lying around all over the countryside. The Iraqis would go grocery shopping for live artillery shells, rig them with fuses, and bury them in the road shoulders as IEDs. You never knew where they were until it was too late. Sometimes the Iraqis used cell phones to detonate the bombs, and sometimes they ran wires from the bomb out to wherever they were hiding in the desert. Either way, the damage these things caused was pretty massive.

I remember one mission I was on in early September 2003. We'd been running a lot of trips out to Camp Ridgeway over by Fallujah. As you can imagine, that was a pretty violent area to operate in[129] what with the insurgency and all. The road to Ridgeway was called Supply Route Zinc. As the insurgency escalated, it became common to see huge, craters all up and down the shoulders of Zinc where the IEDs had detonated. The site was enough to make your pucker factor shoot up a few notches.[130]

It was mid morning. We'd dropped the supplies at Ridgeway and were heading back along Zinc to Camp Dogwood, but our convoy had to stop because another convoy ahead of us had stalled and was blocking the road. One of their vehicles had been hit by a roadside bomb. I know for a fact that one of their men was wounded, because I saw him ride by in a Humvee. He had blood on his face, but didn't seem seri-

---

129. Fallujah became a particular hotbed of insurgent activity after Baghdad fell.
130. When asked what this meant, Sergeant Vance laughed and said by way of explanation: "Your ass."

ously wounded. They shipped him back to Ridgeway for medical attention.

Well, we sat in our vehicles and waited for the road to clear, but after forty-five minutes, our convoy commander decided it wasn't a safe position to linger in. He ordered us to turn back around. We had lunch at Ridgeway and struck out for Dogwood later that afternoon.

Everything was going fine until we got to an area where we had to make a right turn at a T-intersection. There was a crowd of Iraqis hanging out at the intersection; they looked like people from the little farming communities we often saw squatting by the sides of the roads, men wearing dishdashas, women and children, probably forty or fifty people in all. They were all smiling and waving at us, which made us nervous. Remember, this was fairly close to Fallujah. In that area, as with most of the country, it was practically impossible to distinguish which Iraqis wanted to sell you something from the ones who wanted to blow you away.

Our convoy was maybe fifteen vehicles long with a gun truck leading the file and another bringing up the rear. I was driving a PLS situated near the middle, my codriver in the passenger seat was Specialist Michelle Downard. We came to the T and made the right turn, proceeded down the road. We'd gone about three-quarters of a mile when I felt the bomb explode behind me.

I didn't hear it so much as I felt the concussion. It was a small *whoomp*, barely noticeable, but when I looked in my side-view mirror, there it was, a huge mushroom cloud about a half mile behind me billowing gray-black smoke into the air. The explosion looked bad. My first thought was that one of my friends had just been killed. Downard was wearing headphones at the time and hadn't noticed the explosion. I got her attention and told her to look in the mirror. She took a long look, blinked, and said, "Oh, shit."

We didn't have a radio in the truck. Our unit usually functioned using handheld walkies distributed throughout the convoy so we'd never go out of range, but we didn't have a walkie that day so I wasn't sure what to do. I didn't know if somebody back there needed help. I slowed down a bit and tried to look behind me, using the mirror to see what was going on, but I wasn't close enough. The trucks ahead of me kept rolling so I just put the hammer down and rolled, too.

A couple more miles down the road, we made a left turn, pulled off to the side and waited. Then I saw the rear gun truck passing all the vehicles in the convoy behind me, coming forward. The gunner, Staff Sergeant Barrett Alexander, was still sitting up on the little bullshit ring mount seat, manning the .50. He seemed okay. But when the gun truck drew closer and stopped, I saw that Barrett had an angry, bewildered look on his face. He climbed down from the rig and I heard him say, "My shoulder's burning!" A couple of guys helped him take off his flak vest, uniform top, and brown T-shirt because he couldn't move his arms enough to do it himself.

That's when I noticed the gun truck. It looked like someone had taken a sledgehammer to it. The front windshield panes were destroyed. The driver's side glass was cracked into a spider-web pattern; thankfully the pane was shatterproof so the shards hadn't exploded into the driver's face. The passenger's side panel had buckled inward, though, and was lying on the passenger's seat. The entire passenger side of the truck was battered. The door had crushed inward and hung off its hinges; we were never able to shut it properly again. In all, the truck was still functional, but it definitely wasn't pretty.

The blast had punched holes in Barrett's shirt. Gravel from the explosion had blown up and hit Barrett on his upper right arm and shoulder blade. All in all he seemed pretty composed, a lot more composed than I would have been, anyway. Like I said, he looked pretty mad. I glanced at the gun truck's driver and he seemed about the same: shaken and angry. They put Barrett in a Humvee and sped him back to Camp Dogwood. The Hummer could get there in twenty minutes while the trucks would take twice that long. After a while the trucks in front of us began to roll slowly out again so we followed them, and that was that.

My company was very lucky, we never suffered serious casualties from IEDs. A few guys like Barrett suffered light wounds, that was all. In all fairness, I'm sure those ordeals were pretty significant to them, but no one lost an arm, no legs were amputated. Two guys in my company won Purple Hearts: SSG Alexander and SPC Jared Willis. I'm thankful nobody got killed. That would have been a huge burden. I can't imagine what it would have been like to lose a friend over there. I feel for those soldiers who see that happen and still have to go out to do their job the next day.

What do I think I contributed to the war in Iraq? Well, a lot of our soldiers received adequate food and water because of my company. That may sound a bit oversimplified and I don't mean to sell short the work we did. In the small picture, I'm glad I was there and I'm proud my company did its job well.

In the larger picture, I'm frustrated. I didn't think then and I don't think now that the war in Iraq needed to be fought. I remember when George Bush was trying to sell the nation on our reasons for attacking Iraq and Colin Powell went before the UN with a bunch of computer-animated cartoons. He said things like, "This is an artist's rendition of what Saddam's mobile chem labs might look like." He held up some drawings. Then he held up a small vial and said, "It's possible that a quantity of certain chemicals this size could wipe out half of a city."

I remember thinking, *Might* look like? It's *possible*? That's *it*? That's the *most* evidence we have? To me it was like, Let me get this straight: we're going to war over a bunch of cartoon drawings and some conjecture? I thought, *If that's all we have, we're in pretty big trouble.* It seemed to me the government was trying to scare the hell out of us in order to justify the war.

Everybody's entitled to an opinion. My bottom-line opinion is that Bush lied. Saddam Hussein was already under American control before the war thanks to the economic sanctions we'd levied against Iraq. His alleged nuclear program was in shambles—he only had rudimentary components and he still didn't have the capability to deliver warheads anywhere close to United States soil. His longest-range missiles were improvised SCUDs that could only reach something like 110 miles. How is that an imminent threat to the United States? Is that what you call hard evidence that justifies going to war? To me, the answer is no.

George Bush lied, and because he lied a lot of young people are paying a heavy price. That kills me, seeing kids lose their lives over there for the reasons given by the Bush administration. When Bush was trying to sell this war, he didn't say, "There *may* be a connection to al Qaeda." He didn't say, "There *might* be weapons of mass destruction." He stated, as if it were fact, "There *is* a connection." He said, "There *are* weapons, we *know* where they are." Now we know that what he said wasn't true. It's been proven. If that's not lying, tell me what is. If he were running a corporation, he'd be put in jail for cooking the books. But because he's our president, we all get sheepish and say, "Oh well. Guess we'll go to war now."

Once the invasion happened, I noticed that even the harshest critics shut up. The American public seemed unwilling to criticize the war since troops had already been deployed. It just didn't seem right to speak out when the troops were already in harm's way, especially when everyone who *did* speak out was branded as unpatriotic by the president and his administration. I think that's the scariest part of the whole deal. America's now set a precedent that preemptive warfare is acceptable. Is that an example we want the rest of the world to follow? I imagine what kind of world it would be if all nations shot first and asked questions later. That vision concerns me a great deal.

My separation date for the National Guard came up this past June [2004]. I chose not to reenlist even though I'd put in fourteen years of service and only needed six more to get full retirement benefits. Before we invaded Iraq? Hell, I would have been a fool to quit so close to retirement. But now, I don't know anybody who's re-upping, regardless of how close they are. Troops are getting called and recalled for duty. The insurgency's hotter than ever. If I sign up for six more years, there's no way around it, I'll redeploy to Iraq at least once, maybe twice. Based on what I saw while I was over there, it's not worth the risk. So I sacrificed my retirement.

I learned a few things while working in Iraq. For instance, I met a few civilian truck drivers for a Halliburton subsidiary, Kellogg, Brown, and Root. These guys were getting paid around $100,000 a year to do the same job as a military truck driver. But when it came time for me to reenlist in the Guard, they wanted me to sign up for three or six more years for a $5,000 or $10,000 bonus. That's insane. If our government is willing to pay civilians so much money for one year of work, why can't soldiers get a $100,000 bonus for six years of service? It seems only fair, especially now, when a U.S. soldier is pretty much guaranteed to see combat in Iraq. I mean, it's all supposedly coming out of the same pot, right? Taxpayer money. So why not spread the wealth?

It smells really foul to me. The government keeps trumpeting, "Our troops are *great*! They're the best in the *world*! Let's hear it for our *troops*!" But when it comes right down to it, they're not putting their money where their mouth is. If the government paid our troops what they pay civilians, I bet they'd have absolutely no problem filling the ranks to the absolute brim. Our military has a proud tradition. In the past, young men and women have joined the service out of a sense of duty to country. I don't want to make this sound like it's *all* about the money, but these days, it's a fact that most people join our military for financial reasons. Considering that a sizeable percentage of today's recruits will end up putting their lives on the line at some point, it seems only fair to give them as much money as the budget allows. If it allows for private contractors to get paid handsomely, why not our soldiers?

I hope that leaving the Guard puts me in the free-and-clear from returning to active service, but really, who can tell? Because of this war, America will have to maintain a massive military presence overseas, 140,000 troops on the ground or thereabouts in the Middle East alone, full time for several years. Call me crazy, but I don't see how we're going to do that without instituting a draft, regardless of what Bush says.

It boils down to hard numbers—and currently? We just don't have the people.

SETTING THE RECORD STRAIGHT

✭

Sergeant Jim Joraleman
327TH INFANTRY REGIMENT, 101ST AIRBORNE DIVISION

Sergeant Joraleman, age 25, hails from Des Moines, Iowa. He and his wife, Cindy, have a two-year-old son, Zeke. Jim joined the army on July 24, 2000 because, "It was something to do. I wasn't really going anywhere with my life, so I decided, Join the army. I wasn't afraid to go to war. My father fought in Vietnam, so I figured I could do it, too."

He spent the first 351 days of the war (from March 1, 2003, to February 14, 2004) on the front lines in Iraq. Sergeant Joraleman served out the duration of his four-year hitch with the army and was honorably discharged.

I want to say this right off the bat: There's a big difference between being stationed in Iraq and these other guys you hear about on the news, the ones who served in Kuwait. It's a *very* big difference, like night and day. I watch the news, I go on the Internet, and I hear these people talk about their tough war experiences like they were out there on the front lines. Uh-uh. They spent the war with their Sony PlayStation, smoking cigarettes, running to the PX, and talking tough. I want to express my dismay over the fact that nobody seems to want to talk to the guys who were there. That's why I'm interested in being in this book. I was there, and I've got a lot to say.

My unit rolled across the Iraqi border March 28, 2003. It took us three days to get to Najaf by truck, and when we arrived, I don't know why, we just sat around, waiting for word to move into the city. We pulled security and watched the Apaches and Kiowas[131] run bombing missions all day.

---

131. The Boeing McDonnell Douglas AH-64A Apache is the army's primary attack helicopter, a quick-reacting, airborne weapon system that can fight close and deep to destroy, disrupt, or delay enemy forces. The Apache is designed to fight and survive during the day, night, and in adverse weather throughout the world. The principal mission of the Apache is the destruction of high-value targets with the Hellfire missile.

Eventually, Third ID moved up to a forward position and our job kicked in. We began to suppress any enemy forces Third ID came into contact with so the division wouldn't have to stop rolling their tanks on up to Baghdad. We did for this for some time until, finally, we got word to move into the city, where our first mission was to take over this tiny university.

We sat around waiting while military intelligence drove up and down the street in trucks with Arabic translators broadcasting messages over loudspeakers. Word came down through the ranks that the translators were saying, "Leave now. If you don't leave, the United States will remove any enemy personnel through whatever means they deem necessary." Civilians in traditional Shiite Muslim dress—long shirt-skirts, sandals, and headdresses—began pouring out of the buildings. Intel moved in to check everyone's identification, though I have no idea what they were looking for. Once the military cleared these people, they were allowed to wander off into the city. This process went on for three hours.

Then I guess some sort of All Clear signal was given because we commenced to attack the university, using total force. Tanks rolled over the gates, metal screeched, and masonry fell. My unit walked in right over the wreckage. We went from building to building and didn't find anyone. Not a single soul. Which made me think that the whole effort had been an utter waste of time.

About a month after we took the university, just as we were getting ready to leave Najaf, we heard from witnesses, our own soldiers, that Iraqis had been seen fleeing out the back of the buildings as we went in the front. I don't know if they were civilians or Iraqi fighting forces or what, but the reports corroborated one another and seemed pretty clear.

It is also capable of employing a 30 mm M-230 chain gun and Hydra 70 (2.75-inch) rockets that are lethal against a wide variety of targets. The Apache has a full range of aircraft survivability equipment and has the ability to withstand hits from rounds up to 23 mm in critical areas.

The OH-58A Kiowa helicopter was first deployed to Vietnam in early autumn of 1969 and operated with air cavalry, attack helicopter, and field artillery units. The versatile helicopter could also be configured as a troop transport, medevac, or for external lift missions using an external hook. Kiowas were commonly paired with the AH-1G Huey Cobra. The Kiowa would fly low to draw enemy fire, trolling for fire, mark the target, and call in the Cobra to attack. After countless modifications over the years, pilots in Iraq were equipped with the latest model of the Kiowa helicopter, the OH-58D Kiowa Warrior, currently replacing the A and C Kiowas. It is a two-seat, single-engine, four-bladed single main rotor light helicopter with a low-light television, thermal imaging system, and laser range finder/designator incorporated into an above the rotor mast-mounted sight (MMS). It is designed to operate autonomously at standoff ranges providing armed reconnaissance, command and control, and target acquisition and designation under day/night, hot, and adverse weather conditions.

Which made me think, *Huh. We just let them get away*. I was right. Big waste of time.

In other words, our own forces watched these people escape and didn't care enough to, say, pick up the radio and let us know about it. Had they done that, we could have cut the Iraqis off and taken care of them by whatever means we deemed necessary like the guy on the loudspeaker said. But that didn't happen and I guess I'm pretty pissed off about it. There's 23,000 enlisted soldiers in the 101st Airborne Division plus officers to supplement the enlisted personnel. It's one of the largest divisions in the army. So what the hell were we there for if not to be of use?

We set up camp in that university and used it as a base of operations to run patrols all day and all night through the city of Najaf. We were basically walking in groups, looking out for signs of hostility, weapons caches, for instance, or combative personnel. As things turned out, we ended up doing more humanitarian work.

The walking patrols felt more like a parade duty to me, anyway. We'd walk for three hours at a time and Iraqis would turn out in droves to wave at us. We shook a lot of hands even though we weren't supposed to. We'd been ordered to keep people away from us, and at first, that's exactly what we did. But gradually, gradually, the civilians kept creeping closer. They were curious. Eventually, they walked right alongside us as we carried out our patrols. I guess you could say they walked patrol with us.

Our next assignment was up north in a place called Kiaro West, about thirty-five miles south of Mosul. At one point the facility had been an Iraqi airbase that saw a lot of use in Desert Storm but it had stood abandoned for ten years or so. We moved in and co-opted the buildings. Our mission was basically the same as it'd been in Najaf. We went to all the surrounding cities and pulled walking tours. We asked the people we saw if they knew where weapons were cached, if they knew who was caching weapons, or which people had supported Saddam's regime.

It was same old, same old, as far as the work was concerned. But let me add this: we didn't get to take a shower our first three months in Iraq. We didn't get hot meals. We didn't get access to e-mail, we didn't get to make phone calls home. In my opinion, we also had this weird habit, as a military force, of ransacking buildings, sometimes partially destroying them, then turning right back around and saying, "Yes, sir! This looks like a fine place to live!"

For a while, the room I lived in was two doors down from a door we'd blown apart with C-4 Plastique. The ceiling tiles of my place were all hanging down, laying on the floor, that kind of thing, consequences of the blast. Keep in mind, these weren't great buildings to begin with, structurally speaking. We certainly didn't improve things any by shelling them.

Days would go by where we walked patrol and nothing happened. Then, for no apparent reason, on no particular day, you'd stumble into a firefight. There was no rhythm to getting attacked over there. It happened when it happened. When I say firefight, I'm talking about two or three idiots who'd pop up suddenly from an abandoned building or an alleyway and start rattling off with AK-47s. We didn't have any sort of intelligence guiding us, no reports saying, "This area's hostile, that area's not." We were just moving along, stumbling over pockets of resistance. Or maybe it's better to say that everywhere was hostile and, at the same time, nowhere was.

Sometimes we'd walk through an area we'd been through many times before, same street, same buildings, same people pretty much. Only this time some idiot wanted to take a shot at us. That was Najaf, at any rate. In Mosul, the idiots popped up out of little mud huts. But aside from that, it was all pretty much the same. We'd clean them up and move on; that was the job.

The firefights may have been sporadic but the routine of soldiering sure wasn't. The word I want to use here is *monotonous*. There'd be days, whole weeks, in fact, where you just did your job because you were used to doing it. Sometimes we drove unarmored Humvees with no doors and open backs. We placed sandbags on the floorboards of the cab in case we ran over something that exploded. And when it was time to go out on patrol, you'd climb into the trucks with the other five to eleven guys who'd pulled duty with you and drive around for a while.

If you rode in the back, you faced out and pulled security, watching for attackers, watching pretty much for anything. Maybe you'd take fire, maybe you wouldn't. When your shift was over, you'd drive back into the hanger, climb off the truck and forget about it. What difference did it make? Soon enough, you'd have to do it all over again.

I'll say this for the army: they train you pretty well. I thought a lot of the drills they made us do back at Fort Campbell[132] were pretty stupid until I saw firsthand how they could be used in practical circumstances. To me, the whole goal of army training is to prepare you mentally for stressful situations you'll face in combat. You don't have time to think in combat. If you think, you panic; if you panic, you die. So you fall back on training. Habits. Ingrained reactions. In combat, a habit allows you to react without your brain having to get involved.

I'll give you an example. One time in Najaf, we were walking patrol at one in the morning. It was going to be our last duty in Najaf; we'd already gotten word we'd be pulling out soon. We were dead tired and anxious to leave. The city'd been relatively quiet so I guess we got lulled. Another patrol, no big deal. We proceeded down the main highway that runs through the city, same as we'd done many times before. Then we heard the cough of an AK and a green tracer round bounced off the road right next to my foot. Everyone dropped and took a knee. It didn't take long to figure out where the shot had come from, an alleyway off the road right next to us. That was all it took.

No one said a word, we didn't have to. Everyone picked up, ran over, and flattened themselves up against the building on either side of the alley opening. We quickly coordinated ourselves and sent a bunch of guys storming down the alley, shooting as they went.

There were ten of us that night. We killed three of them and started pushing deeper into the alley. But then we looked up and saw that sandbags had been set up on top of the buildings. These were fortified positions. Through the windows, we thought we saw more people running in and out of the houses. Not a good situation. So we backed out of the alley and called in the incident.

Our base commander issued orders for us to head back and enter the

132. Fort Campbell, home of the 101st Air Division, lies on the Kentucky-Tennessee border, sixty miles northwest of Nashville.

buildings, but our patrol lieutenant shook his head. He said, "No, sir. This is not a good idea." We all had the feeling we were being set up. We were ten guys, sure, but who knew how many were hiding in those buildings? Plus our training tells us to engage enemies on a three-to-one show of strength in numbers. Based on that figure, we were pretty certain we'd be outnumbered by book standards. We radioed in this explanation, "It's an ambush." The base commander repeated his orders over the course of three or four radio transactions, but the lieutenant held firm. Finally there was a pause on the other end of the line and the commander said, "Forget it. Abort. Head to the extraction site and we'll pick you up."

See, training ruled the day in that instance. Training woke us up and caused us to react instantly under attack. It showed us how to form the proper counter maneuver for that situation without engaging in discussion and allowed us to destroy our initial attackers. Best of all, training informed us as to which situations were advisable to pursue and which ones clearly were not. Our training kept us alive, which is what it's supposed to do.

Yes, we killed those three men. That was just one incident I'm telling you about. We killed a lot more that I'm not mentioning. I don't know how graphic you want me to be or what point it would prove. It's a weird feeling, I can tell you that. It's a very difficult thing to describe. When you boil it all down, when killing somebody happens, it's just your job, that's it. You do it when you have to. If you don't? You don't go home. Period. End of story.

You don't think much of it at the time. Thinking comes later, when you realize that this isn't a video game, this is real life. It's a moment, a situation, that you'll probably never be in again.

Water was always a problem. For the first six months we lived on two bottles of Aquafina a day, the same types of bottles you'd buy here in the U.S. at a grocery store or a gas station, say, for $1.25. Total fluid content for two bottles: 1.5 liters. That's all we were allowed per day. Evidently the army was having supply problems.

You used your water for bathing and drinking both, rationing it according to your own personal system. I guess most guys used about half a bottle to one full bottle for bathing but, again, it was a matter of personal taste and whatever mood you found yourself in on a day-to-day basis. You also saved a little water for brushing your teeth.

I guess the consensus at the time was unanimous: as far as water went, we could have used a lot more.

Despite the initial hardships, we were pretty well set up by October. By that I mean that our base had Internet access and a phone. We didn't get a PX installed until December so, in lieu of that, a bunch of Iraqi civilians were carefully screened and allowed on the base to set up little shops. A friend and I split the cost of a nice twenty-one-inch color TV that we bought off one vendor for $125 American. I forget the actual brand, but it worked fine, nothing like you'd find here in the States, though. Then we went online and ordered a PlayStation 2 plus a whole bunch of games from Amazon.com. Most things you ordered online could be sent to the APO [army post office] address that the army issued you when you shipped overseas. You ordered it with a credit card, same as you'd do here in the States. A lot of guys carried credit cards into combat. They had their wallets in their pockets as if they were making a trip to the corner store for a loaf of bread and some butter instead of walking into a firefight. I never did that. I wrote my credit card number down on a slip of paper and carried that with me instead.

It took a month for the PlayStation to arrive. Man, it was worth it. We hooked it up to the TV we bought, and every day we came in off patrol, we'd settle in and start playing tournaments of NCAA Football 2003 to get our minds off everything.

Once everything got set up, you could go to the post's finance department and have up to $200 out of your monthly check issued to you in cash. Mostly you used cash to buy personal hygiene equipment and food. A lot of the Iraqis came on base to set up tiny restaurants where they'd cook traditional Arabic cuisine, but they'd make up American words for each selection. A "hero," for instance wasn't a hero [sandwich, a.k.a. a submarine or grinder] as we know it here, it was sliced lamb and beef with salad vegetables on a pita shell. It was really good food and you couldn't beat the price. You could fill yourself up for one dollar American.

We were a little worried the first time we bought food off an Iraqi. Not that they were going to poison us or anything, no, we were more concerned about the cooking standards and preparation hygiene than anything else. We take a lot of things for granted here in the United States about how food is prepared. Iraqis don't know a thing about USDA standards. There aren't any health agencies overseeing how they cook their meat. Luckily, no one ever got sick.

We weren't on base the first time we bought food off an Iraqi, we were on patrol. We stumbled across this local restaurant out in the country-side. Picture this: a bunch of armed American soldiers pull their truck off a road, hit a dirt parking lot, and walk into an Iraqi restaurant in the middle of nowhere. Sounds like the start of a joke, doesn't it?

The building was low slung, made out of clay. It looked like a ratty gas station you'd find in America. There were plastic patio tables and chairs set up out front, and the locals seemed friendly enough. By that point we were all hungry. We'd been eating a steady diet of MREs out of foil bags for four or five months and, let me tell you, that gets old real quick. Those things are so bad some of us cut down to eating less than one a day. I dropped at least twenty pounds working in Iraq. The bad food, the lack of water, plus the heat. It got up to 140 degrees in the summertime.

That restaurant was surreal. They served us Pepsi. Pepsi in Arabia [*sic*]. At that point, we'd been given orders not to eat Iraqi food but we knew that a lot of the higher-ups were going against the order, so that was that. We did it, and it was the best choice we ever made.

I want to take a moment and recall this because September 11, 2001, had a huge impact on me as a soldier. I remember when it happened very clearly. We were out on the training field at Fort Campbell, Kentucky, that morning. We got a call in over the unit radio that somebody'd bombed the Pentagon. To which we said, "Right. Ha-ha. Very funny. Sick joke." We continued with our exercises.

Then we got another call saying that somebody'd bombed the Twin Towers. To which we said, "Come on. Quit playing with us. It's not funny." But one of our officers went to his civilian vehicle and turned on the car radio. We all went over to listen and there it was. The announcers confirmed everything we'd heard.

We sat in silence, listening for a long time. This, too, was surreal. Nobody knew what to say or do. Then somebody broke the silence by asking, "How in the world could anybody bomb all those places?" After that a couple guys jumped up and started pumping themselves up: "We're going to war! We're going to war!"

They locked down the base that day, wouldn't let any trucks out the gate, so we had to hike back in from the training field. They made a big deal out of checking our military IDs before letting us back on post. Once everyone was accounted for, Command handed down orders that we'd have to stand guard over the barracks and company areas until further notice. Seemed crazy to me. They were already guarding the post's outer perimeter. Aside from keeping us busy and making us paranoid, what good did it do to have us guard every hallway, every room, and every door to every building in the fort?

One time in Iraq we got word from Command that we'd be going on a mission in the middle of the desert. We loaded ourselves into helicopters and flew northwest over miles and miles of empty sand. They gave us our orders on the way over. We'd be taking out a terrorist camp.

After about three hours in the air, we flew over a ridge and saw a unit of about forty army rangers. They were already on the ground taking fire from insurgents hiding in the surrounding hills. We landed, climbed out of the birds, and set about reinforcing the rangers. In the middle of the fighting, a stray AK round somehow made it through the windshield of a hovering Apache helicopter and took out the pilot.

Evidently the copilot took over. He landed the chopper behind a hill, pulled the pilot out, and burned the chopper, which I guess is standard procedure so the enemy can't capture the vehicle. Then the copilot started fighting off the Iraqis with his 9 mm sidearm, one pistol against two platoons firing AK-47s, RPGs, and RPKs.[133]

We moved in to assist. My unit and the rangers, about 120 men all told, swarmed over the hill and found this poor guy out there, alone, taking cover behind the burnt shell of his helicopter, completely outnumbered. We surrounded the wreck while the rangers evacuated the copilot. Again, the only thing going through your mind in a situation like that is, "Follow your training, follow your training. Watch your back and

---

133. Ruchnoi Pulemet Kalashnikov—the Soviet-made, crew-manned machine guns equivalent to the American M-60 or M-240 Bravos.

watch your buddy's back. Hopefully, your buddy's doing the same for you." We killed everybody we found and didn't suffer a single casualty. Actually—scratch that. I think one of the rangers was injured but not killed.

Finally the fight was over. About ten minutes after we got word that the area was clear, a wing of seven or eight Black Hawks swooped in and landed. Officers began piling out of the helos, nobody ranked lower than a colonel. Military intelligence was there, too. The brass walked around the area as if it was no big deal and they took lots of pictures of the downed helicopter, the dead bodies lying all over the place, everything.

They searched the bodies and word filtered down pretty quick: none of the men we'd killed were Iraqi. They were Syrian, Saudi, and Jordanian natives. Exactly how the intelligence guys determined that is beyond me. Personally, I couldn't tell one Middle Eastern man from another. And another thing didn't make sense to me: they'd said this place was a terrorist camp, but there weren't any buildings, I didn't see any tents. Apparently the men we'd fought had been living out in the middle of the desert without shelter.

See, I tell this story because people are always saying, "Should we have invaded Iraq or not?" I think we should have. Not because Saddam Hussein was so powerful. Personally, I don't think he pulled much weight as far as the organization of terrorist cells in his own country. If you want my opinion, I think he turned out to be a patsy for Osama bin Laden. Bin Laden used Iraqi soil for training purposes and to hide weapons. I don't think Hussein participated in that at all. I think, if anything, he was just guilty of covering it up.

But here we were in the middle of Iraq. We'd busted a terrorist camp where you couldn't find a single Iraqi among the sixty-five men or so we killed that day. What does that tell you?

Is it right that we're over there? Here we go again. Look, I'll spell it out for you. The reasons we were given for going to Iraq were bogus. President Bush said there were weapons of mass destruction in Iraq and we had to destroy them. Well, the UN weapons inspectors have already confirmed it—there weren't any WMDs. I spent a year over there and I never saw one, neither did any of the people I talked to. So the whole reason for declaring war was wrong.

He should have just told us the truth. He should have said something like this: Saddam Hussein is helping Osama bin Laden. That's only my opinion, but I believe it strongly. I have no problem removing Saddam Hussein from power. The fact that we're in Iraq and performing our mission? I have no problem with that, either. But I do take issue with the propaganda that sent us to war in the first place. I take issue with the fact that a United States president would lie so boldly to his own people in order to manipulate them.

How long do I think it'll go on? Based on what I saw while I was in Iraq, I would've said maybe a couple of years. Based on the news I've seen lately [in January 2005]? I can't say for sure. Mind you, the news is going to report what it wants to report, but things sure look a lot worse. So I'll have to say "quite a while." Let's say it'll be quite a while.

By the way, I base this opinion on something particular I noticed a lot over there. The Iraqi culture is all about paternal bullying. The father is the patriarch and everyone else in the family does as he says because he'll bully them into it. If the United States pulled out now, the insurgents would take over Iraq in a heartbeat. Their rule would be no better, no worse than Saddam Hussein's. There'd be civil war and terrorist rule and the region would be an even bigger mess than it is now. No, we need to begin a gradual pullout while continuing to train the Iraqis to look after themselves. That's the way I see it.

The biggest thing I want to impress on people? It was our job to go over there. I've heard a lot of guys who've come back home feeding negative images of soldiers to the press. They say they were wronged, for instance, or they say that they shouldn't have been sent over there, that they want their lives back, the lives that they had before they shipped out. I get so aggravated when I hear this.

You know what? *Somebody* had to go over there. *Somebody* had to do something. I want to tell these whiners, "You're a soldier in the United States military. Your job is to fight for your country." I say, "Do it well and be proud of that. Whether you think it was right or not—and maybe it wasn't—you've got to lift your head up high and portray the truth to people: that you were given a job and you did it. You did it well, you did it to the best of your ability. That's what being a soldier—that's what being an *American*—is all about. Nobody wants to hear you whine about how you missed your family. Everyone did. Get over it."

I want to speak personally to those soldiers who've come back and behaved like that. Or better yet, I want to reach all those soldiers who maybe are about to leave Iraq. Please: don't give us all a negative image. If you do that, pretty soon people will stop supporting soldiers. They'll start to say, "Well, if the soldiers don't want to go, we shouldn't be in Iraq." The fact is, we're over there now. Right or wrong, we're there and we need support. We're getting done what needs to get done, and hopefully we'll all be home soon.

My battle buddy's name was Sam and he's a year younger than me. He's from Sweetwater, Texas, down by Lubbock, and we got along well because we'd led similar lives before meeting each other in the army. We had the same sort of upbringing. We even looked about the same, same height, six feet or so, same weight, same brown hair. We're both pretty well-built, athletic guys. Sam had brown eyes, my eyes are blue, but that's pretty much the only difference between us.

I learned all kinds of stuff about Sam during the year we served together in Iraq. I heard about his family so often I felt like I knew them. I knew what his parents do for a living, I knew their favorite meals, I knew what his brother liked to do on the weekends, I felt like I was a part of the family. Having Sam as my buddy was an especially good thing because I found out pretty quick that I only got along with maybe four or five guys in my unit.

See, when guys are forced to live so close together for so long, your personalities are either going to get along well or not. For the most part, I experienced not. I got into a lot of fights over stupid stuff, the kind of things you'd fight about when you live with your brother or sister, say: "You're bed's too close to me, move it. Get your stuff away from mine! Why are you always hanging around me? Geez! Can't you give me some space?"

Looking back, it's funny. With everything that was going on all around us, we still made time to squabble over the small stuff. I never fought once with Sam, though. And we never said very much to one another before going into combat. Just "Here we go" and that was enough. "Here we go" seemed to pretty much sum everything up. You didn't have to say things like, "Be careful" or "Watch my back." That kind of stuff was understood. And words didn't help you do your job.

I've been out of the army since July. Sam and I still talk to each other two or three times a week, and I hope that never goes away. The rest of the guys I met in the army, I don't keep in touch with them. But I think about them a lot. I find myself thinking about them all the time.

Now I'm back home in Des Moines and I've got a job working at the John Deere works. Our plant builds farm machines like tillers and so forth. I had trouble sleeping my first month back. I'd wake up almost nightly with my head all filled with visions. It was like I was reliving all the stuff that had happened over there. For a while it was hell but then it subsided. Now it only happens once every couple of weeks or so, and I get through it by reminding myself that I'm back in the United States where I feel safe. I don't have to sleep with my rifle anymore.

Once you leave the army, you have no choice but to go back to who you were before you left. The way I see it, my military training actually helped me here, too. It prepared me to become a civilian again. One of the mottos we used in army training was, "Do what you have to do." The way I see it, my mission now is to make the transition back to being a private citizen and to provide for my family. I love my family. I missed a year of their lives, so I spend all the time I can with them and make sure that my transition doesn't affect them in a negative way.

At John Deere, I run a shot blast machine. It's sort of like a sand blaster but it uses metal shot. You use it to remove rust from metal. I like my job a lot because, if I do my job well, then the rust comes off and the machine gets handed to the welders who can do *their* jobs well. When the welders do *their* jobs, the machine can go back out into the fields, which helps the farmers do their jobs, so people have food to do their jobs. And so on. You see what I mean? That's happiness. To me, that's a good day's work.

HUMAN NATURE IN A WAR ZONE

✭

Staff Sergeant Justin MacEwen
U.S. ARMY, 513TH MILITARY INTELLIGENCE BRIGADE

MacEwen, age 32, hails from the Jacksonville, Florida, area and always knew he'd join the military. He trained for four years in a high school Navy/Marine Corps ROTC program and later signed up with the U.S. Marine Corps Reserve, where he eventually made the rank of sergeant E-5, serving as communications chief for an amphibious assault company.

Justin left the marines after seven years to pursue a job with a civilian firm which, unfortunately, downsized and let him go. "I would never have left the Marine Corps if I knew it was going to happen," he says. At that time, he had a wife and two kids to provide for. Justin considered returning to the marines but was told that, due to his absence, he would reenter the corps as a lance corporal (E-3). "And that," he says, "would have been a real hefty pay cut."

Instead, Justin began exploring career options with the U.S. Army. An army recruitment officer took note of Justin's ASVAB[134] and ACT[135] scores and proclaimed him eligible for military intelligence work. Plus the army would admit him as a specialist, E-4. Justin was thrilled with this proposal and accepted.

Staff Sergeant MacEwen has been deployed to Iraq twice. He worked as the senior intelligence analyst for the Brigade Operations Center (BOC) out of Camp Doha, running missions into Kuwait and southern Iraq from September 2002 through June 2003. Then, after a brief trip home,

---

134. Armed Services Vocational Aptitude Battery—a multipart test given to all incoming military trainees to measure a soldier's skills in areas such as general science; arithmetic reasoning; word knowledge; paragraph comprehension; mathematics knowledge; electronics information; auto and shop information; and mechanical comprehension.

135. American College Test—an exam designed to assess the general educational development of high school students, as well as their ability to complete undergraduate college-level work. Some American colleges and universities require applicants to take the ACT, the SAT, or both exams.

he was redeployed to Baghdad's Camp Victory[136] where he served with the
Operations Counterintelligence Cell for the INSCOM[137] Theater Detach-
ment (ITD) from January 2004 to August 2004.

Currently, Justin MacEwen is posted at Fort Gordon, Georgia, where
he struggles to cope with one of the personal nightmares unique to soldiers
returning from the Gulf: the dissolution of a marriage.

A lot of people don't know what military intelligence is, so let me explain.
I ran source operations that attempted to ferret out foreign operatives
practicing subversion, espionage, and terrorism. We tracked money-
laundering schemes, conducted interrogations, and tried to pinpoint the
hierarchical structures of key insurgency groups. We did a lot of other
stuff besides that, but it's still considered classified and, I'm sorry, I can't
discuss it.

Overall? It was a bewildering situation. Picture any scene from *Apoc-
alypse Now* and that should give you the proper flavor. There were no
rules where I was working. One minute, everything was fine; the next
minute? Total chaos. When we drove around Baghdad, for instance, we
never knew if the next corner we turned would open us up to a barrage
of enemy weapons fire or maybe an IED going off under our truck.
When we met with the local population, we never knew if we'd get a
handshake and a smile or a gun in our faces. We stayed on pins and needles all the time.

War is a circumstance of social instability but human nature is a constant. Human nature will always be about vulnerability and feeling and
everyone wanting to save their own skin and the skins of their families
and loved ones. For the average citizen of any country, war makes these
wants difficult to obtain. So war and human nature go together like bu-
tane and an open flame. They meet, they react, and neither one wins

---

136. Camp Victory is located at the southwest corner of Baghdad City on the grounds of Baghdad International Airport. Via Humvee, the Camp is fifteen minutes' drive into downtown Baghdad. The Camp Victory
site was once a presidential palace area (the Al Faw palace) which American troops have modified for their
encampment. MacEwen describes the palace as "immaculate, beautiful and huge. The place has something
like sixty-two rooms. Saddam Hussein had his own zoo there, so empty cages are still all over the property.
It's a large enough facility to stage several brigades of armor and infantry." According to Sergeant MacEwen,
Camp Victory is also the location where Saddam Hussein was being held after his capture and a majority of
high-echelon multinational commanders are housed.

137. U.S. Army Intelligence and Security Command—a global command (composed of four brigades) that is
charged with "providing the warfighter the seamless intelligence needed to understand the battlefield and to
focus and leverage combat power" (according to the INSCOM official Web site).

out. Instead, they form some kind of weird, explosive hybrid which is very, very hot and consumes itself quickly.

Iraq was complicated. The locals we tried to tap as intelligence sources were hesitant to assist. They were worried about retributive action from insurgency groups. Justifiably so. Anyone who committed themselves to the Coalition point of view was laying his life and the lives of his entire family on the line. As far as my job was concerned, that was the biggest problem we faced in Baghdad: the utter lack of cooperation from the Iraqi population, military or police forces, the same people we were trying to help.

They just didn't have the backbone. When things get tough for American armed forces, we take casualties, but we keep up the fight, for better or worse. We have the resources to sustain a long run. The Iraqis don't. When things got tough for them, they turned tail and ran every time. Police and Iraqi National Guard units would give up their weapons to insurgency leaders—this happened a lot, for instance, during the big uprising in southern Iraq at An Najaf during Sadr's big push in April of '04.

When the people you're trying to liberate turn tail and run to the men you're trying to save them from, that's no way to build an infrastructure.

My unit had a very diverse mission. For instance, we were attached to Abu Ghraib prison after the scandal broke out there, and that's all I'll say about that apart from mentioning that no members, soldiers, officers, or NCOs from my group were involved in the abuse. For the most part, I served as an analyst, which meant that I found myself practicing the art of flexibility as a rule. You had to, because the intelligence network in Iraq was, for the most part, thrown together at the last minute. INSCOM dropped us into the mix with the general idea of assisting field commanders to gain an overall knowledge of everything. Sounds like a big job, right? Well, it was. But when you involve yourself in military action within a foreign country, command personnel has to get brought up to speed on a lot of stuff, and most of it's stuff you're just figuring our for yourself on the fly.

For instance, we had infantry units hiring translators. The translators, being part of the local population, often maintained their own sources for information. Well, this isn't by the book, but it's pretty tantalizing for a foreign army unit to have their very own insider. It became fairly common practice for U.S. units to trade money or other means with Iraqi informants in exchange for the location and identities of insurgency members. The deal was simple: You gave informants a couple of bucks and said, "Who's starting the trouble? Who should we look out for?"

Was it effective? Sometimes. But you had to be careful. Think about it. Giving an Iraqi citizen several hundred American dollars is equivalent to giving him more money than he's earned in his entire lifetime. Once he has it in his hands, what's stopping him from dealing you bogus information? Or setting you up for an ambush in order to earn bonus points with insurgency leaders? That'd be a perfect double score as far as some Iraqis were concerned: get the Americans' money and stay in the good graces of the insurgency. Personally, I never trusted payoffs.

When using nonmilitary translators, you always had to ask yourself some questions: Who are they really working for? What are they doing with the information they translate? Are they translating it correctly and giving us all the facts? Suddenly the simple act of translation presents its own security nightmares. In fact, I went so far as to double up on my translators. I had an Egyptian translator eavesdrop on my Iraqi translators to verify the Iraqis' work. You know how the old saying goes, "You're not paranoid if they really *are* out to get you."

Maybe I should have had another guy verifying the Egyptian's work, but there's only so much you can do, right? I decided to trust him. He was a naturalized U.S. citizen with government clearance to read classified material. And I assure you, he had no love for the Iraqi people. Over there, the overall population supported the idea of a free Iraqi nation but there were definitely some Iraqis who supported or looked the other way when insurgents attacked U.S. troops. My Egyptian wasn't one of them.

One thing that made me trust this guy: he was always worried about *our* security. He kept telling me, "Listen. If we're overrun and there's a firefight, I want a weapon. If we're captured, they'll hack my head off just like they'll hack off yours. Probably with more glee, because I'm helping you."

He was right about that. It made perfect sense. But we're not allowed to arm civilians. There's a number of reasons for that, but let's just say we don't want to endanger them. As a condolence prize, I told my Egyptian that, if I ever got hit, he was welcome to pull my sidearm from my holster and start blasting away at anything that moved. He wasn't happy with that answer, but he accepted it.

Either way, this whole conversation put me at ease. Guys who have an inside track with the enemy rarely worry about getting their heads cut off.

Specific examples of what my job entailed? Okay, here we go. Example Number One: I sat in on a lot of meetings with tribal leaders and discussed various issues related to the comfort level of the Iraqi people, their needs, and the possibility of their participation against elements who sought to discourage the creation of a free society in the new Iraqi nation. Okay?

I can only describe those meetings as incredibly frustrating. For instance, one time we interviewed this woman. She came to us saying she knew where weapons were being cached and she could lead us to them. Obviously, this interested us a great deal.

The conversation started out normally; it wasn't interrogation like you'd see in the movies, bright lights, lit cigarettes, violence, and bullshit. It was civil and respectful. We treated this woman as if she were one of our own, like an American citizen. We got her food from the dining facility and even brought food for one of her friends. We made sure she was comfortable. We talked. She talked. We listened. We learned. Everything was going fine.

As the conversation progressed, though, we asked her for some personal information. Nothing unreasonable, just information to verify her identity so we could keep her in our files. It was information that would allow us to insure her safety more than anything else. All at once she became extremely belligerent. In fact, I've misspoken. Let me use the word *hostile*. She threatened our lives. She told us she had friends in the insurgency movement who'd seek us out and cut our throats in the middle of the night. Then they'd hunt down our families in the United States and do the same to our wives and children. And that was just a warm-up. After that, things went downhill.

It turned out to be an awful afternoon. Remember, this woman had come to *us* and asked *us* to talk. It's not like we picked her up off the streets, threw her in the back of a truck, beat her, and starved her half to death. But that, in a nutshell, is what the situation was like over there. You could feed those people, give them money, try to help them using whatever means you had available. It didn't make any difference. You'd offer a guy medical supplies to help his sickly daughter. The next thing you knew, he was launching mortar rounds at your tent.

I don't know how else to describe the dynamic. Call it a lack of trust. I guess that's another thing about human nature. It's never satisfied.

The teams from the Intelligence Brigade usually got assigned to infantry or artillery units. Command would slice out a piece of that unit like they were carving up an apple pie and insert members of Intel to replace them. We had guys on the ground everywhere, Fallujah, Tikrit, Taji, Mosul, it all depended on where the military wanted access to information. Once they had us on the ground feeding them real-time information, they'd task us to perform different missions based on their overall druthers for the region. Example Two of what my job entailed: sometimes we were tapped to study a certain area of terrain for possible troop routes. Example Three: we'd be asked to search out an enigmatic enemy unit. Example Four: we be tasked to hunt a particular group of insurgents operating in northern Iraq.

From day to day, you took whatever got thrown at you down the pipe and tried to make sense of it. In Baghdad we directly supported Coalition Joint Task Force 7.[138] Then we switched over and supported MNC[139] as strategic CIPs [counterintelligence personnel] for more elevated issues, stuff that was being handled by generals and the State De-

138. CJTF 7 replaced Coalition Forces Land Component Command around mid-June 2003 and thereafter had operational control of all forces within Iraq, including a multinational force of over 130,000 soldiers from Spain, England, Australia, and other countries. It was disbanded less than a year later and replaced by Multinational Corps–Iraq and Multinational Force–Iraq. The decision to disband came after it was determined that different commanders could monitor strategic day-to-day concerns with more efficiency than one. CJTF 7 ran offensive operations to neutralize and secure the area in preparation for the coming Coalition Provisional Authority. It was also responsible for organizing, training, and certifying the Iraqi Armed Forces.
139. Multi national Corps (in this specific instance, Multinational Corps–Iraq) conducts offensive operations to defeat remaining non-compliant forces and neutralize destabilizing influences in Iraq in order to create a secure environment. It simultaneously conducts stability operations to support the establishment of government, the restoration of essential services, and economic development in order to set the conditions for a transfer of sovereignty and operations to designated follow-on authorities.

partment. Luckily, we were high enough up in the food chain to remain autonomous so a lot of times we were left to our own devices. We did our business as best we knew how and didn't talk about it much.

We kept our profiles low. Most of the time we wore civilian clothes so no one could tell who we were. A guy wearing civvies in a war zone might be a contractor with one of the many Western firms operating in the area like CACI, Titan, Blackwater, and so forth.[140] Maybe he's a construction executive or a personal security envoy for any number of private groups including higher-echelon members of the Iraqi government. Maybe we were military in disguise, CIA, FBI, or some other part of the intelligence sector. The point is, we left it vague. We never sought attention, we avoided it.

That's not to say that we *never* dressed in uniform; it largely depended on the issue of safety. If we were going into a really hot zone— Sadr City when the insurgency was in full swing, for instance—we wore uniforms because, what difference did it make? The insurgents shot at you no mater what you looked like.

A lot of times we dressed as civilians in order to influence the behavior of our own troops. A guy dressed in civilian clothes has the advantage when he approaches an officer of the U.S. armed forces. The same ambiguity that worked against the Iraqis could be useful on our own troops. When you dress in civies, the brass doesn't know who you are, so they don't take chances. They have to respect you. Again, it's human nature. Normally, a colonel won't deal with sergeants. They treat them like peasants; that's military hierarchy. But put a specialist in plain clothes and suddenly everything changes. The brass starts listening to you closely. They don't know if you outrank them and, anyway, it's obvious that you have the ear of someone higher up and no one wants to get a phone call from a pissed-off general who's calling to say, "Hello, Major. Our man in the field says that you acted like a complete prick to him and wouldn't provide information pertaining to your own safety."

140. Both CACI International, Inc. from Arlington, Virginia and Titan of San Diego, California, fell under investigation in May 2004 for the role their employees allegedly played in the Abu Ghraib prison torture scandal ("Private Contractors and Torture at Abu Ghraib, Iraq" by Pratap Chatterjee and A. C. Thompson, special to CorpsWatch, May 7, 2004). Blackwater Security Consulting of Moyocock, North Carolina— according to its Web site, "is a strategic division of Blackwater USA. Blackwater USA has historically provided a spectrum of support to military, government agencies, law enforcement and civilian entities in training, targets and range operations as a solution provider. Blackwater Security Consulting has its roots in the Special Operations community and continues to sustain the skills acquired over the years."

Mind you, we never tried to scare or intimidate anyone; that's not useful, either. No, you kept things on the level first and foremost by making it clear to the officers that you were not there to fuck around. "Our mission," you'd say, "is to install antiterrorism measures that will protect your men." Who could have a problem with that? See, when you showed you were useful, the brass didn't tend to care if you were FBI, CIA, or the Avon lady. Your rank didn't add up to a tinker's damn, either, you refrained from mentioning it. For all anyone knew, or cared, you were a warrant officer,[141] a staff NCO, a Rudy-Pooh Private, or Bozo the Clown. In the end, what mattered was how you did your job.

Sometimes you put your life on the line for nothing. Example Five: one time we were driving around in unmarked Mitsubishi Pajeros. They didn't have armor, but we had our pistols and we had the SAW in the back; I was manning it. We also had a pile of grenades close at hand, which turned out to be fortunate. We were driving along when this car suddenly slid out on our tail and accelerated toward us as fast as the driver could punch it. I could see the people inside, kids mostly. Didn't matter. Suicide bombers were a day-to-day threat. That's not human nature as far as we know it here in the U.S., but it's a very real factor in Iraq.

There was no way I could let them get close enough to open fire or blow themselves and us to kingdom come. I prayed they wouldn't get any closer. The SAW was loaded. I thumbed it off safety. All sorts of weird shit was going through my head: *I am not going home in a body bag, not today. I am not going home in a body bag, keep your head on straight. . . .*

They kept on coming.

Usually I wouldn't wait for instructions. But in this case I wanted to let the convoy and the driver of my vehicle know that we had a potential situation. Calling out all threats and possible threats is standard proce-

---

141. Warrant officers comprise a small but vital group of technicians and specialists who serve in the army, navy, and Marine Corps. They do not ordinarily assume officer command responsibilities. In contrast to commissioned officers, their careers emphasize depth rather than breadth of experience. The status and duties of these experts, trainers, and specialty managers have grown and otherwise changed since their grades were established around 1920. Today, they can be found advancing within military careers such as aviation, physicians' assistant, nuclear weapons, and administration.

dures in the war zone, so I popped on the radio and said, "We have a vehicle approaching from the rear, repeat, fast vehicle, request orders immediately." The car pulled closer.

Static. Then: "If you see it as a threat—permission granted to open fire." It's either me or the kids, no way to avoid it. Please don't come any closer. I pointed the weapon and shouted at them over the roar of the engines, "Stop! Goddamit, stop or I have to shoot you!"

They kept on coming.

I could see the driver grinning at me through the dusty windshield. I could feel the trigger under my finger, ready to be squeezed, ready to let loose and carve that car up into jagged, little metal bits. It's funny the ideas that come to you in tense situations like that. I don't know why I did this, I reached over to my side and picked up a grenade. I sort of brandished it. I made as if I was going to toss it out the back, which seemed to change the driver's opinion of me immediately because he slammed on his brakes and twisted the steering wheel. Within a few seconds, we'd pulled away and were gone.

I have no idea what that asshole was thinking. Maybe he was attacking. Maybe he had no common sense in his head whatsoever and was trying to test us. It doesn't matter. What matters is that he got to live another day and so did I. By the way, it was only a smoke grenade.[142] But I'm glad he didn't know that.

I was a section leader, which meant I had young troopers under me. It was their first time in a war zone—hell, it was their first time overseas—and everything was, for lack of a better word, new to them. To a man, my troopers really wanted to help the Iraqi people. They knew the Iraqis had been screwed by Saddam and they wanted to do what was right for them. But they could get very disheartened. Sometimes we watched English translations of Arab news spots and, let me tell you, Al Jazeera[143] reporters do their propaganda work well. They make it sound like

142. Not all grenades are of the lethal fragmentation variety. The M-18 colored smoke grenade is used for ground-to-ground or ground-to-air signaling as in the case of marking landing zones or screening devices for troop movement.

143. The largest and most controversial Arabic news channel in the Middle East. Based in Qatar and founded in 1996, Al Jazeera offers 24-hour news coverage from around the world and focuses on the hottest conflicts in the region.

Americans are only in the Gulf to generate a high body count. If you didn't know any better, you'd start hating yourself for being an American.

One night at Camp Victory, we were all in our quarters, a tent city just inside the camp's triple-thick concrete outer wall. We occupied military-issue general-purpose tents, nothing fancy, but we'd souped them up as best we could, reinforcing the walls with wood timbers and laying down carpeting. We installed interior paneling to section off private sleeping cubbies, and there was a living room area furnished with one of those tiny college dorm-room refrigerators, a beautiful couch and some chairs we'd borrowed from one of Saddam's palaces. He wasn't going to need them anymore. The tents became our own mini-apartment complex for me and five other guys. It wasn't luxury but it was okay. The best part about the place was we'd built it ourselves using good old American ingenuity. We called the complex Whoville[144] and our own tent was called Ghetto Tent because apparently we were the only guys living in canvas when most everyone else was bunking in the modular two-man trailers that became the norm for personnel.

One night we got hit with a barrage of very sudden, very intense mortar fire. Shells landed right by our tent. One second we were all sitting around talking, the next moment we could hear the hollow *shunk* of the rounds being dropped into their tubes; that's how close they were. Next we heard the screech of the air as the shots zoomed in. I screamed, "Incoming! Gear! Gear!" You should have seen the looks on those kids' faces. Pure panic. They were motionless. Frozen. I had to grab one of them and jam my face into his. "Look at me," I said. "Look alive. You're okay. Stay down."

But just then, the shell hit and the blast knocked us all up into the air. Shrapnel started blowing through the tent. My soldiers were frightened before the shells hit, the explosions certainly weren't helping them gain composure. Not that it mattered. The truth is, in a situation like that? It's like being on a roller-coaster ride from hell. The best you can do is hang on tight and ride it out.

We got down on our bellies and low-crawled out of the tent toward the sand bags. More shells came in. One round fell into a tent where

---

144. From Dr. Seuss's *The Grinch Who Stole Christmas.*

some buddies of ours lived; thank God they were out getting dinner just then—the explosion would have killed all six of them. The rounds kept walking in, coming closer and closer, like they were trying to zero in on us specifically. Who knows? Maybe they were.

The situation sucked. There was nothing we could do. We couldn't fire back, we had no idea where the rounds were coming from. Our only alternative was to pray the bastards had crappy aim. And here were these young kids sitting in the pit with me. The fear on their faces was awful, but worse than that—the expectancy. They looked up to me. Their eyes were full of hope that I'd know what to do, I'd get them through it. Keep them alive. I was just as scared as they were. All I could say was, "Stay calm. Nobody move." And we stayed there for a long time like that, motionless in the bottom of the pit.

In March of 2003, my brigade commander, a colonel, led a five-vehicle convoy to the town of Um Qsar. Um Qsar is located in the extreme southern quadrant of Iraq, very close to the border with Kuwait. We were there to attend a meeting with a tribal leader, a local cleric. It was a reasonably secure time in the country; the military had just succeeded in securing a lot of areas. We got stopped at a checkpoint and suddenly the local population swarmed toward us, full force. Hundreds and hundreds of very hungry people looking for food.

I'm going to try to describe this as best I can to you, but I know I'm not going to succeed.

Bear with me.

You've heard a lot of American citizens being critical about the war, right? They say that the suffering in Iraq was caused by this war, they say that our bombs have killed civilian populations. Well, listen closely to what I'm about to tell you: war is war and, yes, people get hurt. That's a truth and it's terrible. But from what I saw on the ground, Iraq's suffering existed a long time before we got there, and one man was responsible. His name is Saddam Hussein. He'd let what little infrastructure that country had turn to crap. The water purification and sewer systems were dilapidated. You could climb in a Humvee at any one of the presidential palaces, these luxurious pleasure domes dedicated to Saddam's sons, and within three or four miles' drive, you'd find whole city blocks where children played in raw sewage flowing down the middle of the street. The smell of the filth would make your knees buckle. Sanitation was nonexistent. You even had bodies in the streets that weren't being disposed of properly. It was a surreal situation in Um Qsar.

These women pressed toward our vehicles lifting two-year-old kids, kids the same age as my youngest, toward the car. The babies were dehydrated. Their skin was chapped and there was crusted salt around their lips. Their eyes were glazed and staring. The people screamed for us to help them. I don't understand Arabic but some things are universal, they require no translation. Human nature. These people crowded in from all sides, seized our vehicles and started to shake them. One kid ran up, grabbed my rifle, and tried to yank the SAW out of the vehicle. I'd already clicked the weapon off safe. There was a round in the chamber. Thank God I'd taken my finger off the trigger, if I hadn't and the kid had pulled hard enough, he'd be dead.

We wanted desperately to do something but we couldn't. We'd given out all the water and food we had. We had to drive on. It made me sick to leave those people like that. Being a father and seeing kids begging for basic items you can buy for nothing on any street in the United States? It hurt. The situation was overwhelming. We had guys who almost broke down. Eventually, we broke through the crowd and continued forward toward our meeting.

When we got there, the cleric was furious with us. "Why don't you have the power working yet?" he demanded. "Why isn't the water working?" I had to tell him, "Sir, we just got here. Your purification system is thirty years old and missing key parts. We can't work magic. We can't create instant, beautiful cities." But when you boil it down, that's what the Iraqis expected of us. We'd waltz right on in, trounce Saddam's brigade, and Boom! All problems solved. Roads would be built. Every home would have an air conditioner. Food would sprout from the gutters. It doesn't work that way. The job we found waiting for us was overwhelming. We'd expected to find a modern Arabic city when we arrived in Baghdad, instead we discovered much of it beneath third-world standards. Oh, certain areas seemed well off enough, mostly the areas where the Sunnis lived. But everyone else? Dear God.

No wonder the Sunnis are so ticked off right now. They'd been the dominant political force for years. They'd allowed the slaughter of the Shiites and the Kurds. Now they've suddenly found themselves in the minority. How would you feel if for decades you had everything you wanted in life at the snap of your fingers. Then, suddenly, you were threatened with having nothing?

The cleric shouted at us and we tried to control ourselves. It was an awful day. When we finally got back to base, I had to take a breather, calm down, and center myself. I was tense, I was stressed out, and I felt bad for everybody involved—them, us, the kids, the parents, everybody. But you shake it off. You move forward. I went to sleep that night thinking, *Well, tomorrow's another day to try and figure this all out.*

It's all about human nature in a war zone. My birthday is June 2. That day I got assigned to run a mission to Camp Snoopy out in the worst part of Sadr City. It started off badly. An IED went off in front of us as we were driving and blew up a semi-truck standing nearby. We hauled ass out of there fast as we could. We thought it was an ambush.

We made it to the post, this facility which at one point had been IIS[145] headquarters. The place had been bombed to hell and back over the past couple of months and the area reeked because some bodies had been left to decay in the rubble and dirt. No one had excavated them, and every time another bomb came in, the rubble would shift and crush the bodies further. The air was so putrid you'd fall to your knees and wretch. By the end of the day, that smell was in my clothes, in my hair; I couldn't shake it and it got me very, very pissed off. This was not the way you'd ever imagine spending your thirty-second birthday. I was a wreck by the time I got back to camp.

I had a friend who was dating a female sergeant at the time. They were both single and there's no rule against dating a fellow soldier, although it certainly wasn't encouraged. She was there when I walked into the tent, threw down my weapon, and just sort of stood there, shaking. They asked me what had happened and I just went off, I was wired. I don't remember what I said. What I shouted, rather. Everything sort of came tumbling out of me and there I was, gasping for breath, angry,

145. Iraqi Intelligence Service—also known as Mukhabarat, the Department of General Intelligence, or the General Directorate of Intelligence. As a quick reference point, it could be called the Iraqi equivalent of the U.S. FBI and CIA rolled into one entity. Many members of the international intelligence community have categorized the IIS's tactics as criminal and barbaric. In 1983, for instance, under the guidance of Barzan al-Tikriti, the IIS organized the massacres of villagers in Al Dujail and Jezan Al Chol, as well as the assassination of ninety members of Ayatollah al-Hakim's family.

ready to cry, ready to explode. I was losing it. This woman got up, slipped behind me and started rubbing my back.

Let me put this into context. I hadn't been intimate with my wife in over a year and a half. Hell, I hadn't been around a woman, not in friendship, for several months. Human nature demands that people be wanted and needed and understood and loved. When you haven't had these things in a long, long while, you actually begin to forget how necessary they are. You forget that you're human at all. Her fingers worked and this woman started saying things to me. Her voice was so calming, so relaxing. I don't remember what she said, but I melted. I gave up. This woman, I swear to God, she drew me back from the brink of a nervous breakdown.

She said, "It's your birthday, right?" I said, "Yeah."

"Well," she said, "I couldn't get you anything. But here's your present. Lie down on your bed and I'll lie down beside you." Which we did. It wasn't anything sexual. How could it have been? I was out cold in minutes. But see, that was a gift in itself. Back then, normally, it took me hours to fall asleep. Sometimes I wonder if I ever really slept at all over there. For that matter, I wondered if I was ever really awake. But this time, with her there even for a little while, everything seemed all right again. Just for that one little moment, it was all right.

I slept deeply that night. The next morning I felt composed. Best birthday present I ever got.

Yeah, I'm back home now. For the moment. What am I doing? I spend a lot of time readjusting.

You know all those stories about Vietnam vets coming back and having a tough time letting go? I never understood where they were coming from until now. It's true. It's all true. Post-traumatic stress disorder is real.

The first thing I noticed when I got home was the quiet. I was used to weapons rattling away at all hours and bombs exploding and enemy rounds dropping down in the middle of the night. Rockets would hit us, mortars would fire, it happened so often that you actually tuned it out. None of that here in the States, though. No screams. No sirens. No gunshots, nobody screaming for medical attention, no nothing. Just quiet. But the quiet didn't soothe me. If anything, it terrified me even more.

You're wound up like a spring over there. You develop some very strange habits. You keep a loaded 9 mm pistol under your pillow, for instance. You stand your rifle by your feet like this lethal exclamation point and learn how to roll out of bed at the barest hint or sound of danger. Grab the gun, pull on your flak vest and helmet, quickly, quickly, all in the dark, all without really being awake. But you're never really awake and you don't really sleep over there. Instead, you sort of drift in and out of consciousness; it's just that sometimes you do it lying down, but that's not really sleep. It's not deep. And all this goes on for however long you're there. You never realize how stressed out you are until you come back home and suddenly the spring is allowed to uncoil.

I can't shake some of these habits. Now, when I hear thunder, I'm up on my feet and diving for phantom sand pits before my brain kicks in and says, *Okay. Bad weather. Stand down.*

You get used to the site of people suffering. Horrific sites. Children in pain or getting killed. Kids in real bad shape. You see these kids and the first thing you notice is, they're the same age as my kids. That's tough to handle. As a father. As a man. Actually, that might be the worst of all of it, the sound of children screaming. It's human nature to loathe the sound of children screaming in pain.

The other night I went out to dinner with a friend at a Cracker Barrel and I lost it. Some little kid slipped out of his seat and started to wail, one of those really deep screams that only a kid can manage. I froze. My fingers locked. I started to shake. In the movie theater of my mind, I was right back there all over again, watching kids get hit, watching them get wounded, not knowing what to do, not knowing where I was. This friend of mine evidently started talking to me. She told me later on. She said she wanted to know if I was all right, if I was there, what was happening to me, I looked funny. But I was gone. Just gone. She even snapped her fingers in front of my nose. Nothing.

Later on, we talked a little. She'd read about it, of course. So had I. The stuff that happens to guys from Korea, Vietnam, and World War II. "Do you have flashbacks?" she asked. As if I somehow knew more about what was happening to me than she did. "Is that what happened?" She asked. "Was it a flashback?"

Tough to answer that one. It was hard to put into words. No, it hadn't been a flashback. It was more like slipping through chinks in the armor of time. For those few seconds, I wasn't here anymore. I was there.

This past New Year's Eve was interesting. I was visiting the apartment of a friend of mine when a weapon opened up maybe five hundred yards away. Somebody shot off twenty rounds or so. In retrospect, maybe it was just firecrackers or something, somebody's way of celebrating, I don't know. I came to face down in the street. Without realizing it, I'd dropped to the ground and low-crawled to the curbside.

Later on I got home and lay on my bed all night listening to my neighbor scream. He's a soldier, too. He got a head wound on his trip to Iraq. I guess they don't really know what's wrong with him, but, man. He screams a lot.

Happy New Year.

I talked to a guy I know, a Vietnam vet, and I asked him, "Does it ever go away?" "Naw," he said. He didn't need to ask what I was talking about. He knew. "Never," he said. "But it does get less intense." I thought, *That's good.*

I have a tough time grilling steaks or meat or anything anymore. I used to love to do that. I was a grill-o-maniac. But now, when I smell that sizzling, popping, fat-over-the-flames burning and dripping and smoke coming up in thick, greasy clouds, I have to throw up. Once, as we were making our rounds, an Iraqi civilian fuel truck got hit by an RPG as we passed by. The cab exploded and started to burn. We were stuck in the middle of the road for a while, watching it go. The smell of a burning human being smells just like meat cooking on a grill. It's a pretty intense odor. So no, I can't eat that stuff anymore. Not for a while, anyway, I guess.

The first time I got back from Iraq my wife told me she wanted a divorce. It was September 2003. She said she'd had enough. I guess it's one of the untold casualties of war, marital relationships. I know this for a fact: I had less than one hundred people in my company the first time I deployed. Not all of them were married but, of that hundred, ten guys got divorced. Some of them had to go through their divorces while they were overseas. That's got to suck. Another half dozen separated from their spouses. Trust me, the numbers don't get any better when your unit redeploys. You go over again and again and again and, each time, more relationships break apart.

Of course it's tough on the spouse who stays home. Male or female, it doesn't matter, it's tough. You're without your husband or wife for six months, a year, maybe more. You plow through your life, waiting for them to come home. When they do, they're different. Maybe they're only home for three months before it's time to head off again for another tour. It's a bleak situation and, in the face of it, a lot of people just give up.

My wife couldn't deal with my long deployments. Sure, we had issues before that. What married couple doesn't? But the deployments were the straw that broke the camel's back. I guess she figured, "This isn't going to end anytime soon, I might have to deal with this for four or five more years." And she made her decision.

My wife and I—my ex-wife and I—have three boys. When I was overseas, I got an e-mail on Father's Day. Apparently my oldest boy had a problem. He was very upset. He'd been crying. My wife begged me to call him, and it was a frustrating situation because there's eight hours' difference between Iraq and home. Plus, you're never guaranteed of getting an open phone line. Connections over there are hoarded like gold.

I wanted so badly to talk to my son it hurt. I tried everything I could think of. Finally, one of my buddies arranged to have me use a satellite phone. I got through to the house. I asked my boy what the problem was and this is what he told me:

"All my friends have their fathers. I don't have mine. What's the point of celebrating Father's Day if my daddy isn't here?" He was eight years old.

When you're a soldier and a father, you have to answer a lot of difficult questions: "Did you hurt anybody? Did you kill anybody, Daddy? Why are you hurting people?" Those questions take a lot of tact and thought and effort to answer. They aren't as bad as this one, though: "When are you coming home?"

I told him something like this: "Your daddy has a mission, son. I don't like it any more than you do. But there's people over here who want to hurt us. They want to hurt me and they want to hurt you. Remember the bad guys who crashed their planes into those towers in New York?" He remembered that. "Well, they want to hurt your brothers and Mommy and we have to stop them, okay?"

He said, "Can't you just tell them to stop?" Kids.

"Son, we've asked them to stop and they won't. So we have to make them stop," I said. And he said, "Well, I don't like it."

"I don't like it any more than you do, kiddo, but Daddy wears a uniform. You've seen my uniform, right?" He'd seen it, all right. "Sometimes we have to use force to keep people from hurting us. We don't want to hurt them, there's just no other way."

"Do you hit them?" he asked. And you can't lie to them. I said, "Yes, son. Sometimes we do."

"Do you hit them so hard that they don't get up?" You can never, ever lie to them. I said, "We don't like to do that, son. But the truth is, sometimes we hit them and no, they don't get up. Sometimes they die."

I remember the line going quiet for a long time. I guess he was thinking it over. Then he said, "When I get older, we'll talk about this more, okay?"

"Yes, son. When you get older, we'll talk about it as much as you want."

My eight-year old's having the hardest time dealing with the divorce. He remembers me being home a lot, before the war. My six- and two-year olds don't. To them, everything that happens to Daddy is normal now. They have no recollection of a time when I put them to bed and tucked them in. They don't remember how I held them or a time when I was normal, when I was me, the person I remember myself being.

Maybe someday that'll change. I hope it'll change. I'm hoping the old me comes back.

ACKNOWLDEGMENTS

Compiling *Heart of War* would not have been possible without enormous contributions from the following people:

Martha Kaplan of the Martha Kaplan Literary Agency. Thank you, Martha, for your constant guidance. Mark Woods, Cynthia Beard, and Senior Chief Petty Officer William Baker, United States Navy (Retired), all of the New River Dramatists project in North Carolina. For luring me away from New York City in January so I could work on the shores of a placid lake. Eric Schmeltzer and Paul Rieckhoff of Iraq and Afghanistan Veterans of America, who offered me the chance to meet soldiers outside my own, tiny circle. The stories of these brave men and women are as powerful as IAVA's mission to present them to the world at large. David Fisher, a mentor in the truest sense of the word. Frank Weimann at the Literary Group. Michaela Hamilton and Gary Goldstein at Kensington-Citadel. My friends and family whom my life would be nothing without, no matter how infrequently I return phone calls. Thank you for understanding. Jessica Pogash. Lastly (and most significantly), this book is possible only through the selfless contributions of American soldiers. Your generosity and enthusiasm for this project overwhelmed me from the start. Thank you for sharing your stories with me and the grateful country you've served.

�֎